A
VISION
FOR
PREACHING

A

VISION

FOR

PREACHING

UNDERSTANDING THE HEART
OF PASTORAL MINISTRY

ABRAHAM KURUVILLA

B
Baker Academic
a division of Baker Publishing Group
Grand Rapids, Michigan

Published by Baker Academic
a division of Baker Publishing Group
P.O. Box 6287, Grand Rapids, MI 49516-6287
www.bakeracademic.com

Printed in the United States of America

Library of Congress Cataloging-in-Publication Data
Kuruvilla, Abraham.
    A vision for preaching : understanding the heart of pastoral ministry / Abraham Kuruvilla.
      pages cm
    Includes bibliographical references and index.
    ISBN 978-0-8010-9674-7 (pbk.)
    1. Preaching. I. Title.
BV4211.3.K87 2015
251—dc23   2015015877

Unless otherwise indicated, translations of ancient texts, including Scripture quotations, are the author's translation.

15   16   17   18   19   20   21   7   6   5   4   3   2   1

In keeping with biblical principles of creation stewardship, Baker Publishing Group advocates the responsible use of our natural resources. As a member of the Green Press Initiative, our company uses recycled paper when possible. The text paper of this book is composed in part of post-consumer waste.

To
Dallas Theological Seminary
whose seal
after almost a century
still bears the words
κήρυξον τὸν λόγον
(2 Timothy 4:2)

Contents

Acknowledgments

To my colleagues, past and present, in the Department of Pastoral Ministries at Dallas Theological Seminary, especially Timothy Warren, Vic Anderson, Ramesh Richard, Tim Ralston, and Reg Grant: thank you for those discussions on a vision for preaching—what it would look like and how it might be articulated.

To my family—my father, brother, sister-in-law, and nephews: thank you for your love, prayers, and constant support.

To Jim Kinney, who has had persistent faith in my productions: thank you for the "megaphone."

To Northwest Bible Church: many thanks to this local assembly of God's people for their encouragement at all times, and especially when I preach.

To Dallas Theological Seminary: I am grateful to God for its noble heritage, for the nine decades of its belief in preaching, and for its people—the faculty, staff, and students who make it a wonderful place to labor for Christ and his church. To this institution I am privileged to dedicate this work.

The solemn responsibility of preaching God's ineffable word (as well as that of teaching preaching to a fresh generation) has impacted me powerfully as I labored through this book. What an honor to partner with God, albeit in a minuscule way, in his glorious purposes for the cosmos and for his church! I am grateful for the divine grace that has entrusted me with an opportunity to participate in God's work.

> I solemnly charge [you] before God and Christ Jesus who is going to judge the living and the dead, and by His appearing and His kingdom: preach the word! (2 Tim. 4:1–2)

May all of us preachers (and teachers of preachers) be faithful to our commission, facilitating the transformation of lives, in the power of the Spirit, to further the kingdom of Christ, for the glory of God.

Abraham Kuruvilla
Dallas, Texas
Pentecost 2014

Introduction

"The Entrance of Thy Words . . ."

The entrance of Thy words giveth light.
Psalm 119:130 KJV

> Biblical preaching, by a leader of the church, in a gathering of Christians for worship, is the communication of the thrust of a pericope of Scripture discerned by theological exegesis, and of its application to that specific body of believers, that they may be conformed to the image of Christ, for the glory of God—all in the power of the Holy Spirit.

It is a fact that all speech is answering speech. We were all spoken to before we uttered our first words, be they "Mama," "Papa," "Mine!" or "No!" Immersed in a sea of words from birth, over a period of months we learned to babble, vocalize, and finally speak. Preaching, too, is always answering speech, a response to what God has already said in the Bible, the Scriptures of the Christian church. There would be no preaching were it not for the word that first came from God. But though it is a response to the utterances of God, preaching is a different kind of response: it is more an *extension* of that divine utterance, an amplified echo that carries God's word to God's people, rather than an answer directed back toward the One who spoke first. By that token, preaching is crucial speech for the body of Christ: it is speaking for God, based upon the word of God, to bring humankind into relationship

1

with God. In other words, preaching leads the world to follow God. "What could be more full of meaning?—for the pulpit is ever this earth's foremost part; all the rest comes in its rear; the pulpit leads the world. . . . Yes, the world's a ship on its passage out, and not a voyage complete; and the pulpit is its prow."[1] With the pulpit for a prow, humanity is led by preaching into a unique world, an ideal world, *God's* world, where it may dwell with him. That makes preaching a kind of address that has no parallel.

But preaching, after all, is just words, is it not? As Eliza Doolittle lamented:

> Words! Words! Words! I'm so sick of words!
> I get words all day through;
> First from him, now from you!
> Is that all you blighters can do?[2]

Is that all preaching is—just words? And is that all we preachers can do—spout words? One might well ask: Whose words are these words originally (preaching is biblical)? By whom are they to be spoken (preaching is pastoral)? In what context (preaching is ecclesial)? What should these words convey (preaching is communicational)? What are these words intended to do (preaching is applicational)? And why (preaching is conformational)? To what ultimate end (preaching is doxological)? By whose power (preaching is spiritual)?

Before the rest of the book attempts to answer these questions in the form of a vision for preaching, glance with me, your tour guide—through my eyes and with lenses I'm familiar with—at how preaching has been conceived at key points in the history of the church.

Preaching through the Ages

From the very early days in the life of the people of God, preaching took the form of a commentary on the sacred text of Scripture. In the mid-fifth century BCE, Ezra's reading of the law, and the Levites' explanation thereof, demonstrates this "preaching" activity.[3]

1. Herman Melville, *Moby-Dick, or The White Whale* (Boston: The St. Botolph Society, 1890), 42.

2. Alan Jay Lerner and Frederick Lowe, *My Fair Lady: A Musical Play in Two Acts Based on Pygmalion by Bernard Shaw* (New York: Coward-McCann, 1956), 146.

3. The description of this momentous event will be considered further in the chapters of this work. Even before Ezra, in the days of Jehoshaphat, king of Judah in the ninth century BCE, the Levites "went to all the cities of Judah, teaching the people" from "the book of the law of Yahweh" (2 Chron. 17:9).

> So Ezra the priest brought the law before the assembly of men, and even women and
> all who could listen with understanding, on the first day of the seventh month. . . .
> And they [the Levites] read from the book, from the law of God, clarifying to give
> the sense so that they [the people] understood the reading. (Neh. 8:2, 8)

Jesus himself adopted that same pattern of reading the text and expounding
it (Luke 4:16–21), as did the New Testament church (Acts 2:42; 13:14–15;
20:7, 11). And, in the millennia that followed, the church has continued to
adhere to Jesus's command that his ideas be spread "to the end of the age"
through preaching:

> Therefore go, make disciples of all nations, baptizing them in the name of the Father
> and the Son and the Holy Spirit, teaching them to obey all that I commanded you.
> And, behold, I Myself am with you always, to the end of the age. (Matt. 28:19–20)

This was "an infinite goal that envisioned enormous, continuing oratorical effort on a world-wide basis," marking a "purposeful corporate
rhetoricality . . . not found in any other community of the ancient world."[4]
Yet for all that, the only major treatise on preaching to appear in the first
millennium of Christianity was *On Christian Doctrine* by Augustine of
Hippo in the late fourth century.[5] Perhaps the reason for this lack of any
formal conception of preaching was that in the early centuries of the church,
soon after the days of firsthand witnesses of Jesus Christ, biblical exposition focused, for the most part, on discriminating between orthodoxy
and heresy; it was mostly apologetic and informational in function. For
instance, Irenaeus, one of several Christian apologists in the second century,
right after reciting a creed, asserted the following about the importance of
preaching right doctrine:

The Church, having received this preaching and this faith [the creed], although
scattered throughout the whole world, yet, as if occupying but one house, carefully preserves it. She also believes these points [of doctrine] just as if she had
but one soul, and one and the same heart, and she preaches them, and teaches
them, and hands them down, as if she possessed only one mouth. . . . As the
sun, that creature of God, is one and the same throughout the whole world, so

---

4. James J. Murphy, *Rhetoric in the Middle Ages: A History of Rhetorical Theory from St.
Augustine to the Renaissance* (Berkeley: University of California Press, 1974), 273, 274.
5. Though it is less focused on preaching, one might add the sixth-century work *The Pastoral Rule* by the Latin church father Gregory the Great; his concern is more with the life of
the preacher and the diversity of audiences. Another is *The Training of the Clergy* by Rabanus
Maurus, a German Benedictine in the ninth century, consisting mostly of passages culled from
Augustine and Gregory.

also the preaching of the truth shines everywhere, and enlightens all men that
are willing to come to a knowledge of the truth. Nor will any one of the rulers
in the Churches, however highly gifted he may be in eloquence, teach doctrines
different from these.[6]

Of course, the decline of the Roman Empire and the beginning of the Dark
Ages in the fourth and fifth centuries did not help the cause of preaching
scholarship; in those days there seems to have been little time for theoriz-
ing about preaching. Even the lone standout, Augustine's treatise (published
partly in 397 and partly in 426), focused for the most part on defending the
adoption of the pagan art of rhetoric into preaching.[7]

Now, the art of rhetoric being available for the persuasion either of truth or
falsehood, who will dare to say that truth in the person of its defenders is to
take its stand unarmed against falsehood? . . . Since, then, the faculty of eloquence is available for both sides, and serves much to persuade either of wrong
or right, why do not good men engage in its study for the cause of truth, when
bad men use it to obtain the triumph of wrong and worthless causes, and to
further iniquity and error?[8]

Later, Thomas of Chobham, a dean of Salisbury Cathedral in the thirteenth
century, also affirmed that "the doctrine of the orator is very necessary for the
office of a preacher."[9] Around the same time, the twelfth-century Cistercian
monk Alan of Lille taught that "preaching is the plain and public instruction
in morals and faith, serving the information of mankind, proceeding by the
path of reason and issuing from the fountainhead of authorities."[10] Thus, the
influence of rhetoric continued to grow, but the style of preaching remained
topical and doctrinal, dealing with felt needs of the hour and serving to uphold
dogma as prescribed by the authorities of the church.

Things began to get fuzzy as the Middle Ages progressed: exegesis became
rather esoteric, with multiple senses of Scripture being expounded. The Benedictine abbot of Nogent, Guibert (1053–1124), famously gave the example of
the fourfold meaning of the word *Jerusalem*:

6. *Against Heresies* 1.10.2, in *The Ante-Nicene Fathers*, ed. Alexander Roberts and James
Donaldson (1885–1887; repr., Peabody, MA: Hendrickson, 1994), 1:331 (hereafter *ANF*).

7. See Murphy, *Rhetoric in the Middle Ages*, 286–92.

8. *On Christian Doctrine* 4.2.3.

9. *Summa de arte praedicandi* ("Essence of the Art of Preaching"), Corpus Christianorum:
Continuatio Mediaevalis 82, ed. Franco Morenzoni (Turnhout, Belgium: Brepols, 1988), 262
(lines 78–79; my translation).

10. *De arte praedicatoria* ("On the Art of the Preacher"), Patrologia Latina 210, ed. J.-P.
Migne (Paris, 1855), column 111 (my translation).

Historically, it represents a specific city; in allegory it represents the holy Church; tropologically, or morally, it is the soul of every faithful man who longs for the vision of eternal peace; and anagogically it refers to the life of the heavenly citizens, who already see the God of Gods, revealed in all His glory in Sion.[11]

Historian of preaching Hughes Oliphant Old explains this lack of clarity in the Middle Ages:

Medieval preachers tried very hard to take their exegesis seriously, but they faced formidable problems. By the year 500 Jesus and his disciples had become figures of long ago and far away. . . . With the fall of the Roman Empire and the barbarian invasions, the New Testament—and in fact the whole Bible—was becoming very difficult to understand. It more and more became a book of mysteries that could only be solved by mystical contemplation. . . . The language barrier also contributed to the difficulty in understanding the Scriptures. How can one do grammatical-historical exegesis when almost no one west of the Adriatic Sea could read Greek, let alone Hebrew? True expository preaching was almost impossible. No wonder the conscientious preacher found allegorical exegesis attractive.[12]

But then came the Reformation in the sixteenth century, and the Bible was once again brought to light, translated into the vernacular from Hebrew and Greek (and Latin), printed for mass distribution, and preached regularly. The emphasis in sermons of this period was necessarily on soteriological truths. This focus on Christ and redemption, after centuries of confusion as to what it took for sins to be forgiven and salvation to be gained, was epochal. No wonder Martin Luther was inclined to see Christ everywhere in Scripture: "[Christ] is the man to whom it [Scripture] all applies, every bit of it."[13] Such a monopolizing focus tended to make sermons largely evangelistic or a recitation of salvation benefits. "[The] concern that every Christian sermon expound its text in relation to Christ and his saving work is solidly rooted in the Reformation and the Protestant heritage that is its legacy."[14] The Reformation's christocentric impact upon homiletics continues to this day.[15]

11. Guibert de Nogent, *A Book about the Way a Sermon Ought to be Given*, in *Readings in Medieval Rhetoric*, ed. Joseph M. Miller, Michael H. Prosser, and Thomas W. Benson (Bloomington: Indiana University Press, 1973), 171.

12. Hughes Oliphant Old, *The Medieval Church*, vol. 3 of *The Reading and Preaching of the Scriptures in the Worship of the Christian Church* (Grand Rapids: Eerdmans, 1999), xv–xvi.

13. "Prefaces to the Old Testament," in *Word and Sacrament I*, vol. 35 of *Luther's Works*, trans. Charles M. Jacobs, rev. E. Theodore Bachmann (Philadelphia: Muhlenberg, 1960), 247.

14. Dennis E. Johnson, *Him We Proclaim: Preaching Christ from All the Scriptures* (Phillipsburg, NJ: P&R, 2007), 49n49 (italics removed).

15. In a later chapter, "Preaching Is Conformational," I will describe an alternative way to make sermons christological. Also see Abraham Kuruvilla, *Privilege the Text! A Theological Hermeneutic for Preaching* (Chicago: Moody, 2013), 238–68.

It is obvious that preachers and scholars of preaching are children of their own ages. Circumstances and the need of the hour determine, to a great extent, the shape of preaching in any era. In the history of the church, there have been many and varied ideas of what preaching is and should be, each emphasizing one facet of this activity or another, some of which I have highlighted here. But an integrated vision that addresses the essentials of this most important activity in the church has been lacking, and that is what this work hopes to provide. In addition, there has been a glaring lacuna in preaching theories over the years: the understanding of how a particular text chosen for preaching dictates specific life change in the lives of Christians. While application was no doubt considered to be important throughout church history (see "Preaching Is Applicational"), guidance as to how to attend to the details and specificities of a particular passage of Scripture, how to discern its theological thrust, and how to discover its specific demand for concrete life change has been unavailable to the preacher. This book, providing an integrated vision for preaching, will thereby also suggest a means to plug that gap in preaching theory.[16]

The Lacuna in Preaching

Through the two millennia of the church age, there has been a striking deficit in conceptions of preaching: a lack of clarity about how to derive valid application for a modern audience from a specific passage in the ancient text. A robust hermeneutic for making this move from text to audience, which places preaching and application within the larger scheme of the spiritual formation and discipleship of God's people, has been sorely wanting. Despite the recognition that "the highest service that men attain on earth is to preach God's word,"[17] this complex—and critical—issue of how the preacher moves from text to sermon has not been explicated; throughout church history it has remained something of a black box. David Buttrick writes:

> Many books have been written on "biblical preaching"; specifically on how preachers can move step by step from the Bible passage to a sermon. . . . But in all such books there seems to be a gap. There's something left out in between. The crucial moment between exegesis and homiletical vision is not described. The shift between the study of a text and the conception of a sermon—perhaps

16. Of course, I too am a child of my times. Conceivably, there will be more holes to be filled in the field of preaching.
17. John Wycliffe (1329–84), "On the Seven Deadly Sins," in *Miscellaneous Works*, vol. 3 of *Select English Works of John Wyclif*, ed. Thomas Arnold (Oxford: Clarendon, 1871), 143.

it occurs in a flash of imagination—is never discussed. So alert readers are left with the odd impression that we move from the Bible to a contemporary sermon by some inexplicable magic![18]

Stanley Porter concurs: "The move from the original text of Scripture, with all of its time-bound character, to theological truths for life today is one of the most demanding intellectual tasks imaginable"—an uphill struggle faced by preachers every time they take to the pulpit.[19] Thomas Long expresses the angst of the preacher incisively:

> Conscientious biblical preachers have long shared the little secret that the classi-cal text-to-sermon exegetical methods produce far more chaff than wheat. If one has the time and patience to stay at the chores of exegesis, theoretically one can find out a great deal of background information about virtually every passage in the Bible, much of it unfortunately quite remote from any conceivable use in a sermon. The preacher's desk can quickly be covered with Ugaritic parallels and details about syncretistic religion in the Phrygian region of Asia Minor. It is hard to find fault here; every scrap of data is potentially valuable, and it is impossible to know in advance which piece of information is to be prized. So, we brace ourselves for the next round of exegesis by saying that it is necessary to pan a lot of earth to find a little gold, and that is true, of course. However, preachers have the nagging suspicion that there is a good deal of wasted energy in the traditional model of exegesis or, worse, that the real business of exegesis is excavation and earth-moving and that any homiletical gold stumbled over along the way is largely coincidental.[20]

This I call the hermeneutic of excavation—the exegetical turning over of tons of earth, debris, rock, boulders, and gravel: a style of interpretation that yields an overload of biblical and Bible-related information, most of it unfortunately not of any particular use for one seeking to preach a relevant message from a specific text. And so, at this frustrating juncture in sermon preparation, one of two things happens: alchemy or distillation.[21]

In the first scenario, the preacher, deprecating the apparent lack of any gold in the Bible, gives up. After all, what relevance is there in the morass

---

18. David Buttrick, *A Captive Voice: The Liberation of Preaching* (Louisville: Westminster John Knox, 1994), 89.

19. Stanley E. Porter, "Hermeneutics, Biblical Interpretation, and Theology: Hunch, Holy Spirit, or Hard Work?," in I. Howard Marshall, *Beyond the Bible: Moving from Scripture to Theology* (Grand Rapids: Baker Academic, 2004), 121.

20. Thomas G. Long, "The Use of Scripture in Contemporary Preaching," *Interpretation* 44 (1990): 343–44.

21. The two scenarios are, no doubt, exaggerations, but they enable me to make a point.

of historical, geographical, and linguistic detail for living life come Monday morning? So the enlightened and modern preacher, the alchemist, turns away from an outdated and seemingly irrelevant book—"a shift away from the canons of classical 'sacred rhetoric' and a move toward psychology and personalism."[22] The only recourse now for the preacher is to preach something that is more emotionally and existentially relevant to the congregation but only tangentially connected to a biblical text. Often the driving force of such sermons is a felt need scavenged from yesterday's newspaper or today's blog, boosted by the latest in media and technology, and bolstered by a smooth delivery with glib humor and pathos that sustains the rapt attention of listeners. After all, the Bible itself has nothing much to say about real life, such preachers conclude. Therefore they transact some sort of alchemy, transmuting the base metal of the remote and rambling text into the noble metal of an entertaining and moving sermon, though the biblical "lead" and sermonic "gold" really have nothing to do with each other: alchemy!

In the second scenario, the preacher, still trying vainly to locate gold in Scripture, performs a distillation of the text into propositions of the sermon that are preached in formulaic fashion, with outlines, points, proofs, and arguments, and with application drawn seemingly at random somewhere along the way. This reflects the tendency toward a sort of eliminative reductionism that breaks things down to their constitutive parts, and these elementary parts—usually bits and bytes of systematic theology—are taken to be more real and more valuable than the whole.[23] Thus, the dross of texts is distilled off to leave behind the precious residue of theological propositions that is then preached. Or, as Fred Craddock puts it, "The minister boils off all the water and then preaches the stain in the bottom of the cup."[24] Such propositions end

---

22. Thomas G. Long, "A New Focus for Teaching Preaching," in *Teaching Preaching as a Christian Practice: A New Approach to Homiletical Pedagogy*, ed. Thomas G. Long and Leonora Tubbs Tisdale (Louisville: Westminster John Knox, 2008), 8.

23. Michael S. Hogue, *The Promise of Religious Naturalism* (Lanham, MD: Rowman and Littlefield, 2010), 213.

24. Fred B. Craddock, *Preaching* (Nashville: Abingdon, 1985), 123. It was perhaps Haddon W. Robinson, whose book *Biblical Preaching* has chaperoned generations of preachers through the field of homiletics since its first publication in 1980, who popularized the use of propositions in preaching in modern times. See *Biblical Preaching: The Development and Delivery of Expository Messages*, 3rd ed. (Grand Rapids: Baker Academic, 2014), 5, 20, 21. Walter C. Kaiser calls for "principlizing the text paragraph by paragraph into timeless *propositions* which call for an immediate response from our listeners." See *Toward an Exegetical Theology: Biblical Exegesis for Teaching and Preaching* (Grand Rapids: Baker 1998), 236 (italics added). Such a distilled extract of the text is the "timeless, transcultural theological *proposition*" that is to be preached (Timothy S. Warren, "The Theological Process in Sermon Preparation," *Bibliotheca sacra* 156 [1999]: 342 [italics added]). Also see Ramesh Richard,

up having a self-contained existence independent of the text and denuded of all its specificity—the gold without the impurity, the kernel without the husk, the candy without the wrapper: distillation! Neither alchemy nor distillation does justice to the text or respects its intricacies and specificities.[25]

Notwithstanding the alchemical and distillatory tendencies of this generation, it is in our current era that the Holy Spirit shows up for the first time in a formal definition of preaching: Haddon Robinson speaks of a proposition derived from the text that "the Holy Spirit first applies to the personality and experience of the preacher, then through him to his hearers."[26] And thus, with this particular attention given to the life-changing work of the Spirit, the practical sanctification phase of Christian life returns to the core of biblical preaching: the gradual transformation of the people of God into the image of Christ.[27] Of course, what kind of life change is called for in the text and how one may discern it from a particular passage, has never been elucidated: the black box continues to work by some "inexplicable magic."

In the vision for preaching propounded here, I seek to address this lacuna by borrowing from the fields of language philosophy that study how language works and what authors do. These areas of scholarship have, in the last few decades, borne much fruit for the understanding of communication, including communication that is textual. With the confluence of these latter developments, I believe a renewed focus on preaching will be profitable, particularly the scrutiny of the theological role of the specific portion of Scripture chosen for a given sermon, and an examination of what *that* text has to say about the transformation of the lives of God's people for God's glory.

Preparing Expository Sermons: A Seven-Step Method for Biblical Preaching (Grand Rapids: Baker Books, 2001), 19, for the same notion.

25. This book will propose an alternative to both these approaches and show that one has neither to transmute the biblical text into something entirely new (alchemy) nor to reduce it into a propositional entity (distillation). See the chapters "Preaching Is Communicational," "Preaching Is Theological," and "Preaching Is Applicational."

26. Robinson, *Biblical Preaching*, 5.

27. See Tony Merida, *Faithful Preaching: Declaring Scripture with Responsibility, Passion, and Authenticity* (Nashville: Broadman and Holman, 2009), 10. See also Richard, *Preparing Expository Sermons*, 19, for his goals of preaching: "to inform minds, instruct hearts, and influence behavior towards godliness." Nevertheless, other contemporary definitions of preaching are less than clear. Many continue to focus exclusively on information and hardly touch on transformation. For example: "Expository preaching is essentially the practice of explaining the meaning of a passage of Scripture" (Graeme Goldsworthy, *Preaching the Whole Bible as Christian Scripture* [Grand Rapids: Eerdmans, 2000], 120); and, "I assert that expository preaching is really exegetical preaching and not so much the homiletical form of the message" (John F. MacArthur Jr., "The Mandate of Biblical Inerrancy: Expository Preaching," *The Master's Seminary Journal* 1 [1990]: 12).

Vision for Preaching

This book seeks to portray what preaching is in an ideal sense and what the characteristics of this unique form of address are. Here is my vision for preaching, in one sentence, individual elements of which will be unpacked chapter by chapter in the pages that follow.[28]

Vision for Preaching	Chapter
Biblical preaching,	1. *Preaching Is Biblical*
by a leader of the church,	2. *Preaching Is Pastoral*
in a gathering of Christians for worship,	3. *Preaching Is Ecclesial*
is the communication of the thrust of a pericope of Scripture	4. *Preaching Is Communicational*
discerned by theological exegesis,	5. *Preaching Is Theological*
and of its application to that specific body of believers,	6. *Preaching Is Applicational*
that they may be conformed to the image of Christ,	7. *Preaching Is Conformational*
for the glory of God	8. *Preaching Is Doxological*
—all in the power of the Holy Spirit.	9. *Preaching Is Spiritual*

I have deliberately refrained from calling this recital a "definition," preferring to label it a "vision." A definition is far too categorical for what I am attempting in this work. My goal is not to provide a precisely demarcated boundary within which is preaching and without which is everything that is not. Rather, I seek to articulate this vision as a target toward which all of us preachers—novices and experts and everyone in between—can work.[29] In other words, this vision is not the prescription of a precise destination with GPS coordinates telling you that you're either there or you aren't. Rather it is more of a road to travel, a direction to take, a momentum to develop. The

---

28. Each chapter tackles a facet of this vision for preaching, validating each element's inclusion in the vision, addressing its implications for preaching today, and exhorting preachers to align their preaching with the call of that particular facet of the vision. A "Reflection" section in each chapter, based upon a portion of the Gospel of Mark, deals with a related theme of the chapter—but with a twist—geared to stimulate thought; these studies from Mark also serve to illustrate the hermeneutic proposed in this work. Also provided in the "Reflection" sections are some ideas and questions for pondering, for further exploration, for prayer, and for the preacher's development. Each chapter may therefore be employed either for personal contemplation or for group discussion in a fellowship of students, ministers, or pastors. Greek and Hebrew terms are used minimally in this work; when employed, they are both translated and transliterated.

29. For the same reason, I have purposely retained the vagueness of some terms in the preaching vision: "gathering" (how many make a gathering and how often should they gather?), "worship" (what constitutes worship?), "leader" (what office of the church does a leader occupy?), etc.

vision is thus an ideal that preachers (and churches) can aim for. If this book helps them advance toward that goal, the intent of this work will have been accomplished.

Such an approach concedes that a spectrum of activities may be labeled "preaching": pastoral preaching during a worship service, guest preaching, preaching at a Bible conference, preaching in a seminary chapel, preaching at a gathering of men (or women, or young adults), and so on. The difference between these activities is one of degree: the extent to which each approximates the vision in being biblical, pastoral, ecclesial, communicational, theological, applicational, conformational, doxological, and spiritual. Of course, it is impossible to provide a metric by which a sermon may be gauged as to *how* biblical, *how* pastoral, *how* ecclesial, or *how* communicational (and so on) it is, and so I won't. This vision for preaching simply exhorts that a sermon be biblical, pastoral, ecclesial, communicational, theological, applicational, conformational, doxological, and spiritual, without dogmatically quantifying each of these facets. That is like providing a vision for parenting that comprises a number of essential elements: love, discipline, protection, nourishment, clothing, education, exercise, fellowship, and so on. Clearly, a variety of models can accomplish each of these elements to varying (and unquantifiable) degrees: parenting in a nuclear family, parenting by separated parents, parenting by a single parent, parenting by adoptive parents, or parenting in a foster family, to name a few. A vision for parenting may therefore simply be an encouragement that parenting be loving, disciplinary, protective, nourishing, and so on. So also with this vision of preaching. It is an encouragement to preachers to keep traveling toward a broadly outlined goal ("vision") rather than to arrive at some precisely pinpointed destination ("definition").

In a sense, then, the vision propounded here is almost a manifesto—a declaration of principles and intentions (i.e., this author's stance on what preaching should tend toward).[30] But rather than it being solely my individualistic and idiosyncratic conception, this vision has sought to integrate the work of many who have faithfully plowed the field of homiletics in ages past. As I stand on the broad and powerful shoulders of those who have gone on before, I have attempted to rearticulate what has been expressed earlier,

---

30. A Protestant evangelical bias will, no doubt, be discernible in this vision of preaching, reflecting my own reading and interpretive practices with regard to Scripture and my concept of and personal engagement with the local and universal church. This perspective, however, does not invalidate my attempt to provide an account of what preaching is all about. A perspectival description is not necessarily rendered unviable or inaccurate simply because it comes from a particular viewpoint. Hopefully the acknowledgment of my particular frame of reference will make these observations complementary to those of others from a variety of traditions.

rediscover what has been forgotten, and resurface what has been lost sight of, by mining church history, teasing out connections, and sifting through biblical theology.[31] In addition, I have reconnoitered some new terrain, particularly the domain of language philosophy, to shed light on how valid application may be derived from a particular passage of Scripture. It is hoped that an integration of all these—elements old and new, observations historical and exploratory, findings theological and secular—into a summative vision for preaching will help sustain and further the role of this preeminent form of public address in the life of the church.

More proximally, my aim is to give future pastors—those who are training to go out into the front end of the battle arena to pastor—a better conception of what it means to preach, a heightened sense of the divinely granted privilege of preaching, and a greater excitement for the preaching ministry. In these days when preachers have to compete with the latest in technology and the ultimate in media, when they have to contend with the trends and fads of culture and the apathy and inattention of a new generation, a fresh look at preaching, the heart of pastoral ministry, is essential. And for those already in the trenches preaching regularly, the ideas in this work hopefully will serve as an encouragement to persist and a goal to strive for as you earnestly and faithfully discharge the responsibility of your divine appointments to proclaim the word of God to the people of God.

I offer this work as a big-picture depiction of the preaching task, to show how it fits in with the rest of pastoral ministry; how it is consistent with biblical and systematic theology; how it incorporates aspects of communication theory, rhetoric, and language philosophy; and how it plays a key role in the spiritual formation of God's people, through Scripture and by the agency of the Holy Spirit, all for the furtherance of Christ's kingdom and the exaltation of God's name.

---

31. The wide range of sources and ideas throughout this work reflects considerable consensus in Christendom, both historical and contemporary, regarding the various concepts of preaching that are discussed here.

1

Preaching Is Biblical

The sum of Your word is truth,
And all Your righteous ordinances are everlasting.
                                        Psalm 119:160

Biblical preaching, by a leader of the church, in a gathering of
Christians for worship, is the communication of the thrust of a
pericope of Scripture discerned by theological exegesis, and of its
application to that specific body of believers, that they may be
conformed to the image of Christ, for the glory of God—all in
the power of the Holy Spirit.

As millions watched on television on January 28, 1986, seventy-three
seconds after liftoff, the mission of space shuttle *Challenger* ended
in a fiery disaster resulting in the death of all seven crew members.
In response, both a congressional house committee and a presidential commission were charged with investigating the catastrophe. Apparently an O-
ring manufactured by Morton Thiokol was at fault. In a statement to the
investigating House Committee on Science and Technology, Charles S. Locke,
chairman and CEO of Morton Thiokol, said:

With the benefit of hindsight, it is clear that some decisions made the evening of January 27 were wrong—that mistakes were made. Our space program experts, confronted with reports that the weather would be substantially colder than for any previous launch, reviewed the available data and initially concluded that a launch should not occur at an O-ring temperature lower than 53 degrees Fahrenheit, the lowest previous launch temperature.[1]

The day of the launch, temperatures were as low as 16°F at Kennedy Space Center in Florida, but NASA officials overrode the objections of Thiokol engineers. During a televised hearing of the Presidential Commission, member and Nobel Prize–winning physicist Richard Feynman stunningly demonstrated that O-rings lost resilience at cold temperatures by immersing one in a Styrofoam cup of ice water. In a memorable understatement, he declared, "I believe that has some significance for our problem."[2] And how!

One disregards manufacturers' instructions at one's own peril. This is why preaching has always sought to be biblical, from the word of God, the Scriptures of the community of God. For therein is the word of the Creator to his creation. Neglecting his directives can have calamitous consequences. Christian preaching over the millennia has therefore consistently been based on the Scriptures of the church: preaching is biblical. "The most notable characteristic of the Christian homily, not only theologically but also rhetorically, is its dependence on the biblical text."[3] The community of God's people holds that this divine discourse that comprises the Christian canon is to be preached as normative for the faith and practice of Christians. In fact, the Bible itself demands to be read this way. In the Old Testament, Joshua declares:

> This Book of the Law shall not depart from your mouth, and you shall meditate on it day and night, so that you may give heed to do according to all that is written in it; for then you will make your way prosperous, and then you will be successful. (Josh. 1:8)

1. "Statement of Charles S. Locke, Chairman and Chief Executive Officer, Morton Thiokol, Inc., Before the Science and Technology Committee, United States House of Representatives (June 17, 1986)," in *Investigation of the Challenger Accident (Volume 1, Part 2): Hearings before the Committee on Science and Technology, House of Representatives, Ninety-Ninth Congress, Second Session (June 10, 11, 12, 17, 18, 25, 1986)* (Washington, DC: Committee on Science and Technology, 1986), 331.

2. Richard P. Feynman, "Testimony of Lawrence B. Mulloy, Project Manager, Solid Rocket Boosters, Marshall Space Flight Center, NASA," in *Report to the President, by the Presidential Commission on the Space Shuttle Challenger Accident, June 6th, 1986, Washington, DC, Volume 4: February 11, 1986 Session,* 679. Available at http://history.nasa.gov/rogersrep/genindex.htm.

3. Jaroslav Pelikan, *Divine Rhetoric: The Sermon on the Mount as Message and as Model in Augustine, Chrysostom and Luther* (Crestwood, NY: St. Vladimir's Seminary Press, 2001), 32.

And in the New Testament, Jesus asserts (citing Deut. 8:3):

> It is written, "Man shall not live by bread alone, but by every word that comes from the mouth of God." (Matt. 4:4)

Why is the Bible so special? What are the unique qualities of this canonical text of the church? After all, all kinds of books exist, as Hugh of St. Victor noted a long time ago (in the eleventh century):

> There are books and books. . . . The books that men write are made of the skins of dead animals or some other corruptible material and, as these last for only a short time, the books themselves grow old and in their own way are reduced to nothing, leaving no vestige of themselves behind. And all who read these books will die some day, and there is no one to be found who lives forever. These, therefore, being made of dead things by mortal beings who are going to die, cannot bestow enduring life on those who read and love them. They are certainly not worthy to be called books of life, but would be termed more fitly books of death, or of the dead or dying.[4]

A couple of millennia before Hugh, a biblical sage warned that "the making of books has no end" (Eccles. 12:12). And not all of those innumerable tomes are worthy of being read. Google has estimated that, as of August 2010, a total of 129,864,880 unique books have been published throughout history.[5] However, only a fraction of these have survived the attrition of time. Even from among these hardy survivors, there are those that stand out—the "classics," works judged over a period of time to be outstanding in quality with recognized and established value for the conceivable future.

The Classic Nature of the Bible

Classics, scholars say, possess philosophical quality and original content, they influence events, they are the foremost examples of a certain category of thought, and they bear extended relevance far beyond the dates of their

4. In Hugh of St. Victor, *Selected Spiritual Writings* (New York: Harper and Row, 1962), 88.

5. See Leonid Taycher, "Books of the World, Stand Up and Be Counted! All 129,864,880 of You," *Google Books Search* (blog), August 5, 2010, http://booksearch.blogspot.com/2010/08/books-of-world-stand-up-and-be-counted.html. Also see reports from the Electronic Frontier Foundation, especially Fred von Lohmann, "Google Book Search Settlement: Updating the Numbers, Part 2," February 23, 2010, https://www.eff.org/deeplinks/2010/02/google-book-search-settlement-updating-numbers-0.

publication.[6] The Bible succeeds in meeting every one of these criteria. However, the peculiar features of this sacred work surpass the qualities of any other classic, whether it be Plato or Shakespeare. What makes this biblical classic unique and particularly pertinent for Christian preaching is that it is abiding, weighty, and binding.

The Bible Is Abiding

For any text, its content is usually consumed at an event of reading subsequent to the event of its writing. However, information conveyed by a text is not necessarily relevant to a readership far away in time and space. That would be like reading a local newspaper from another city, a decade after its publication. In other words, the "literature of knowledge," which merely conveys information, usually becomes outdated in direct proportion to the distance in time and space between the event of writing and event of reading. Ancient texts are therefore less relevant to the modern-day reader. Likewise, today's grocery lists, bank statements, inane blog posts, Twitter feeds, emails, and a whole host of other published works that have only parochial concerns, provincial consequences, and personal value will never interest anyone but the odd historian in a few years. Pure information rarely transcends time and space to provide direction for future application and behavior. Such informational texts (literature of knowledge) merely tell us how things *were* or *are*, not necessarily how things *can* or *should be*. On the other hand, the "literature of power" never grows outdated.[7] Texts in this category (i.e., the classics) retain the power to say something relevant across the span of ages, making recommendations for *all* time: they have abiding value. Such abiding texts that possess value for the future—advocating for how things *can* or *should be*—are rightly labeled "classics," specimens of the literature of power.

Authors of classics are usually conscious of the future-directedness of their work and typically intend their meanings to go beyond what is attended to at the moment and place of writing. The effects of such classic texts are therefore boundlessly extended in time and space into the "always" and the "everywhere": they are abiding—perennial in relevance. Psalm 102:18 explicitly marks Scripture as being recorded for all time: "Let this be written for a generation to come." Thus this abiding quality, an inherent property of classics, characterizes the Bible as well. This book has amply proven its abiding nature over the millennia, for it has been preached gainfully to every

6. Michael Levin, "What Makes a Classic in Political Theory?," *Political Science Quarterly* 88 (1973): 463.

7. E. D. Hirsch, "Past Intentions and Present Meanings," *Essays in Criticism* 33 (1983): 88.

generation of God's people, and its profit has accrued to many, even those situated far from the original event and location of writing.[8] Things written over a thousand years before the time of Paul's readers remained relevant to them, as they still are to current readers.

> For whatever was written in former times was written for our instruction. (Rom. 15:4; see also 1 Cor. 10:11)

That the Bible is an abiding classic is not just an a priori assumption. Rather, it demonstrates itself to be abiding—relevant and material in every new generation, addressing every age and era with immediacy and urgency. This is not to say that the Bible is outside the boundary of time, but that it is inside the perimeter of *all* time: the Bible is abiding.[9]

> Forever, Yahweh, is Your word;
> It is established in heaven.
>   Ps. 119:89

Why is Scripture so abiding? The reason for its endurance is its unique *weightiness*: it concerns matters of critical importance to humankind in every era and thus remains vital and potent across the span of time.

The Bible Is Weighty

Dealing as it does with matters concerning its main character, God, and his relationship to humankind, the Bible addresses issues of immense significance, both temporal and eternal. It is weighty—substantial in content. It provides direction for entering into a relationship with God (Heb. 2:3; 2 Tim. 3:15), and it guides the maintenance of this relationship with the Creator as it gives the child of God "training in righteousness." Only in the Scriptures can one discover how to be "complete, equipped for every good work"—weighty matters, indeed.

> All Scripture is God-inspired and profitable for teaching, for reproof, for correction, for training in righteousness; that the man of God may be complete, equipped for every good work. (2 Tim. 3:16–17)

8. See, e.g., 1 Pet. 1:25 (Isa. 50:8). Though dealing specifically with Jesus's own words, Matt. 24:35 (Mark 13:31; Luke 21:33) echoes the same sentiments about the divine word—its abiding quality. How the Bible's guidance for the future—i.e., God's direction for how things *can* or *should be*—may be discerned for preaching will be dealt with in "Preaching Is Theological."

9. See Hans-Georg Gadamer, *Truth and Method*, 2nd rev. ed., trans. Joel Weinsheimer and Donald G. Marshall (London: Continuum, 2004), 288, 290.

Therefore, Athanasius of Alexandria, in the fourth century CE, could declare:

> They who thirst may be satisfied with the living words they [the Scriptures] contain. In these alone is proclaimed the doctrine of godliness. Let no man add to these, neither let him take aught from these.[10]

No wonder Paul concludes his description of inspired Scripture by giving Timothy a sacred commission: "preach the word" at all times (2 Tim. 4:1–2). The sort of discourse found in the Bible, the philosopher Paul Ricoeur wagered, is worthy of study "because something is said that is not said by other kinds of discourse."[11] The Bible is uniquely weighty, and because of the gravity of its content—God and his relationship with humans—it has supreme priority for the life of the Christian. Preaching, therefore, is necessarily biblical.

The reverence and respect that God's people have accorded Scripture, and the resulting responsibility with which its preaching has been undertaken over the centuries, testify to the weightiness of the Bible. The proliferation of interpretive works on Scripture—innumerable commentaries, homilies, and tracts—reflects this preeminence. The prodigious output of Origen, an early Christian theologian of the third century CE, for instance, amounted to 6,000 writings, including homilies on almost the entire Bible (over 200 preserved).[12] John Chrysostom, a church father of the late third century, bequeathed over 900 sermons (i.e., those that survive).[13] Equally significant in attesting to the weighty quality of the Bible is the abundance of manuscript copies extant, as well as the plethora of translations and versions of Scripture created in the past and that continue to be produced today. Portions of the New Testament, for instance, are preserved in more ancient manuscripts than is any other ancient writing—around 6,000 in Greek, 10,000 in Latin, and another 10,000 in Armenian, Ethiopic, Coptic, Syriac, and other languages. Ironically, even the myriad controversies over interpretations of Scripture that have dogged the church throughout its existence testify to the weighty content of the Bible. This book and its interpretation mattered enough to be vigorously, sometimes even violently, defended.

---

10. *Festal Letters* 39.6, in *The Nicene and Post-Nicene Fathers*, series 1, ed. Philip Schaff (1886–1889; repr., Peabody, MA: Hendrickson, 1994), 4:552 (hereafter *NPNF*[1]).

11. Paul Ricoeur, "Philosophy and Religious Language," *Journal of Religion* 54 (1974): 71.

12. This is recorded by Epiphanius, a fourth-century bishop in Cyprus, in *Refutation of All Heresies* 64.63.8. Also see Henri Crouzel, *Origen*, trans. A. S. Worrall (Edinburgh: T&T Clark, 1989), 37–39.

13. See Wendy Mayer and Pauline Allen, *John Chrysostom* (London: Routledge, 2000), 7; and J. N. D. Kelly, *Golden Mouth: The Story of John Chrysostom—Ascetic, Preacher, Bishop* (London: Duckworth, 1995), 132–33.

Not just the entire collection as a whole, but individual texts and pericopes that compose Scripture are weighty as well, no portion of it trivial.[14] For instance, in 1 Corinthians 9:9 Paul considers Deuteronomy 25:4, a relatively minor text in the Old Testament, as being significant for the current practice of the community of believers. In fact, it is the weightiness of every part of the Bible that promotes the serviceability of pericopes for preaching. The density of the canonical text, packed as it is with substantial matters, makes it advisable to engage the Scriptures in smaller, bite-sized segments for weekly church use. Hence the use of pericopes.

The Bible is, indeed, a text of great consequence; therefore this abiding and weighty work, in all of its parts, is not to be neglected but rather preached and applied. The substantiality of Scripture mandates a surrender by readers and listeners to the gravity of the text and to the will of God that it expresses—a willingness to align themselves to divine demand. Thus the Bible is not only abiding and weighty, but it is also *binding* for the faith and practice of the church.

The Bible Is Binding

Classics are generally considered prescriptive, to one extent or another. The philosopher Hans-Georg Gadamer declared that "the most important thing about the concept of the classical . . . is the normative sense."[15] But whether that prescription is authoritative enough to demand compliance is another matter. For Scripture, however, the community of God holds that this text is binding in a manner that no other classic ever has been, is, or ever can be, because the Bible is divine discourse. In other words, the binding nature of the Bible is a consequence of its construal as a divine communiqué, making it authoritative for the faith and practice of the church. This divine discourse, the word of God, must therefore be preached as binding upon the people of God, bidding them to hear it and to apply it—it is normative in quality.

To assert that Scripture is binding, then, is to acknowledge it as divine discourse. For most of its history, the church has affirmed that Scripture is God's word. "All Scripture," 2 Timothy 3:16 affirms, "is God-inspired." John 10:35 uses "word of God" in parallel with "Scripture." In Mark 7:9–13 "commandment of God," what "Moses said," and "word of God" are interchangeably

14. Though "pericope" has a technical sense of a demarcated portion of the Gospels, I use the word in this work simply to designate a preaching text, irrespective of genre or length (see "Preaching Is Theological").

15. Gadamer, *Truth and Method*, 288.

employed, attesting to the nature of the Bible as divine discourse—its human authors guided by the divine Author, the Holy Spirit, to produce the word of God (2 Pet. 1:21).[16] The first-century church father Clement of Rome called Scripture "the true utterances of the Holy Spirit" and "the oracles of God."[17] Origen also held "the holy Scriptures to be no human compositions, but to be written by inspiration of the Holy Spirit."[18] Augustine of Hippo expounded on this divine agency working through human authors:

> All that he [God] intended to give for our perusal on the matter of his own doings and sayings, he commanded to be written by those disciples, whom he thus used as if they were his own hands.[19]

The fact that no ancient creed incorporates the idea of inspiration (or inerrancy) is simply because inspiration was an accepted fact and was never challenged in the early church. It was never a controversy to be adjudicated or a heresy to be countered. As Bruce Vawter sums up, "The language of the Fathers both in the East and in the West, as well as their habitual handling of the Scripture, leaves little doubt that for many if not most of them God was . . . the *literary* author of the Bible."[20]

Well beyond the age of the fathers, the church held it to be dogma that Scripture was divine discourse. The Dominican theologian Thomas Aquinas (1225–74) declared that "the author of Holy Scripture is God."[21] During the Reformation era, Luther was explicit: "Thus you are to deal with Scripture: consider it as God himself speaking."[22] It was this notion of Scripture as divine discourse that led the church to construe Scripture as binding.

16. Nicholas Wolterstorff, *Divine Discourse: Philosophical Reflections on the Claim That God Speaks* (Cambridge: Cambridge University Press, 1995), 53. Also see William Lane Craig, "'Men Moved by the Holy Spirit Spoke from God' (2 Peter 1:21): A Middle Knowledge Perspective on Biblical Inspiration," in *Providence, Scripture, and Resurrection*, vol. 2 of *Readings in Philosophical Theology*, ed. Michael Rea (Oxford: Oxford University Press, 2009), 157–91. In this work I will consider Scripture the joint product of both human and divine authors, without differentiating between the two.

17. *1 Clement* 45, 53 (ANF 1:39, 44–45). He also introduced Jer. 9:23 with "the Holy Spirit says" (*1 Clement* 13 [ANF 1:16, 41]). Equally, Paul's writings, Clement claimed, were inspired by the Holy Spirit (*1 Clement* 13, 47).

18. *First Principles* 4.9 (ANF 4:357).

19. *Harmony of the Gospels* 1.35.54 (NPNF[1] 6:101).

20. Bruce Vawter, *Biblical Inspiration* (Louisville: Westminster, 1972), 96.

21. *Summa Theologica* 1.1.10.

22. *Predigten über das erste Buch Mosis und Auslegungen über die folgenden biblischen Bücher bis zu den Psalmen*, vol. 3 of *D. Martin Luthers sämtliche Schriften*, trans. (from the original Latin to German) Johann Georg Walch (St. Louis: Concordia, 1894), 21 (my translation into English).

It is to the canonical Scriptures alone that I am bound to yield such implicit sub-jection as to follow their teaching, without admitting the slightest suspicion that in them any mistake or any statement intended to mislead could find a place.[23]

That it is divine discourse renders the Christian canon binding in a manner unique to itself; no other classic shares that property. Given this binding and prescriptive status of the Bible for believers, preaching is to be, first and foremost, biblical.

Another consequence of the binding nature of the canon, one that is perti-nent to preaching, is the demarcation of what is acceptable as "Scripture" and what is not. In effect, the canon is an ancient form of "copyright" protecting the Bible as a whole from distortion and deformation.[24] And so, for the purposes of preaching, the canon also delineates what texts may be employed for the edification of the church. It confers (and thereby restricts) binding author-ity to these particular texts. Only these may be preached from to bring the corporate life of the community and the lives of the individuals it comprises into alignment with the will of God.[25]

There was a good reason for this limitation of which texts could be included in the canon of Scripture and be preached from. The church in the second century recognized that without a *written* binding norm its station in time was too distant from the apostolic age for it to be able to guard the purity of what had been *orally* handed down. Neither Jesus nor any of the apostles were around at that time for consultation. Besides, all kinds of spurious lit-erature was floating around and being championed as normative for God's people. There needed to be a clear demarcation, a line, a "rule"—which is what κανών (*kanōn*) means: "rule/canon." This principle of canon was an acknowledgment by the community of God's people that thenceforth every act of preaching would be submitted to the control of the authoritative apostolic tradition that was textually fixed within the canon of Scripture.

Not only did the canon establish which texts could be employed in preach-ing but this principle had yet another implication: no one passage of Scripture could be so expounded in preaching "that it be repugnant to another" (article 20 of the Thirty-Nine Articles of Religion [1563], the defining statement of the doctrines of the Church of England). In other words, the bounding of the

23. Augustine, *Epistle to Jerome* 82.3.24 (*NPNF*[1] 1:358).

24. George Aichele, *The Control of Biblical Meaning: Canon as Semiotic Mechanism* (Har-risburg, PA: Trinity, 2001), 20.

25. I am avoiding any debate here about the specific composition of the canon. The faith and practice of a particular Christian tradition will, no doubt, be dependent upon the boundaries of the canon that it submits to.

canon mandates that the interpretation of one biblical text not be inconsistent with that of any other, for they all together make one book of God.[26] In the second century, Irenaeus wisely noted:

> All Scripture, which has been given to us by God, shall be found by us perfectly consistent; . . . and through the many diversified utterances [of Scripture] there shall be heard one harmonious melody in us, praising in hymns that God who created all things.[27]

The canon thus renders the Bible cohesive and congruent in all its parts. This settled and stable body of written texts was deemed binding, and so it became the authoritative norm for regulating preaching in the church.[28] Nothing else would carry as much authority for preaching as would the canon of Scripture.[29] Therefore, nothing else is to be preached but this binding text.

In sum, the canonical classic of Scripture—abiding, weighty, and binding—demands to be preached and applied. One might go so far as to say that a willingness to be subject to the abiding, weighty, and binding claims of Scripture marks a member of God's community. Because the Bible is abiding, weighty, and binding, it is to be preached, for it alone is efficacious for the alignment of individual and community to the will of God: all Scripture is profitable for application, to render God's people complete, competent, and capable for every good work (2 Tim. 3:16–17). The obligation for the preacher is therefore equally serious because the Bible is abiding, weighty, and binding: preaching must be biblical, comprehensively and exclusively.

26. Cyril of Alexandria, a fifth-century church father, declared: "The entire Scripture is one book and was spoken by the one Holy Spirit" (*Commentary on Isaiah*, on 29:11–12 [my translation]).

27. *Against Heresies* 2.28.3 (*ANF* 1:400). So also Irenaeus's contemporary, Justin Martyr: "I am entirely convinced that no Scripture contradicts another" (*Dialogue with Trypho* 65.2, [*ANF* 2:177]). See Abraham Kuruvilla, *Privilege the Text! A Theological Hermeneutic for Preaching* (Chicago: Moody, 2013), 71–76.

28. Oscar Cullman, *The Early Church* (London: SCM, 1956), 90–91.

29. Formal acceptance of the canonical texts of Scripture occurred early in the life of the church; Paul credits the Thessalonians, for instance, with having received his word as the word of God (1 Thess. 2:13). The designation of Luke's Gospel as "Scripture" also acknowledges its canonical reception by the church from early days (and 1 Tim. 5:18 expressly labels Luke's Gospel as such, citing Luke 10:7; also see 2 Pet. 3:15–16). As well, these accepted biblical documents were widely acknowledged to be relevant to the community of God's people. Indeed, the Colossians are asked to have their letter passed on to other Christian assemblies (Col. 4:16). Tertullian, the second-century Christian apologist, could therefore ask rhetorically: "But of what consequence are the titles [of the letters], since in writing to a certain church the apostle did in fact write to all?" (*Against Marcion* 5.17 [*ANF* 3:465]). So also, Rev. 1:3 assumes a wider readership than the seven churches to which John wrote.

Preaching Biblically, Reading Continuously

If preaching is to be biblical, respecting the abiding, weighty, and binding nature of Scripture, then every part of Scripture is valuable and every text of Scripture must be preached from. How can one begin to accomplish this?

While most of the evidence about the liturgical practices of the synagogue comes from the second century CE onward, it is clear that quite early on, the pattern of communal utilization of Scripture in measured doses came to be directed by Jewish lectionaries that prescribed which passages of the Bible were to be read and preached on, on a given day. Appropriately divided sections of the text (pericopes) were read in continuous fashion (*lectio continua*, "reading continuously") from week to week, each subsequent reading taking up from where the previous one had left off. This was the oldest approach to the exposition of Scripture, and it was the standard practice on nonfestival Sabbaths in Jewish synagogues.[30] In all likelihood, this protocol of continual reading was bequeathed to the church; this sequential assimilation of Scripture, *lectio continua*, appears to have been the norm for most of early church history.

By the time of the fifth century, however, the proliferation of feasts and special days in the church calendar and the allotment of specific biblical texts for each of those days rendered readings almost entirely *lectio selecta* ("reading selectively"): the textual assignments for these occasions were based upon the significance of the particular saint or that special day being celebrated. Such selections of the biblical text were rarely contiguous, and thus *lectio continua* fell into disuse. Soon the complexity of the festal calendar required that texts allocated for particular occasions be listed formally, and so Christian lectionaries configured for this purpose came into existence.[31] Unlike for most of church history, the Middle Ages therefore suffered a dearth of *lectio continua* sermons. It was not until the Reformers that this practice returned to popularity in churches. Luther advised: "One of the books should be selected and one or two chapters, or half a chapter, be read, until the book is finished.

---

30. The Babylonian Talmud tractate *Megillah* 4 refers to interruptions from the "regular order" of reading for festival/special days and returning to the set pattern afterward. This rabbinical writing also points to "the people of Palestine, who complete the reading of the Pentateuch in three years"—*lectio continua* in action. As quoted in Jacob Neusner, *The Comparative Hermeneutics of Rabbinic Judaism*, vol. 1, *Introduction and the Hermeneutics of Berakhot and Seder Mo'ed* (Binghamton, NY: Academic Studies in the History of Judaism, 2000), 544. Skipping passages of the Torah was looked upon with disfavor.

31. See Hughes Oliphant Old, *The Medieval Church*, vol. 3 of *The Reading and Preaching of the Scriptures in the Worship of the Christian Church* (Grand Rapids: Eerdmans, 1999), 85, 289; and John Reumann, "A History of Lectionaries: From the Synagogue at Nazareth to Post–Vatican II," *Interpretation* 31 (1977): 124.

After that another book should be selected, and so on, until the entire Bible has been read through."[32] Huldrych Zwingli, the Swiss Reformer, explained that he followed *lectio continua*: Matthew for a whole year, then Acts, then the letters to Timothy, the letters of Peter, and Hebrews.[33] So also John Calvin, the great Reformer:

> What order must pastors then keep in teaching? First, let them not esteem at their pleasure what is profitable to be uttered and what to be omitted; but let them leave that to God alone to be ordered at his pleasure. . . . Mortal man shall not be so bold as to mangle the Scripture and to pull it in pieces, that he may diminish this or that at his pleasure, that he may obscure something and suppress many things; but shall deliver whatsoever is revealed in the Scripture, though wisely and appropriately for the edifying of the people, yet plainly and without guile, as becomes a faithful and true interpreter of God.[34]

Several crucial assumptions operate in the practice of *lectio continua*. First, *all* portions of the abiding, weighty, and binding text of Scripture are valuable and worthy of being preached. The tendency to pick and choose texts based on preacher's fancy, significance of event, or ease of exposition is to be strongly resisted. Second, individual pericopes are properly interpreted only in the context of the rest of the book, and it is continual reading and preaching that emphasizes this relationship of part to the whole. While the pericope is the smallest unit of text attended to in a given gathering of God's people, preaching by *lectio continua* affirms the pericope's indissoluble unity with its textual neighborhood.[35] Thus the integrity of a whole book may not be disrupted by preaching noncontiguous pericopes.

What, then, is the role of topical preaching that necessarily deals with diverse texts of Scripture in a single sermon? There is undoubtedly a place in the life of the church for ad hoc sermons (i.e., those that are topical in nature) to meet the needs of particular situations and circumstances, be they national in scope (to address wars, terrorism, special days), or local (to address celebrations, bereavements, weddings), or theological (to address

---

32. Martin Luther, "Concerning the Order of Public Worship (1523)," in *Liturgy and Hymns*, vol. 53 of *Luther's Works*, trans. Paul Zeller Strodach, rev. Ulrich S. Leupold (Philadelphia: Fortress, 1965), 12.

33. Gottfried Locher, *Zwingli's Thought: New Perspectives* (Leiden: Brill, 1981), 27.

34. John Calvin, *Commentary upon the Acts of the Apostles,* vol. 2, trans. Henry Beveridge (Edinburgh: Calvin Translation Society, 1844), 251–52.

35. Again, by "pericope," I intend only a small, preachable portion of Scripture. To a great extent, what is preachable will depend upon the preacher. Too narrow a slice will result in texts with theological thrusts not very different from each other week by week; too large a cut will result in specific theological thrusts being overlooked. See "Preaching Is Theological."

doctrinal weaknesses, spiritual issues, festivals on the church calendar). Such sermons may be biblical in the sense that their ideas are drawn from the Bible. However, I submit that to be biblical, not only do ideas have to be from Scripture, but also the sequential development of Scripture's ideas (i.e., the trajectory of a particular book incrementally developed pericope by pericope) has to be respected. Thus the preaching of sequential pericopes in any given book is essential and ought to be the staple (and stable) practice of preachers. Only then can one catch the thrust of a text, the agenda of the author, in its fullest sense. Jesus's healings of the blind men in Mark 8 and 10 are often preached in isolated fashion as proving Jesus's divinity and omnipotence (as systematic theology topical sermons that expound Jesus's control over the optic apparatus and exhort listeners to trust in the Great Physician). But Mark's thrust with each of these texts is different and may be caught only as one moves through the book, pericope by pericope.[36] Thus, while not discounting the value of the occasional topical sermon, I would strongly recommend that the regular diet of the congregation be sequential sermons through books of the Bible—*lectio continua*. One scholar with a particular aversion to topical messages advised his students "to preach a topical sermon only once every *five* years—and then immediately to repent and ask God's forgiveness!"[37] I have to confess there is some merit to this recommendation.

In short, to preach pericopes sequentially through books is therefore a significant part of what it means to preach biblically.[38] *Lectio continua* requires the interpreter to seek application in every portion of the canon, pericope by pericope, week by week, and to catch the sequential development of ideas within a given book.[39]

36. For the interpretation of these passages, see the Reflection section of "Preaching Is Communicational." Also see Abraham Kuruvilla, *Mark: A Theological Commentary for Preachers* (Eugene, OR: Cascade, 2012), 155–68, 226–37. Each of the two healings has a specific intent and seeks to elucidate discrete facets of Mark's overall theme of discipleship. So also do each of the two crowd feedings in Mark 6 and Mark 8: they too are distinct in their theological thrusts (see ibid., 129–41, 155–68).

37. Walter C. Kaiser, *Toward an Exegetical Theology: Biblical Exegesis for Preaching and Teaching* (Grand Rapids: Baker, 1981), 19.

38. Of course, the choice of which book to preach from will depend upon a number of factors, including the preacher's pastoral vision and goals, and the congregation's spiritual status and maturity. Preaching through each chapter of a book may not work with those portions of the Scriptures that are collections of songs and sayings—the Psalms and Proverbs, for instance—as these are not necessarily organized with a broader arc of meaning and an interpretive trajectory from verse to verse or chapter to chapter.

39. The benefits of *lectio continua* are further developed in "Preaching Is Theological," with the introduction of the concept of the *world in front of the text*.

Summary

What does it mean to affirm that preaching is biblical? We have seen that Scripture, divine discourse, is to be the source material for sermons in the church, for the Bible is abiding, weighty, and binding upon the people of God for their faith and practice. Therefore, preaching that is biblical will ensure that every part of Scripture is preached over a period of time (ideally by reading continuously, *lectio continua*), for "all Scripture" is profitable for the body of Christ (2 Tim. 3:16). Biblical preaching by *lectio continua* guarantees that the voice of every pericope is heard, and heard sequentially, enabling successive sermons to gradually develop the trajectory of a whole book. Needless to say, biblical preaching "allows a text from the Bible to serve as the leading force in shaping the content and purpose of the sermon."[40] In other words, the "force" of the biblical text being handled—its *thrust*, as this vision for preaching has it (see "Preaching Is Communicational")—is what must be preached, not a catchy illustration on which the preacher can build a whole sermon, or a snippet of systematic theology gleaned from the text. In other words, it is Scripture itself that must be preached to the people of God, for it alone is divine discourse, abiding, weighty, and binding. *Preaching is biblical!*

Reflection

Mark 7:1–30—Disciples and God's Word[41]

> And in vain they worship Me teaching as doctrines the precepts of men. Neglecting the commandment of God, you hold the tradition of men. (Mark 7:7–8)

The subject of this pericope, Mark 7:1–30, is purity and acceptability before God, the issue of what is clean versus unclean. The first episode of the pericope (7:1–23) stages the issue and culminates in a list of sinful elements coming from the heart that render one unacceptable before God. The second episode (7:24–30) illustrates what is acceptable to God and worthy of commendation by Jesus. In short, what is important to God is obedience to his commandments stemming from an inward, heartfelt devotion rather than the outward observance of man-made regulations. Thus, the outward

40. Thomas G. Long, *The Witness of Preaching*, 2nd ed. (Louisville: Westminster John Knox, 2005), 52.
41. For more details on this pericope, see Kuruvilla, *Mark*, 142–54. These studies on Mark's Gospel in the Reflection sections in each chapter are intended not only to stimulate thought but also to serve as illustrations of the hermeneutic proposed in this work.

observance of man-made rules without inward, heartfelt compliance to the commandments of God renders one unacceptable before him.

The pericope commences with the disciples eating with unwashed hands. This galls the Pharisees, who question Jesus about the adherence of his disciples to tradition. While hand washing was enjoined only of priests in the Old Testament (Exod. 30:17–21; 40:30–32), ritual washings in the context of prayer are mentioned in several nonbiblical Jewish writings. These latter "traditions of the elders" (Mark 7:5) were supposed to have been delivered to Moses from God at Mount Sinai. Mark's pointing to "many other things" (7:4) and "many similar things" (7:13) indicates that this imposition of humanly devised rules involved more than just hand-washing rituals. The long and short of it is that wherever they may come from, traditional human regulations, being outside the word of God, cannot constitute divine standards for morality.

On the other hand, Jesus's concern is with the priority of obedience to divine commands arising from an inward, from-the-heart morality (7:6, 19, 21) over outward, self-righteous adherence to man-made laws. Three sets of antitheses expressed by Jesus bring this argument to the fore (7:8, 9, 13):

Antithesis 1 (Mark 7:8)	Neglecting	the commandment	of God
	Holding	the traditions	of men
Antithesis 2 (Mark 7:9)	Rejecting	the commandment	of God
	Establishing	tradition	your
Antithesis 3 (Mark 7:13)	Annulling	the word	of God
	Passing down	tradition	your

The issue was not whether the disciples should obey the Old Testament laws but rather whether they needed to adhere to those nonbiblical rules developed in Pharisaical Judaism. What the Pharisees called the "tradition of elders" (in their question to Jesus in 7:5), Jesus labeled "precepts of *men*," "tradition of *men*," and "*your* tradition" (7:7, 8, 9, 13). In other words, Jesus challenged the default assumption of authority in those human traditions. So the fundamental contrast in this episode is the one in the last column of the table above: "of God" versus "of men/your." It was clear which one was to be held preeminent. Unfortunately, the adoption of tradition by the Pharisees was producing a disregard for God's commands. Theirs was an escalating degree of abandonment of God's word: from "neglecting" (7:8) to "rejecting" (7:9) to "annulling" (7:13). Jesus's stern accusation is that the commandments of God in his word have been rendered secondary to tradition. The Bible no longer came first!

Jesus provides an example in 7:10–11 of the contrast between "Moses said" and "you say," the antithesis between God's word and man's tradition. The stakes are raised considerably with the citation of a specific item of law from the Ten Commandments, the breaking of which incurred the death penalty: "Honor your father and your mother" (Exod. 20:12; Deut. 5:16). Here, a son's resources, from which parents could reasonably expect support, were (apparently with Pharisaical approval) being declared "Corban," an exclusive "offering" to God as "divine property." This made it no longer accessible for such philanthropic purposes as parental support. Very cleverly, the vow was being used to avoid one's responsibility to one's parents so as to keep one's own property intact. Thus the son calculatedly (and callously) evaded his *divinely* mandated responsibility to honor his parents by seeking refuge in a practice of *human* tradition.[42] This was a rejection of God's commandment while adhering to a man-made regulation, all in the service of selfish gain: adherence to human tradition rather than devotion to God's word.

It is interesting that the Pharisees, while feeling free "to abandon" (ἀφίημι, *aphiēmi*) God's commandment (Mark 7:8), found it necessary not "to permit" (also ἀφίημι) the son to honor his parents in any fashion (7:12). In other words, for them, it was acceptable to reject God's word but not acceptable to support one's parents! The use of the same verb makes the hypocrisy of the Pharisees more vivid. What was a capital offense in the Mosaic law is not just being allowed but is being demanded by these tradition-bound officials.[43] This was a case of misplaced priorities, man-made regulations trumping God-ordained rules, man's word surpassing God's word. But no amount of punctilious keeping of human codes would find acceptability with God without submission to the mandates of the divine word. Acceptability to God begins with an inward attitude of devotion to divine commandments (7:19, 21); it is not the result of an outward, self-righteous adherence to human regulations.

In a striking juxtaposition of narratives, in 7:24–30 Mark provides an illustration of a woman—a gentile mother whose daughter had an unclean spirit (7:25–26), not one the Pharisees would ever have dreamed of considering pure. But with the healing of her daughter, this unlikely individual is found acceptable to Jesus because of her "answer" (λόγος, *logos*, 7:29), clearly a wordplay on what the tradition-bound Pharisees were "neglecting," "rejecting," and "annulling": the "word" (also λόγος) of God (7:13; also 7:8, 9). It was not what unclean things went into the woman, or what her "unclean" genetic background was, or what unclean spirits lurked in her abode, that

---

42. Adela Yarbro Collins, *Mark: A Commentary*, Hermeneia (Minneapolis: Fortress, 2007), 352; R. T. France, *The Gospel of Mark: A Commentary on the Greek Text*, New International Greek Testament Commentary (Grand Rapids: Eerdmans, 2002), 286.

43. Robert H. Stein, *Mark*, Baker Exegetical Commentary on the New Testament (Grand Rapids: Baker Academic, 2008), 342.

mattered, but what clean things came out of her, in this case the λόγος, reflecting her inward attitude. This is Mark's way of pointing out the devotion of this woman to God and his λόγος: in the only words she speaks, she herself produces λόγος, exactly what those Pharisees had been abandoning. And Jesus, in response, proclaims her daughter healed; and the woman, with her attitude of faith in Jesus, instantly obeys, departing for her house (7:28–30). She trusts in the only act of telemedicine that Jesus performs in this Gospel as she goes as Jesus commanded (7:29). This woman is the one who becomes acceptable to God, her inward, heartfelt devotion manifesting in obedience: she was a disciple, indeed, abiding by God's word!

Clearly, the Bible is to be what is preached and applied, heeded and obeyed, not tradition, not the rules of man, not the stipulations of culture. God takes a dim view of any attempt at the subversion and devaluation of his word. So, first and foremost, *preaching is biblical.* The centrality of Scripture in the life of the community of God cannot be overstated. Every facet of that community's faith and every one of its practices are to be biblical. Preachers have the primary responsibility of keeping Scripture at the forefront of all of their ministerial activities. The pulpit is the venue for this, the most public of preachers' responsibilities: it is here that the word is opened, read, exposited, and applied into the lives of listeners. And that activity must be wholly biblical.

- We must work hard at the discipline of studying the text. This, of course, means *time*! Do we budget adequate chunks of time for this endeavor? Are we conscientious in planning and working way ahead for our sermons? All kinds of exigencies will derail the preacher if preparation is put off till the last week and the last minute. Let's take the task of preaching seriously, respecting the text as God's word.

- How conscientious are we in ensuring that every pericope of Scripture is preached? It is easy to fall into the habit of preaching topically, catering to what is felt to be the need of the hour (or the comfort of the preacher). Part of what it means to affirm that preaching is biblical is to "read continuously" (*lectio continua*), respecting each pericope and the momentum of the book it is part of.

- If asked by an outsider, would our listeners say that we, their preachers, keep the Bible front and center in our sermons? Is that obvious to all who listen to us? Perhaps we should work to make it more obvious, both in our treatment of Scripture from the pulpit and by explicit statements to that effect in our sermons, prayers, and conversations.

- Our focus on Scripture must extend beyond the preaching endeavor. As preachers and leaders of our congregations, we must set this tone for all the other activities that go on in the church—children's ministries, midweek Bible studies, missions activities, and so on. All of pastoral ministry, not just preaching, must be biblical.

Preaching Is Biblical!

2

Preaching Is Pastoral

May those who fear You turn to me,
And they will know Your testimonies.
Psalm 119:79

Biblical preaching, *by a leader of the church*, in a gathering of Christians for worship, is the communication of the thrust of a pericope of Scripture discerned by theological exegesis, and of its application to that specific body of believers, that they may be conformed to the image of Christ, for the glory of God—all in the power of the Holy Spirit.

The newest iterations of the iPhone at this writing have Touch ID, Apple's fingerprint-scanning security system. Gone are the days of passwords to unlock your phones. Now all you need to do is put one of your fingers on the sensor and—*voilà!*—your device is instantly accessible. Notwithstanding fears that the system can be hacked, one must admit that it does enhance the security of the phone: only the one whose fingerprints were recorded during setup can use the device. In other words, there is a rightful person authorized to operate that iPhone. No one else can. And no one else should.

Not only are there fingerprints; there are also voiceprints. Barclays Bank in Britain is not satisfied with account numbers and other proofs of identity when you call in. They now have a program that analyzes your voice, and if yours does not match a voiceprint on file, you cannot log in. And vein-prints are in vogue, too, at some ATMs in Japan. Cards and passwords are not sufficient—the machine will scan the vein patterns in your palms before giving you your cash. Only the appropriate individual can get at your hard-earned money. No one else can. And no one else should.

In this chapter I claim that preaching has similar constraints. Not all can preach. Not all should preach. Biblically and historically, preaching has always been pastoral; that is, an ideal vision for preaching has the shepherd of the flock, the pastor, engaging in the formal and corporate ministry of the word. In other words, there is an authorized person for this important task.[1] Not everyone can be preaching. And not everyone should.

Pastoral Nature of the Preacher's Task

In Nehemiah 7:73b–8:18, when the Israelites returning from exile in the fifth century BCE assemble for the reading and exposition of the divine law, it is the leaders of the assembly who are at the forefront of this endeavor. Thirteen named leaders of the community stand by Ezra the protagonist, on his right and his left, as Ezra does his thing. These leaders are the prime activators of the reading of God's word for God's people. Subsequently, another group of thirteen named leaders (Levites) explains this reading to the people. And thus the Bible is preached.

> Ezra the scribe stood at a wooden podium that they had made for the purpose. And beside him stood Mattithiah, Shema, Anaiah, Uriah, Hilkiah, and Maaseiah on his right hand; and Pedaiah, Mishael, Malchijah, Hashum, Hashbaddanah, Zechariah, and Meshullam on his left hand. . . . And Jeshua, and Bani, and Sherebiah, Jamin, Akkub, Shabbethai, Hodiah, Maaseiah, Kelita, Azariah, Jozabad, Hanan, Pelaiah—the Levites—explained the law to the people as the people remained standing. And they read from the book, from the law of God, clarifying to give the sense so that they understood what was read. (Neh. 8:4, 7–8)

This was a significant event in the life of the community, as is preaching always, the exposition of the word of God for the people of God.[2] The world is, as we heard Herman Melville declare, "a ship on its passage . . . and the

1. There is also a proper *context* for this activity: see "Preaching Is Ecclesial."
2. The event and circumstances of the reading and explanation of God's law in Neh. 8 are helpful for reflecting upon preaching and its various aspects. Therefore this Old Testament account, functioning almost as a paradigm for preaching, will show up again in subsequent chapters of this book.

pulpit is its prow."[3] Every ship needs a captain, and every pulpit a pastor—not just anybody can, or should, captain or preach.

Why is it the pastoral leader's task to preach? Because the regular exposition of Scripture is part of the task of shepherding, it devolves upon the one who is tasked with shepherding the congregation to preach: preaching is essential for spiritual formation. There cannot be a severance between preaching and pastoring, between the exposition of God's word and the shepherding of God's people. The two form an inseparable and integral unity, and so it is a leader of the church who must preach. Preaching is the most visible manifestation of pastoral leadership, from which, to some extent at least, the leader derives authority, casts vision, and provides guidance for the faith and practice of the church. Preaching is, in its essence, spiritual formation from the pulpit—truly a pastoral ministry.

This pastoral nature of preaching was documented very early in church history. Justin Martyr in the third century recorded a typical worship service, with the leader taking the responsibility for preaching:

> And on the day called Sunday, all who live in cities or in the country come together to the same place, and the memoirs of the apostles or the writings of the prophets are read, as long as time permits; then, when the reader has ceased, the leader[4] verbally instructs and exhorts the imitation of these good things.[5]

And so Paul urges Timothy, the pastor-preacher of the church at Ephesus, to focus upon the exposition of Scripture:

> Prescribe and teach these things. . . . Until I come, give attention to the public reading of Scripture, to exhortation and teaching. (1 Tim. 4:11, 13)

As the primary mode of address to the body of Christ gathered for worship, the public discourse of preaching has a unique significance and plays a key role in the life of the church. "Preaching is a vital part of pastoral work in that it permits both preacher and parishioners to weigh, submit to theological examination, integrate, bring to clarity, and express issues that are scattered through the many pastoral contacts and activities. In this sense, preaching can bring to completion and closure matters that otherwise would

---

3. Herman Melville, *Moby-Dick or The White Whale* (Boston: The St. Botolph Society, 1890), 42.

4. Or "presider," the one presiding over the gathering. The verb is also found in 1 Thess. 5:12 and refers to pastoral/teaching authority: "those who are *over you/presiding/leading*."

5. *First Apology* 67.

remain fragmented and dangling."[6] It is preaching that, undertaken for the long term, sets the vision (i.e., the image of Christ) for that local body, the direction it should move (i.e., toward Christlikeness), and the shape it should take (i.e., conformity to that image of Christ).[7] The pulpit is not just the prow of the world; it is, particularly, the prow of God's ship, the church! And pastor-preachers stand at the bow, bearing the burden of edifying the people of God. It is the responsibility of these, who have immersed themselves in the word of God and the things of God, to convey to the children of God, with discernment and sensitivity, what a particular text means for their lives and how they might align themselves to the will of God, the divine call in that text. At bottom, of course, is a pastoral love and concern for one's flock—the dynamo that drives the preacher's passion. Karl Barth once said: "Preachers must love their congregations. . . . It will not help to speak with the tongue of either men or angels if this love is missing."[8] It is this lover of the congregation who must necessarily engage in the primary task of preaching.

Pastoral Appointment to the Preacher's Office

Many decades ago, Phillips Brooks, an American Episcopal preacher, declared that "Truth through Personality is our description of real preaching"—that is, *divine* Truth through *human* Personality.[9] God, in his inscrutable wisdom, has chosen human vessels to bear the divine voice (2 Cor. 4:7). And so the person and personality of the vessel, the preacher, is indispensable in the enterprise of preaching.

Who can be a preacher? Obviously not anyone and everyone; the gifts of the Spirit are not universally distributed in monotonous uniformity, "but to each is given the manifestation of the Spirit for the common good" (1 Cor. 12:7).

> Now you are the body of Christ, and individually members. And God has appointed in the church, first apostles, second prophets, third teachers, then [workers of] miracles, then gifts of healings, helps, gifts of leadership, [different] kinds of tongues. Not all are apostles, are they? Not all are prophets, are they? Not all are teachers, are they? Not all are [workers of] miracles, are they? Not all have gifts

6. Fred B. Craddock, *Preaching* (Nashville: Abingdon, 1985), 40.

7. See "Preaching Is Conformational."

8. Karl Barth, *Homiletics* (Louisville: Westminster John Knox, 1991), 84. William Perkins (*The Arte of Prophecying; or, A Treatise concerning the Sacred and Onely True Manner and Methode of Preaching*, trans. Thomas Tuke [London: Felix Kyngston, 1607], 141) also affirmed that one of the qualities of the preacher is "love of the people."

9. Phillips Brooks, *Lectures on Preaching: Delivered before the Divinity School of Yale College in January and February 1877* (New York: E. P. Dutton, 1877), 8.

> of healings, do they? Not all speak with tongues, do they? Not all interpret, do they? (1 Cor. 12:27–30)

No, not everyone is identically gifted, and therefore "not all" engage in these activities; so also for preaching (Rom. 12:7; 1 Cor. 12:28; Eph. 4:11; 1 Pet. 4:10–11).[10] The New Testament clearly asserts that it is the "elder" who is to teach the Scriptures to the church.

> The elders who rule well are to be considered worthy of double honor, especially those who work hard at preaching and teaching. (1 Tim. 5:17)

I have used "leader" in my vision for preaching quite deliberately: "Biblical preaching, by a *leader* of the church"—whether pastor or teaching elder or one bearing another title. Irrespective of label, the preacher must be one who shepherds the flock (or a part thereof) and is involved with people and their lives on a consistent basis.[11]

A preacher must also possess knowledge of Scripture, soundness of doctrine, and capacity for public speech—all of which are essential for the public proclamation of God's word. Ezra's reading of the law, referred to earlier, was an undertaking of great moment, executed by one upon whom was the "hand of Yahweh." Not only that, Ezra was "skilled in the law of Moses" (Ezra 7:6, 10) and was expressly commissioned by King Artaxerxes I of Persia (ruled 465–424 BCE) as one who possessed "the wisdom of your God" to teach the "laws of your God" (7:25–26). Clearly an ability to preach was assumed in those who were appointed to proclaim and teach God's word. So also noted Philo, the Jewish philosopher of the first century, regarding synagogal instruction on the Sabbath:

Some of those who are experienced instruct [the assembly] in what is good and profitable, by which the whole of their lives may be dedicated to uprightness.[12]

Philo's description of teachers as "those who are experienced" points to those who are "mature, who because of practice have their senses trained to discern good and evil" (Heb. 5:14). The ability to teach God's word effectively is an essential biblical criterion of church leadership (1 Tim. 3:2; 5:17; 2 Tim. 2:24;

---

10. And, for that matter, not everyone who works in a hospital is a nurse; neither is everyone who plays on the football field a linebacker.

11. This also eliminates, at least in this work, the debate over whether there is to be any gender discrimination for preachers. I leave that to readers' systems of ecclesiology. If their reading of Scripture permits women to be elders in the church, then women can preach.

12. *On the Special Laws* 2.15.62.

Titus 1:9). All this to say, some fundamental qualifications mark the one set apart to preach, relating to one's gifting, abilities, and character.[13] Not all can preach; not all should preach.

Ordination

The criteria regarding gifting, abilities, and character necessarily imply that to function in a formal fashion in the corporate assembly as a preacher, an official recognition of the individual is called for. Such a formality is encompassed in the concept of ordination. Calvin called ordination "a special rite for a certain function."[14] While the ambiguity, diversity, and paucity of scriptural references to ordination make it difficult to specify an exact process for this transaction, it is nonetheless helpful to reflect on a couple of examples of "ordination" from the Old Testament and the New Testament.

One of the earliest accounts of what appears to be an ordination process of community leaders is that of Moses's appointment of surrogates to take over part of his leadership/judging roles. This delegating was conducted at the advice of Moses's father-in-law, Jethro, and is detailed in Exodus 18:13–27. A later account of the same event in Deuteronomy 1:5–15 provides, in conjunction with the Exodus description, an informative composite of the process.[15] In Exodus 18:21, Moses is advised to "see" (i.e., "pick") qualified men out of all the people and "place" them as leaders. Jethro notes that "God commands you" to do this (18:23), reassuring Moses that this was not just a human endeavor. Moses proceeds to "choose" appropriate individuals and "set" them as heads over the people (18:25). Here, in Exodus, the people are not shown to be involved in the undertaking. But in Deuteronomy 1:5–15, Moses apparently first asked the people to "select" his deputies, and then he "placed" them in office (1:13)—"taken" and "set" by Moses as heads and leaders of the assembly (1:15). Here, however, God's command finds no mention. In any case, the variety of verbs employed in these parallel accounts—see, choose, set, select, take, place—and the number of subjects involved in the process—God, Moses, the people—all indicate this as being a joint affair between deity, leader, candidates, and congregation. In both accounts the character of the men appointed as Moses's deputies is specifically noted: "capable men who

13. For the character qualities of a preacher, see below and also "Preaching Is Spiritual."

14. *Institutes of the Christian Religion*, 4.19.28, trans. Henry Beveridge (Edinburgh: Calvin Translation Society, 1845), 3:509. Though preaching is the focus of this book, there is nothing stopping the church from ordaining individuals for other leadership roles and functions.

15. The ordination of priests in the Old Testament, an inherited office, will not be considered here.

fear God, men of truth, those who hate bribes" (Exod. 18:21), and "wise and understanding and experienced men" (Deut. 1:13, 15).

A similar situation occurs in Acts 6, where the apostles delegate some of their functions to deacons. Here also, the people are asked to "select" appropriate individuals ("men of good repute, full of the Spirit and wisdom" and "full of faith"), whom the apostles "appoint" to office (6:3, 5; both these verbs of commissioning are used in the LXX, in Exod. 18:21 and in Deut. 1:13, 15). Accordingly, in Acts 6:5–6, the people proceed to "choose" their leaders, and these deacon candidates are "set" before the apostles, who appoint them, praying and laying their hands on them. A formal appointment with laying on of hands is also found in Acts 13:3; 1 Timothy 4:14; 5:22; and 2 Timothy 1:6, likely signifying a transfer of authority and legitimacy, as well as an invocation of divine empowerment upon those ordained.[16]

While much of this points to human appointment, the ancients were quite clear about the divine initiative in ordination. For instance, Chrysostom declared:

> The hand of man is laid on, but God performs everything, and it is his hand which touches the head of the one ordained, if he is truly ordained.[17]

The third-century *Apostolic Tradition* (attributed to Hippolytus) recommends the prayer that is to be uttered at the ordination of a bishop. In part it says:

> God and Father of our Lord Jesus Christ, . . . who from the beginning of the world has been pleased to be glorified by those whom you have chosen, pour out upon him [the candidate being ordained] the power which is from you, the princely Spirit, which you gave to your beloved Son Jesus Christ, which he gave to your holy apostles, who founded the Church in every place as your sanctuary, for the glory and endless praise of your name. Grant, Father who knows the heart, to your servant whom you chose for the office, that he will feed your holy flock, that he will wear your high priesthood without reproach, serving night and day.[18]

The prayer explicitly recognizes the hand of God in the entire process and in the continuing ministry of the one being ordained.[19]

---

16. Such a pattern is also followed in the appointment of Joshua as the successor to Moses: Num. 27:15–23; Deut. 31:7–8, 14–15, 23; 34:9. These texts describe Joshua's "appointment," his choice as a Spirit-filled person, and the laying of hands upon him.

17. *Homilies on Acts* 14 (*NPNF*[1] 11:90).

18. *Apostolic Tradition* 3 (*ANF* 7:482).

19. Likewise, the fourth-century *Apostolic Constitutions* 8.5: "For not every one that desires is ordained, . . . but he only who is called of God" (*ANF* 7:499).

In the sixteenth century, Lutheran Reformer Martin Chemnitz observed:

> For through laying on of hands the person called is set before God, as it were,
> so that there might be a public and outward testimony that the call is not only
> a human matter, but that God himself calls, sends, and appoints that person
> for ministry, though by regular and legitimate means.[20]

Thus, ordination has two facets representing the two primary entities who
act in this transaction: a divine appointment and a human affirmation of that
divine appointment. Ordination for preaching is, therefore, the endorsement
by the body of Christ of those among them as being gifted and qualified
for the public ministry of God's word. It involves the extended process during which the congregation receives the ministry of the candidate (prior to
ordination) and acknowledges the person as divinely endowed, capable, and
impassioned for the opportunity to serve the church selflessly, for God's glory
and his people's edification. The actual act of ordination is the culmination
of this extended endorsement process, as the candidate is formally appointed
to office. Such legitimization furthers the stability, continuity, and orthodoxy
of that body of believers.

Needless to say, there is a priority of divine action: God is the one who gifts
those whom he is giving to the church.[21] Often it is the representatives of the
body who oversee much of the ordination process, but it is important that
"the local church itself . . . always be present at ordination, since precisely *it*
is the human subject of ordination," affirming/empowering the one divinely
gifted.[22] The sixteenth-century Baptist John Smyth, considered the founder
of that branch of Christendom, concluded: "They are sent by God to preach,
whom the church sendeth."[23]

Some important consequences are implicit in ordination. Responding to the
corporate charge to undertake the responsibilities of the office faithfully, the
ordinand commits to discharging this responsibility and to living in a manner
worthy of the calling of a leader in the church and a minister of God's word.
Also implicit in ordination is the ongoing responsibility of the congregation
toward their ordained leaders. Not only are they called to submit to them

20. Martin Chemnitz, *Ministry of Word and Sacrament: An Enchiridion* (St. Louis: Concordia, 1981), 36–37.
21. Ephesians 4:11 makes it clear that such gifted leaders are themselves gifted to the church
by Christ: "He gave some as . . . pastors and teachers."
22. Miroslav Volf, *After Our Likeness: The Church as the Image of the Trinity* (Grand
Rapids: Eerdmans, 1998), 249.
23. John Smyth, *The Works of John Smyth*, 2 vols., ed. W. T. Whitley (Cambridge: Cambridge University Press, 1915), 1:256.

(Heb. 13:17; 1 Pet. 2:13); they also are to be in prayer for them (1 Thess. 5:25; 2 Thess. 3:1; Heb. 13:18), invoking the Spirit to continue his gifting, to empower and bless their ministries.[24]

Ordained Ministry vs. Lay Ministry

Gerhard Forde, lamenting the general tendency to see just any Christian as capable of performing most or all of the functions of those ordained, observes:

> It is ironic that the state turns out to be one of the last holdouts here. The state, clinging to the vestigial remains of the public office will not allow just any lay person to marry or get tax exemptions or serve as chaplain or do visitation in institutions and so on. For [these] more "public" functions the state wants the assurance of ordination. The state, at least, recognizes a public office when it sees one.[25]

The question of why certain believers should be ordained to ministry, when the priesthood of all believers is a core doctrine of Reformation church practice, has often been raised. Ordination does not distinguish between two types of priesthood, or two types of gifting; after all, all the gifts, irrespective of kind, are from God the Spirit, and every believer, in that sense, is a "professional" gifted in one way or another to serve the church. Rather, ordination refers to "two dimensions in the service of every member of the church," a public dimension and a more private one. Miroslav Volf notes that the significance of ordination lies in the fact that the public dimension of the service of those ordained pertains to the entirety of the local church. The ordained one represents the congregation as a whole, serves the congregation as a whole, acts toward God on behalf of the congregation as a whole, and acts in the name of Christ toward the congregation as a whole.[26] It is the public nature of that ministry that requires the public act of ordination. As Luther wryly put it:

> Every Christian has the same power that the pope, bishop, or priest has. [Someone will say,] "Ah, so now I will hear confessions, baptize, preach, and administer

---

24. Thomas C. Oden, *Pastoral Theology: Essentials of Ministry* (San Francisco: HarperSanFrancisco, 1983), 30. Besides the commitment by the congregation to the ordinand, and vice versa, ordination affords some degree of permanence (and perhaps remuneration?) and a setting apart in dignity, honor, and authority, as well as legal standing as a representative of the church to those outside it. See Bengt Holmberg, *Paul and Power: The Structure of Authority in the Primitive Church as Reflected in the Pauline Epistles* (Philadelphia: Fortress, 1978), 108.

25. Gerhard O. Forde, "The Ordained Ministry," in *Called and Ordained: Lutheran Perspectives on the Office of the Ministry*, ed. Todd Nichol and Mark Kolden (Minneapolis: Fortress, 1990), 126–27.

26. Volf, *After Our Likeness*, 246–47, 249.

the Sacraments?" No! St. Paul says, "All things should be done according to order" [1 Cor. 14:40]. If everyone wanted to hear confessions and distribute the sacrament, how would that work? If everyone wanted to preach, who would want to listen? If they preached at the same time, it would become like a racket made by frogs: "Croak, croak, croak!" Instead, it should happen in this way: the congregation should set in place someone who is competent for it to preach, distribute the sacrament, etc. We all have the power, but no one should presume to exercise it publicly except for him who is chosen by the congregation. Privately, however, I may indeed make use of it. For example, when my neighbor comes, saying, "Dear friend, my conscience is burdened, speak an absolution [prayer of forgiveness] to me," I may do that freely, but it must happen privately.[27]

This is perhaps the significant difference between ordained and unordained ministry—the public versus private nature of these activities. Thus, to ordain to the ministry of God's word is, likewise, to distinguish between the gift and the authority to use that gift in the larger assembly of God, in a public setting. Others may have the gift, but not all have been legitimized to exercise it on behalf of the church as a whole.[28] Such legitimation comes with ordination that the body of Christ performs on behalf of its head. Therefore, ordination is an essential requirement for the public ministry of preaching.

In sum, as Thomas Oden observes, "There remains a line as thin as a hair, but as hard as a diamond, between ordained ministry and the faithful layperson."[29] The reason for a corporate act of ordination of preachers is commensurate with preachers' august role of expositing Scripture. Luther declared: "The public ministry of the word, I hold, by which the mysteries of God are made known, ought to be established by holy ordination," for upon such ministry the church depends, "since the church is nothing without the word and everything in it exists by virtue of the word alone."[30] Thomas Long agrees:

> The church knows that its life depends upon hearing the truth of God's promise
> and claim through Scripture, and it has set the preacher apart for the crucial

27. Martin Luther, "Sermon for the First Sunday after Easter, John 20:21–29," in *Sermons on the Gospel of St. John Chapters 17–20*, vol. 69 of *Luther's Works*, ed. Christopher Boyd Brown, trans. Kenneth E. F. Howes (St. Louis: Concordia, 2009), 330–31.

28. Volf, *After Our Likeness*, 248. Gifted individuals who do not hold the pastoral office may legitimately be exercising their teaching gifts at other venues: Bible studies, Sunday schools, adult Bible fellowships, home groups, etc. The issue in this work is the public act of preaching in the corporate gathering of the church in worship (see "Preaching Is Ecclesial").

29. Oden, *Pastoral Theology*, 88.

30. Martin Luther, "Concerning the Ministry," in *Church and Ministry II*, vol. 40 of *Luther's Works*, trans. Conrad Bergendoff, ed. Helmut Lehmann and Jaroslav Pelikan (Philadelphia: Muhlenberg, 1958), 11.

activity of going to the Scripture to listen for that truth. The authority of the preacher, then, is the authority of ordination, the authority of being identified by the faithful community as the one called to preach and the one who has been prayerfully set apart for this ministry, the authority that comes from being "sworn in" as a witness.[31]

Thus the appointment of a pastor-preacher is a sacred trust, and the responsibility of preaching one of immense gravity for the preacher, as emphasized in the mandate to Timothy:

> O Timothy, guard what has been entrusted to you. . . .
>   I solemnly charge you in the presence of God and of Christ Jesus . . . preach the word. (1 Tim. 6:20; 2 Tim. 4:1–2)

And, in light of this august mandate, hard work and diligence are expected of the one recognized and endorsed by the body of Christ as divinely called and gifted to preach.

> We proclaim Him [Christ], instructing all people and teaching all people with all wisdom, so that we may present all people mature in Christ. For this also I *labor, striving* according to His *working* that *works powerfully* in me. (Col. 1:28–29)

"Labor," "striving," "working," and "works powerfully" all indicate the painstaking and strenuous nature of this ministry, albeit enabled by God. It is a grave responsibility of preachers, entrusted to them by their God and by their congregations. And so preachers are the ones to whom parishioners implicitly appeal at ordination:

We are going to ordain you to this ministry, and we want your vow that you will stick to it. This is not a temporary job assignment but a way of life that we need lived out in our community. We know you are launched on the same difficult belief venture in the same dangerous world as we are. We know your emotions are as fickle as ours, and that your mind can play the same tricks on you as ours. That is why we are going to *ordain* you and why we are going to exact a *vow* from you. We know that there are going to be days and months, maybe even years, when we won't feel like we are believing anything and won't want to hear it from you. And we know there will be days and weeks and maybe even years when you won't feel like saying it. It doesn't matter. Do it. You are ordained to this ministry, vowed to it. There may be times when we come to

31. Thomas G. Long, *The Witness of Preaching*, 2nd ed. (Louisville: Westminster John Knox, 2005), 48. See "Preaching Is Communicational" for this notion of the preacher as a "witness."

you as a committee or delegation and demand that you tell us something else than what we are telling you now. Promise right now that you won't give in to what we demand of you. You are not the minister of our changing desires, or our time-conditioned understanding of our needs, or our secularized hopes for something better. With these vows of ordination we are lashing you fast to the mast of word and sacrament so you will be unable to respond to the siren voices.[32]

Indeed, even in the paradigmatic account in Nehemiah 8 discussed earlier, it is the *people* who specifically asked Ezra "to bring the book of the Law of Moses which Yahweh commanded Israel" (8:1)—the word of God for the people of God, with a formally recognized intermediary to perform the public reading and proclamation. "It is not the preacher who goes to the Scripture; it is the church that goes to the Scripture by means of the preacher. The preacher is a member of the community, set apart by them and sent to Scripture to search, to study, and to listen obediently on their behalf."[33] This is the functional and pragmatic consequence of ordination.

Pastoral Character of the Preacher's Life

In the fourth century BCE, Aristotle observed that in public speech there were three elements upon which persuasion depended: the *logos* of the event (the words uttered and content offered), the *pathos* of the speaker (the emotions and passions of both the one speaking and the audience that is stirred up), and the *ethos* of the speaker (his character and credibility before his listeners). Indeed, Aristotle went on to note that of the three, *ethos* was the most effective.

> For it is not the case, as some writers of rhetorical treatises lay down in their "art," that the goodness of the speaker in no way contributes to his persuasiveness; on the contrary, character [*ēthos*] may almost be designated as the most powerful means of persuasion.[34]

The communicator's character, he noted, must be constituted by "good sense, virtue, and kindness."[35] Two centuries later, rhetoricians would still be addressing the same issue of the speaker's virtue. One of the most prominent of

32. Eugene H. Peterson, *Working the Angles: The Shape of Pastoral Integrity* (Grand Rapids: Eerdmans, 1987), 24–25.
33. Long, *Witness of Preaching*, 49.
34. *Rhetoric* 1.2.135.
35. *Rhetoric* 2.1.1378a.

them, the Roman philosopher Cicero (106–43 BCE), asserted that "wisdom without eloquence does too little for the good of [city] states, but eloquence without wisdom is generally highly disadvantageous and is never helpful."[36] In the first century another Roman rhetorician, Quintilian (ca. 35–100 CE), adopted the same sentiments, declaring a "perfect orator" could be none but "a good man."[37] Thus rhetoric, in the right sense, is not simply the art of persuasion but the art of persuading *for good*, accomplished only by one who is morally *good*. Augustine, in the fourth century, agreed with Aristotle and the rest: "Whatever the grandness of style [of the preaching], the life of the speaker carries more weight to gain the obedience of the hearer."[38] Without *ethos*, without the moral grounding of a speaker, every rhetorical transaction, including preaching, though it be a powerful communication, is only demagoguery. Wayne Booth, the noted rhetorician, labeled such operations "rhetrickery"—the work of an unscrupulous speaker, one without a moral compass, one who is not "good" but skilled in "the art of producing misunderstanding" for nefarious purposes.[39] How much more important, then, that the Christian preacher, handling the ineffable word of God, be morally upright!

John Quincy Adams, Boylston Professor of Rhetoric and Oratory at Harvard in the early nineteenth century, declared, "It is unquestionably true, that in forming the ideal model of an all-accomplished orator, that perfect master of the art, . . . the first quality, with which he should be endowed, is uprightness of heart. . . . We cannot separate the moral character from the oratorical power." Adams, like Aristotle, considered the orator's "reputation of unsullied virtue" as one of the "most efficient engines of persuasion." This, he noted, was particularly true for preachers: "To men of this vocation the maxim of Quinctilian [*sic*] might be applied in its utmost extent. The orator of heaven must be a saint upon earth."[40] Perhaps it is not surprising that Paul echoed those same ideas.

> Our gospel did not come to you in word only [i.e., *logos*], but also in power and in the Holy Spirit and with full conviction [i.e., *pathos*], just as you know the kind of men we were among you for your sake [i.e., *ethos*]. (1 Thess. 1:5)

---

36. *On Invention* 1.1, in *On Invention, Best Kind of Orator, Topics*, trans. H. M. Hubbell, Loeb Classical Library 386 (Cambridge: Harvard University Press, 1970), 4.

37. Quintilian, *Institutes of Oratory* 1.1.9. He added, "No man can ever become an orator unless he be a good man" (12.1.3).

38. *On Christian Doctrine* 4.27.59.

39. Wayne C. Booth, *The Rhetoric of Rhetoric: The Quest for Effective Communication* (Malden, MA: Blackwell, 2004), x, 11.

40. John Quincy Adams, *Lectures on Rhetoric and Oratory* (Cambridge, MA: Hilliard and Metcalf, 1810), 345, 352, 355. Adams also served as the sixth president of the United States.

The consequence of such proclamation was dramatic change in the lives of Paul's listeners: they became imitators of Paul and of Jesus Christ, and exemplars of true disciples.

> And you became imitators of us and of the Lord, having received the word in much tribulation with the joy of the Holy Spirit, so that you became an example to all the believers in Macedonia and in Achaia. (1 Thess. 5:7)

Thus, without a doubt, the character of the one ordained for preaching is critical to the ministry of the word, for its efficacy and for its power. Again, here is Paul to Timothy, the preacher-pastor of the church at Ephesus:

> In speech, conduct, love, faith, and purity, show yourself an example of those who believe. (1 Tim. 4:12)

The pastor and preacher is to be an exemplar of spirituality, walking with God, entrusting the preaching endeavor to the Almighty in prayer, relying upon the Holy Spirit in every aspect of sermon preparation and delivery and, indeed, in all aspects of life. This one must be a believer in whose life there is constant, perceptible spiritual growth, the defeat of the flesh by the Spirit, ongoing maturity of character, and progressive development of Christlikeness. Spiritual formation by shepherding goes beyond words uttered in the pulpit, though that may be the most public and prominent of the activities of the pastor. The Aristotelian *ethos* demands that preachers' lives also reflect their words. They should be models, to the best of their abilities and in the power of the Spirit, as they portray what it means to be faithfully obedient.[41] Gregory the Great, in his magisterial handbook for pastors, exhorts:

> The ruler [i.e., leader] should be exemplary in his conduct, that by his manner of life he may show the way of life to his subjects, and that the flock, following the teaching and conduct of its shepherd, may proceed the better through example rather than words. For one who by the exigency of his position must propose the highest ideals, is bound by that same exigency to give a demonstration of those ideals. His voice penetrates the hearts of his hearers the more readily, if his way of life commends what he says.[42]

The voice of words spoken and the "voice" of life lived must work in tandem in the pastor-preacher. Richard Baxter puts it well:

41. Also see "Preaching Is Spiritual."
42. *The Pastoral Rule* 2.3, in St. Gregory the Great, *Pastoral Care*, trans. Henry Davis, Ancient Christian Writers 11 (Westminister, MD: Newman, 1950), 48.

It is a palpable error in those ministers that make such a disproportion be- tween their preaching and their living, that they will study hard to preach exactly, and study little or not at all to live exactly. . . . O how curiously [i.e., carefully] have I heard some men preach, and how carelessly have I seen them live! . . . When it came to matter of practice, and they were once out of church, how incurious [i.e., not careful] were the men, and how little did they regard what they said or did, so it were not so palpably gross as to dishonor them! They that preached precisely, would not live precisely! . . . We must study as hard how to live well, as how to preach well. We must think and think again how to compose our lives as may most tend to men's salvation, as well as our sermons.[43]

In other words, the text of Scripture must do its work in the preacher by the power of the Holy Spirit, and this work must be manifest in the life and character of the preacher.

Summary

What does it mean to say that preaching is pastoral? From the days of the Old Testament onward, the responsibility for the preaching of Scripture was primarily entrusted to the leader of the community of God's people. It is the shepherd of the flock who is commissioned to exposit the word of God, to guide the lives of God's people into alignment to God's demands. Thus, the exposition of Scripture is an integral part of shepherding, and the task of pastoring may not be divorced from the responsibility of preach- ing, for they operate together: lives changed by word and by example, by public proclamation and by private counsel. The one to whom these duties pertain is necessarily one gifted by God to pastor and to teach and preach. Such a person is to be ordained, that is to say, endorsed by the local church as being divinely gifted and qualified to undertake the task of preaching. This formal appointment to the office, whether of pastor, elder, or minister, recognizes the public nature of the task of preaching in the church. As the leader of the body, and as its shepherd, the preacher must live in a man- ner worthy of this august calling, demonstrating Christlike character and spirituality, without which all the effort of preaching is in vain, for lives are changed not only by the words spoken by the preacher but also by the life lived by this one. All this to say: not all can preach; not all should preach. *Preaching is pastoral!*

43. Richard Baxter, *The Reformed Pastor*, vol. 14 of *The Practical Works of the Rev. Richard Baxter* (London: James Duncan, 1830), 59–60.

Reflection

Mark 9:30–42—Greatest or Least?[44]

> If anyone wishes to be first, he shall be last of all and servant of all. (Mark 9:35)

The second passion prediction of Jesus occurs in this section (Mark 9:31). As in the first (8:31), the disciples demonstrate their blindness to kingdom values (9:33–34), a deficit Jesus attempts to correct (9:35–37). The entire section unveils a facet of discipleship essential for those who would be leaders in God's economy—humility in service to others.

The irony of the Son of Man being delivered into the hands of men (9:31) must not be lost: the one to whom all authority is given (Dan. 7:13–14) is now to be given over to the authority of men. It turns all earthly values of greatness upside down. Jesus employs the verb παραδίδωμι (*paradidōmi*, "to betray," literally "to give over/deliver," Mark 9:31): not only is it in the present tense (a "futuristic" present), indicating certainty of the event yet to happen; it is also a divine passive, underscoring God's sovereign will in the whole enterprise. That same verb had already indicated the fate of John the Baptist (1:14) and anticipated Judas's betrayal (3:19), and it would indicate Jesus's betrayal by Judas in the next passion prediction (10:33 [2×]). It also shows up frequently in Mark in the actual account of Jesus's passion (14:10, 11, 18, 21, 41, 42, 44; 15:1, 10, 15). In spite of this deluge of explicit hints, the disciples fail to accept Jesus's suffering mission: suffering is the last thing on their minds. Their lack of discernment depicted in earlier chapters of Mark is now a full-blown refusal to accept Jesus's mission of death. The painful pathway of suffering was not going to be theirs.

Instead, they were looking out for themselves and contending about who would be the greatest (9:33–34). They, like the rest of us, would rather have glory—an affliction that has become an epidemic among leaders in God's community. Here in Mark 9, perhaps this question of who was the greatest was provoked by the choice of Peter, James, and John to accompany Jesus to the mountaintop to observe the transfiguration (9:2). And this perceived slight to those remaining below may have been aggravated by their weakness and inability to perform an exorcism—a humiliation in front of a crowd (9:18–19, 28–29). So now they are quarreling over which of them is the greatest (9:34). Incredibly, this question of status is consuming the disciples even as Jesus

44. For more details on this pericope, see Abraham Kuruvilla, *Mark: A Theological Commentary for Preachers* (Eugene, OR: Cascade, 2012), 188–201.

is anticipating his martyrdom. All disciples, but especially church leaders, must be vigilant against such arrogance. The privileges of ordination and of publicly handling Scripture, and the authority inherent in the office, can easily go to one's head. We are never to forget that the leader is but a servant of God and of the people of God.

In reply to the disciples' self-engrossment and ambition, Jesus makes a profound statement (9:35–37): the highest status in the kingdom of God is appointed for those who are servants of all. On the social scale, the lowest were children, who were under the authority and care of others and without the right of self-determination—last and least of all. Yet a disciple who wants to be great is to go one step further: to become the lowest of the low by *serving* those who, like the child whom Jesus took into his arms, are last and least (9:35). This was a drastic reversal of the conventional scale of values, a complete overturning of the disciples' prideful pursuit of greatness. Serving and receiving the last and least was to be done by the disciple "in My name" (9:37), that is, as though the last and least were representing Jesus himself. To receive the child, therefore, was to receive Jesus; and since Jesus represents God, to receive Jesus was to receive God (9:37). In other words, being a servant to the last and least is perhaps the most significant attitude a disciple could adopt, a stark contrast to the brazen pursuit of prestige and honor. Augustine's observation is apt:

> Consider a tree: first it trends downward, that it may then grow upward. It fixes its root low in the ground, that it may extend its top toward heaven. Is it not from humility that it endeavors to rise? And would you then . . . extend toward heaven without a root? This is a ruin, not a growth.[45]

A most interesting comment from John follows in 9:38; it sounds like a non sequitur, unconnected with what precedes it. But after Jesus's object lesson with a child, John's exclusivism emphatically demonstrates that he had not grasped what Jesus was talking about. Exorcism was a special commission to the disciples (3:14–15; 6:7, 13), and the discovery of others performing such healings stung their egos, particularly when they themselves had just been unable to perform one successfully in the episode before this one. John is unwilling to surrender his "special" status, and his use of the first-person plural suggests that his fellow disciples agreed with this breach of protocol: "*we* saw," "*we* prevented" (9:38). But even more striking is John's accusation that that unknown exorcist was "not following *us*." One would think

---

45. *Sermons on Selected Lessons of the New Testament* 67.17 (NPNF[1] 6:464–65).

he (and the rest) would have caught on by now that disciples follow *Jesus*, not the Twelve: the verb "to follow" elsewhere in Mark is almost always used of following Jesus.[46] John's "we prevented him" (9:38) is expressly countered by Jesus's "Do *not* prevent him" (9:39). Presumption and pomposity had gotten the better of these disciples, who now thought themselves royalty to be followed after! Such a conceited attitude was exactly what Jesus had been attempting to disabuse them of. The love of hierarchy, status, and position appears to have been a deeply ingrained problem for these disciples; and, I dare say, it is so for many church leaders as well—a danger we must be vigilant against. God-given status and authority of disciples, particularly of leaders in the church, are not intrinsic to any individual, and neither do they indicate spiritual superiority. Rather, since the source of the calling and gifting and ongoing ministry is God himself, there can be no primacy or elevated status based upon one's own self.

The consequences for *not* having a heart of humility are serious. Jesus sternly adjures disciples to be proactive in the care of the last and the least, the "little ones." If, instead of being received, those "little ones" are led astray or "caused to stumble" (9:42), the punitive ramifications will be considerable. The one who so causes others to stumble is, in effect, disabling another's discipleship. To cause another's downfall is, in Jesus's eyes, a very serious offense, and nothing less than dangerous hubris.

In sum, the entire discussion has established a trajectory toward Jesus's self-identification later, in Mark 10:45, as the one who came not to be served "but to serve and to give his life as a ransom for many." Thus, this section of Mark's Gospel turns out to be a lesson in humility patterned after Jesus himself. The humble disciple serves the least, without being arrogant or assuming oneself to be great. The task of remaining servantlike is crucial to discipleship—and particularly essential for all leaders in the church, who should diligently and conscientiously cultivate this attitude, removing everything that stands in the way of such servanthood.

- Do we really consider ourselves as servants—to God and to the people of God? The test for servanthood is our reaction when others actually treat us as servants. How do we respond? With indignation, frustration, and self-righteousness, or with humility, gentleness, and self-sacrifice?
- One way to guard against such hubris in leaders is to ensure that we have trusted people close to us who have the permission to be brutally honest with us when the need arises. A lack of such accountability is

46. Mark 14:13 is another exception.

frequently the first step toward the disaster that comes with a swollen head. Perhaps that accountability partner could be a faithful friend, a mentor, or a fellow pastor, in addition, of course, to one's spouse/family, fellow elders, and church board.

- What is our attitude to the last and least in the local body of Christ of which we serve as leaders—the disabled, the mentally challenged, the poor, the refugees, the children, the aged . . . ? Do we spend time with them? Does our preaching reflect our care and concern for these, as Jesus exhorted? Do we regularly pray for them, in private and in public?

- It is a privilege (not a right) to be ordained to minister God's word to God's people. Let us be thankful for that sacred trust that has been bestowed on us preachers, and let us handle it with reverence and fear.

Preaching Is Pastoral!

3

Preaching Is Ecclesial

I am a companion of all those who fear You
And of those who keep Your precepts.
                                    Psalm 119:63

Biblical preaching, by a leader of the church, *in a gathering of Christians for worship*, is the communication of the thrust of a pericope of Scripture discerned by theological exegesis, and of its application to that specific body of believers, that they may be conformed to the image of Christ, for the glory of God—all in the power of the Holy Spirit.

In the annals of the institution where I teach, there is a (true) story of a graduating student who chose to wear shorts at the commencement exercises. He was not allowed to "walk" on stage to receive his diploma (he did graduate, though). The relevant authorities saw fit to determine that some items of attire were out of place for such a solemn occasion. The graduate collected his diploma in private, no doubt shod in the gear of his own choice. But a formal pair of pants was deemed appropriate at public ceremonies such as graduations. Likewise, one doesn't jump into a swimming pool in a jacket and tie or a fancy gown. There is a place for everything. And there is an appropriate place for certain activities too. One doesn't do jumping jacks during worship. I don't do ballet in my dermatology clinic as I see patients. You don't send text messages while driving a car.

So also for preaching. There is a proper locus for that activity. Extracting the activity from its proper locus, conducting it anywhere and everywhere, divorcing it from the biblical, historical, and pastoral contexts of which it is an integral part, renders preaching, to a great extent, devoid of its significance and its potency.

One question that does not often figure in discussions of preaching is: *Where (or in what context) should preaching take place?* Perhaps in the earlier days, when gatherings of God's people occurred exclusively for worship services, it was taken for granted that preaching occurred only in such assemblies, in "church." But these days, with all kinds of situations and a multiplicity of occasions when Christians assemble, both formally and informally, this question is a valid one. Is my speaking at a Bible conference (usually calling for four or five talks during the single week of these gatherings) "preaching"? How about the sermon I delivered in the chapel of my institution the other day? What about the monologue I offered at a Bible study for medical students during their lunch hour? Or a discussion at a gathering of singles in my church? Do these discourses constitute preaching? Where can/should/must preaching occur? Based on the standard definitions of preaching (including some that I provided in the introduction), you could probably even fit a one-on-one with a fellow believer at a coffee shop into the category of "preaching"—as long as it communicates a truth from the Bible, exhorts application, and so on.

I submit in this chapter that preaching is ecclesial. That is to say, a vision for preaching sees this activity as ideally occurring in the regular gathering of a local body of Christ for worship. Karl Barth asserted that "preaching must be done in the sphere of the church, i.e., in concrete connection with the existence and mission of the church. . . . Only in this place where we are set by revelation can there be legitimate preaching."[1] Constituted by the word of God, the church is the proper place for the exposition of Scripture. The Bible is, without doubt, the church's book, and therefore the arena of its exposition is the congregation of God's people, the church, "the pillar and support of the truth" (1 Tim. 3:15). Thus the primary locus for the preaching of Scripture is the church, the assembly of God's people, a setting that provides the direction and thrust for its interpretation.

Of course, such an assertion could be taken to mean that preaching should occur in the presence of God's people, however many or few they

---

1. Karl Barth, *Homiletics* (Louisville: Westminster John Knox, 1991), 56, 57.

may be, and for whatever purpose they are gathered, whenever and wherever this might take place. But I would like to argue that the label "preaching," in the ideal sense, be reserved for that activity conducted in the context of the regular worship service of the gathered faithful. Preaching ought not to be divorced from the worship event and experience, for, as I explore here, the people of God hear him loudest and clearest in such a context, and Christ's presence occurs in a special way in these assemblies, particularly in conjunction with the Lord's Supper. This formal worship gathering of the church is the liturgical locus where ordinances are practiced, praises are sung, prayers are made, offerings are given, and sermons delivered. After all, worship, in its entirety, is the proper and primary response of the people of God to the voice of God.

A Definitional Aside

Because the goal of preaching is to conform human beings to the image of Christ (Rom. 8:29; see "Preaching Is Conformational"), and because the first step of such conformation is the placing of one's trust in Jesus Christ as only God and Savior, the proclamation of the good news of salvation has also generally been considered (and translated in the New Testament as) "preaching" (from κηρύσσω, klēryssō).[2] However, in the Bible, evangelistic "preaching" is never a formal exposition of a specific biblical text that contextually interprets authorial thrust, discerns divine demand, and draws out relevant application. And rarely is κηρύσσω itself textually sourced; more often than not, the verb is used in the New Testament in the generic sense of "announcing/proclaiming" as, for instance, in Revelation 5:2.[3]

> And I saw a mighty angel proclaiming [κηρύσσω] in a loud voice, "Who is worthy to open the scroll and to break its seals?"

With the establishment of the canon and the institutionalization of the church, and with the attendant need for direction on how life was to be lived by believers, it is easy to see how the divergence between evangelistic proclamation (heralding the good news) and edifying preaching (guidance

2. Another verb employed in the New Testament for such announcements of the gospel is εὐαγγελίζω, euangelizō, "to proclaim the good news" (1 Cor. 9:16; Gal. 1:16; etc.).
3. There are a few exceptions where κηρύσσω is actually employed for textual exposition, for instance in Rom. 2:21–22. There, "preaching" deals with the Decalogue, a specific text of the Mosaic law. Also see 2 Tim. 4:2 (in connection with 3:16), where κηρύσσω is rightly "preaching," an exposition of a source text.

for Christian life based upon a specific biblical text) came about. The former deals with the announcement to nonbelievers about an accomplished act—the atoning work of Christ (with evidence from Scripture, perhaps). Thus the message and application in such evangelistic proclamations remains the same in every iteration: *Trust Jesus Christ as your only God and Savior!* Edifying preaching, on the other hand, involves the exposition of a particular biblical text and the specific demand of *that* text upon the life of the Christian. The message and application in such preaching varies from sermon to sermon, depending on the text used. So, on the whole, "missionary preaching is not to be confused with preaching within the assembly since the two activities have different aims and different audiences."[4] In other words, the methods, emphases, and goals of employing Scripture for proclamation of the gospel and using it for preaching are distinct.

Therefore, in this work "preaching" will deal with the exposition of a particular biblical text to discern divine will regarding Christian living. Such a narrowing not only reflects the use of a specific portion of Scripture as the basis of preaching, but also makes another distinction: "preaching" refers to the ministry of the word to those who are *already* part of God's people. Evangelistic proclamation—essentially an announcement of the same message each time (the redemptive work of Jesus Christ, God incarnate)—is a call to faith for those outside the perimeter of the church. Thus it falls into a distinct category and will not be considered in this work.[5]

Preaching in Biblical History

A brief overview of preaching in biblical history establishes it as an integral part of the liturgical events constituting the ecclesial, corporate worship of God's people.

Preaching—a Liturgical Event in the Old Testament

Preaching as a historical practice conducted among God's people at worship has its origins in the Old Testament. The primary text for this is Nehemiah

4. Alistair Stewart-Sykes, *From Prophecy to Preaching: A Search for the Origins of the Christian Homily*, Supplement to *Vigiliae christianae* 59 (Leiden: Brill, 2001), 24.
5. This does not mean that one should not present the gospel when preaching; I often do so myself, but not necessarily because the text I'm preaching calls for it—i.e., it is not a hermeneutical constraint imposed upon the preacher by the chosen text of Scripture. Rather, I present the gospel frequently simply because I'm uncertain if everyone in my audience is a believer—i.e., it is a pragmatic constraint that I choose to abide by. See "Preaching Is Conformational."

7:73b–8:12, which records the reading and interpretation of Torah in the context of a liturgical assembly.

> So Ezra the priest brought the law before the assembly [קָהָל, *qahal*; LXX: ἐκκλησία, *ekklēsia*] of men, and even women and all who could listen with understanding, on the first day of the seventh month. . . . And Ezra blessed Yahweh the great God, and all the people responded, "Amen, Amen!" while lifting their hands; and they bowed down and worshiped Yahweh, their faces to the ground. . . . And they [the Levites] read from the book, from the law of God, clarifying to give the sense so that they understood the reading. (Neh. 8:2, 6, 8)

It is in the gathering of God's people that Scripture is expounded by Ezra and his associates. The word "assembly" is most frequently used in the Old Testament of the gathering of the congregation of Israel in the presence of God. This coming together of God's people is mentioned sixteen times in the account in Nehemiah 7:73b–8:12, and in different terms: "sons of Israel" (7:73); "all the people" (8:1, 3, 5 [2×], 6, 9, 11, 12); "as one man" (8:1); "the assembly" (8:2); "men, and women, and all who could listen with understanding" (8:2); "men and women, those who could understand" (8:3); and "the people" (8:7 [2×], 9). In fact, the account is bracketed on either end by a gathering of "all the people" (8:1, 12). This focus on the corporate assemblage of the people of God is remarkable; such a gathering serves as the primary context of the ministry of God's word. And this event, at which the Torah was read and explained, is explicitly labeled as an act of worship (8:6)—the appropriate accompaniment to the exposition of Scripture. The preaching of the word of God, the book of the people of God, is rightly ecclesial. Such practices of reading and interpreting Scripture were codified in later Jewish custom, as evident in writings of the first century CE and later. For instance, Philo writes:

> What then did he [Moses] do? On these seventh days [the Sabbaths], he required them [the people] to gather together in the same place and, sitting with one another, to listen to the laws in a respectful and orderly manner, so that no one should be ignorant. . . . And then some priest who is present, or one of the elders, reads the sacred laws to them, and interprets each of them individually until almost late afternoon; and then they depart, having gained knowledge in the sacred laws, and having made much advance in piety.[6]

Later, such routines were incorporated into the early church.

6. *Hypothetica* 7.12–13.

Preaching—a Liturgical Event in the New Testament
and the Early Church

There is evidence in the New Testament of the "reading" of Scripture, almost always linked to an interpretation thereof (i.e., preaching), occurring in a formal gathering of God's people for worship, as the verses below indicate.[7]

> And they [Paul and his company] went into the synagogue on the Sabbath day and sat down. And after the reading of the Law and the Prophets the officers of the synagogue sent [a message] to them, saying, "Brothers, if you have in you any word of exhortation for the people, say it." (Acts 13:14–15)

The liturgical nature of the preaching event is also evident in its juxtaposition with the Lord's Supper, prayer, and other key elements of worship of the early church.

> On the first [day] of the week, when we were gathered together to break bread, Paul began speaking to them and, intending to leave the next day, he prolonged his message until midnight. . . . He went back up, and after breaking the bread and eating, he talked [ὁμιλέω, *homileō*[8]] with them for a long while. (Acts 20:7, 11)

> They were devoting themselves to the apostles' teaching and to fellowship, to the breaking of bread and to prayer. (Acts 2:42)

Even the readings of the Pauline Letters, which assume the gathered people of God in place, would have resounded with liturgical words and acts, bespeaking their public proclamation in a ritual context: "Amen!" (Rom. 16:27; 1 Cor. 16:24; Gal. 6:18), "*Maranatha!*" (1 Cor. 16:22), the holy kiss (1 Cor. 16:20; 2 Cor. 13:12; 1 Thess. 5:26), the many benedictions (1 Cor. 16:23; 2 Cor. 13:14; Gal. 6:18; Eph. 6:23–24; Phil. 4:23; 1 Thess. 5:23, 28; 2 Thess. 3:18), and the prayer formulas at the commencement of several of these epistles (Rom. 1:8; 1 Cor. 1:4; 2 Cor. 1:3–4; Gal. 1:3–5; Eph. 1:3–14; Phil. 1:3–5; Col. 1:3; etc.).[9] In short, exposition of Scripture was an integral element of such formal worship gatherings of the people of God, alongside other liturgical elements that even today

---

7. Also see Acts 15:21. Jesus's own practice is described in Luke 4:16–21 as occurring in the synagogue on the Sabbath: Jesus reads and interprets Scripture (preaches). In fact, "reading" by itself may be a synecdoche (i.e., a figure of speech specifying a particular element but signifying the entire operation of which that element is a part) for the whole process of exposition that involves reading + interpretation. That seems to be the case in 2 Cor. 3:14; Col. 4:16; and 1 Thess. 5:27.
8. We get "homily" from this word.
9. Gordon Lathrop, *Holy Things: A Liturgical Theology* (Minneapolis: Fortress, 1993), 44n19.

are important aspects of the worship of the church: prayer, singing, offerings, the Lord's Supper, and so on. Several second-century CE Christian writings attest to preaching being an indispensable part of these worship activities.

> And on the day called Sunday, all who live in cities or in the country come together to the same place, and the memoirs of the apostles or the writings of the prophets are read, as long as time permits; then, when the reader has ceased, the leader[10] verbally instructs and exhorts to the imitation of these good things. Then we all rise together and prayer is offered, and, as we said before, when our prayer is ended, bread and wine and water are brought, and the leader likewise offers prayers and thanksgivings as he is able, and the people assent, saying "Amen!"[11]

Tertullian includes in worship services the "reading of Scriptures," "chanting of psalms," "preaching of sermons," and "offering of prayers."[12] All of this suggests that preaching was an element of worship in the early church.

While there seems to be no question about the primary derivation of the church's preaching from the corresponding Jewish liturgical practices of the synagogue, in the New Testament church there was also a striking tendency to employ metaphors borrowed from temple praxis, particularly in the frequent employment of the language of sacrifice. The community was to offer itself to God as a "living sacrifice" (Rom. 12:1). Individual lives were to be sacrifices as well (Phil. 2:17; 4:18; 2 Cor. 2:14–17; 4:10–11). The people of God formed a "royal priesthood" (1 Pet. 2:9; Rev. 1:6; 5:10), entering the holy place through the flesh/blood of Christ, the veil (Heb. 10:19–20). And, of course, Christ was their high priest (Heb. 2:17; 4:14–5:10; 8:1; 9:11). In fact, even the individual components of the church's liturgy were portrayed in the metaphor of sacrifice: prayer and praise (Heb. 13:14–15; 1 Pet. 2:5, 9; Rev. 8:3–5), offerings (Phil. 4:18; Heb. 13:16), and the Lord's Supper. Not surprisingly then—and this is where our interest lies—the ministry of the word also had the same connotation of sacrifice.

> For the word of God is living and active and sharper than any double-edged sword, and piercing even to the division of soul and spirit, of both joints and marrow, and able to judge the thoughts and intentions of the heart. (Heb. 4:12)

"References to bones and marrow being cut by a double-edged sword place us in the realm of sacrificial imagery. The word is the cutting sword that dismembers

---

10. Or "presider," the one presiding over the gathering.
11. Justin Martyr, *First Apology* 67.
12. *The Soul* 9 (*ANF* 3:188).

us so that we may offer ourselves as sacrifices in praise and thanksgiving and prayer."[13] It is striking that the function of Scripture is described in terms of sacrifice. Indeed, the author of Hebrews immediately reverts to the high priestly image in 4:14–15, sustaining this liturgical analogy. Chrysostom also emphasized this metaphor of the ministry of the word as he imagined Paul declaring: "For me this is the priesthood, preaching and proclaiming; this is the sacrifice I offer. . . . For even my knife is the gospel . . . the word of preaching."[14] Thus even in the terminology of preaching, its connection with liturgy is substantial, placing it firmly within the worship activities of God's people.

If preaching is an integral part of the worship, and if it is frequently juxtaposed to other liturgical elements, particularly the Lord's Supper, is the exposition of God's word sacramental like that ordinance is?

Preaching: A Sacramental Act

"Sacrament" is derived from the Latin *sacrâre*, "to consecrate, to set apart as sacred, to devote to deity"; the root *sacer* also shows up in the English "sacred." There can be no doubt that the exposition of Scripture is a "consecrated" activity—concerning itself with the consecrated word, conducted by a consecrated individual (see "Preaching Is Pastoral"), in a consecrated event, the gathering for worship of a consecrated people, the saints of God. If we begin with the straightforward definition of "sacrament" as a "[visible] form of invisible grace" that affects, impacts, and transforms people,[15] surely it would be hard to disagree that the "visible" exposition of Scripture is an "invisible" divine impartation of grace. Here is Ben Witherington on the same notion:

> While "de jure" baptism and the Lord's Supper are the Protestant sacraments, "de facto" there has always been another one, and in fact one that has been seen and believed to have a far more regular and enduring effect—namely the Word of God. . . . If a sacrament is a means of grace, by which is meant a means of divine influence and change in a person's life, then surely the Word of God and its proclamation, reading, hearing, learning, [and] memorizing is a sacrament.[16]

13. Peter J. Leithart, "Synagogue or Temple? Models for the Christian Worship," *Westminster Theological Journal* 64 (2002): 132. Note the other references equating Scripture to a sword: Eph. 6:17; Rev. 1:16; 2:12.

14. John Chrysostom, *Homilies on Romans* 29 (NPNF[1] 11:543). For Paul's own use of liturgical terms to describe his ministry, see Rom. 15:15–16; 2 Cor. 4:7–12; Gal. 6:17; Phil. 2:17; 2 Tim. 4:6; etc.

15. "A sacrament that is properly so called is the sign of grace and the [visible] form of invisible grace" (Peter Lombard, *Book of Sentences* 4.1 [twelfth century CE]).

16. "Word as Sacrament," *Ben Witherington* (blog), November 9, 2007, http://benwithering ton.blogspot.com/2007/11/word-as-sacrament.html. "Sacrament" generally focuses on the *divine*

Notice the similarities between the Lord's Supper and preaching. Both are proclamations of Christ as 1 Corinthians 11:26 and Colossians 1:28 affirm, employing the same verb.[17]

> For as often as you eat this bread and drink the cup, you *proclaim* the death of the Lord till He comes. (1 Cor. 11:26)

> . . . whom [i.e., Christ] we *proclaim*, instructing everyone and teaching everyone with all wisdom, so that we may present everyone complete in Christ. (Col. 1:28)

Besides, both need the mediation of divine activity to be efficacious. As Calvin noted:

> Both in the preaching of the Word and in the use of the sacraments [the Lord's Supper], there are two ministers, who have distinct offices. The external [human] minister administers the vocal word, and the sacred signs [elements of the Lord's Supper] which are external, earthly and fallible. But the internal [divine] minister, who is the Holy Spirit, freely works internally, while by his secret virtue he effects in the hearts of whomsoever he will their union with Christ through one faith (1 Cor. 3:5–7; Acts 16:14).[18]

In other words, preaching is no less sacramental than the ordinances, making the prime locus of the former the same as that of the latter—the gathered body of Christ in worship. Since both the Lord's Supper and baptism ideally occur in the context of such assemblies, so also should preaching.

Word and Sacrament

In times ancient and modern, "word and sacrament" have existed side by side. Such a tendency is visible even in the Old Testament, though of course it was not the Lord's Supper that was juxtaposed to the interpretation of God's word, but sacrifices and the communal meal that usually followed the

---

act involved—God's offering grace to those participating in the Lord's Supper and baptism. In that case, the exposition of Scripture must also be sacramental: note the "activity" of the Scripture as God extends grace to humankind through it: 1 Thess. 2:13 (it "works"); Acts 6:7 and 12:24 (it "grows"); Col. 3:16 (it "dwells"). The more common Protestant term "ordinance" focuses upon the actions of *believers* in these events—their partaking of the bread and cup and their undergoing baptism.

17. How preaching is a proclamation of Christ will be considered in "Preaching Is Conformational."

18. John Calvin, *Summary of Doctrine concerning the Ministry of the Word and the Sacraments*, article 5, in *Theological Treatises*, ed. J. K. S. Reid, Library of Christian Classics 22 (Philadelphia: Westminster, 1954), 173.

sacrifices.[19] In the very first establishment of the word of God as law given to Moses, word and sacrifice occur together in the context of worship. In Exodus 3:12, Moses and the people are commanded by God to "worship God at this mountain." That worship is carried out in Exodus 24 (see 24:1, which reflects 3:12). In other words, what happens in 24:1–11 is what Yahweh intended as worship in 3:12. Notice the careful structuring of 24:1–11, the content of this divinely mandated worship:

A Moses and elders instructed to ascend and worship (24:1–2)

   B Word of Yahweh and affirmation of the people (24:3)

      C Words written by Moses (24:4a)

         D Sacrifices and blood ceremony (24:4b–6)

      C′ Book read by Moses (24:7a)

   B′ Word of Yahweh and affirmation of the people (24:7b–8)

A′ Moses and elders ascend and worship (24:9–11)

The liturgical elements are clear: the bulk of the structure (B, C, D, C′, B′) is made up of dealings with God's word and with sacrifices.[20] Thus the gathering for worship in conjunction with sacrifices has biblical precedent for being the primary context of the sacramental exposition of God's word. Of course, after the redemptive work of Jesus Christ, it is no longer sacrifices as in the older dispensation; now the completed ultimate sacrifice of Christ is reflected in the Lord's Supper.

Thus, all throughout biblical history and onward, preaching (the ministry of God's word) seems to have been firmly rooted in worship liturgy and considered sacramental along with the ordinances.[21] Calvin, therefore, declares

19. The culmination of Old Testament sacrifices, reflected later in the Lord's Supper, was often a sacred meal shared by devotees (see Exod. 24:8; Jer. 31:31; Lev. 1–7; 1 Cor. 10:16–18).

20. John W. Hilber, "Theology of Worship in Exodus 24," *Journal of the Evangelical Theological Society* 39 (1996): 178–79. Similar transactions, where readings of God's word are coupled with sacrifices (or mentions of sacrifices at altars), are found in Deut. 27:1–10 and Josh. 8:30–35. In Neh. 7:73b–8:18, discussed earlier, a communal meal takes place in lieu of sacrifices (8:10, 12, 18).

21. Rather than label preaching a "sacrament," I consider preaching as sacrament*al*, "to express the reality of God's presence through human instrumentation or divine activity through human labor." Such a use of "sacramental" affirms that it is *God* working, through the agency of his people, in and with the ordinances (and preaching). That God deigns to use fallible human modalities to accomplish his purposes and to proffer grace is a wonder in itself (2 Cor. 4:7). See J. Mark Beach, "The Real Presence of Christ in the Preaching of the Gospel: Luther and Calvin on the Nature of Preaching," *Mid-America Journal of Theology* 10 (199): 81, 92n38.

that preaching and the Lord's Supper are part of the signs of a true church: "Wherever we see the word of God sincerely preached and heard, wherever we see the sacraments administered according to the institution of Christ, there we cannot have any doubt that the Church of God has some existence."[22] Likewise, article 19 of the Thirty-Nine Articles of the Church of England defines the church as a congregation of the faithful "in the which the pure word of God is preached, and the Sacraments be duly administered."[23]

Preaching, thus, is a sacramental and liturgical act. Its ideal locus is the gathering of God's people for worship, where the voice of God is most powerfully heard. In other words, God is not merely the Subject under discussion in a sermon; he is a live voice, the One who introduces the discussion, graciously addressing his people as to how they should live in covenant fellowship with him (also see "Preaching Is Theological").[24] In fact, Jesus equated the speech of his disciples to his own words:

> The one who listens to you listens to Me, and the one who rejects you rejects Me; and the one who rejects Me rejects the One who sent Me. (Luke 10:16)

This raises the issue of the presence of God in the sacramental and liturgical act of preaching.

Presence of Christ in the Sermon and the Supper[25]

It is evident in Exodus 24 that the presence of God was manifested in a special way during the word + sacrifice worship of the Israelites: the altar (standing for Yahweh) and the twelve pillars (standing for the twelve tribes, 24:4) signified the presence of both parties to the covenant; both of the signatories were sprinkled with blood (the altar, 24:6; the people, 24:8); and both sides partook of the sacrifices (24:5), with a communal meal for humans (24:11) and consumption of the offering by fire for deity (24:5), signifying covenant fellowship between worshipers and God. "In Exodus 24 worship is response to the covenant relationship, which is characterized by God's presence

22. *Institutes of the Christian Religion*, 4.1.9, trans. Henry Beveridge (Edinburgh: Calvin Translation Society, 1845), 3:21.

23. W. H. Griffith Thomas, *The Principles of Theology: An Introduction to the Thirty-Nine Articles*, 6th rev. ed. (London: Vine, 1978), 265.

24. See Thomas H. Keir, *The Word in Worship: Preaching and Its Setting in Common Worship* (Oxford: Oxford University Press, 1962), 3.

25. "Sermon and Supper go together," quipped Hughes Oliphant Old (*Worship: Reformed according to Scripture* [Louisville: Westminster John Knox, 2002], 128). Adding the other ordinance, I'd rather say, "Bible, Bread, and Bath go together."

[24:16–17], defined by his word [24:3–4a, 7–8] and mediated through sacrifice [24:4b–6]."[26] It is impossible to get away from the impression that all of this is one package: worship, word and sacrifice, *and* divine presence.

Perhaps the one aspect of similarity between the sacramental acts of preaching and the Lord's Supper that has been forgotten in the modern era is the fact of Christ's presence in both.[27] Calvin declared: "Wherefore, let it be a fixed point that the office of the sacraments differs not from the word of God; and this is to hold forth and offer Christ to us, and, in him, the treasures of heavenly grace."[28] In other words, both of these liturgical activities, the Lord's Supper and preaching, in a special sense, evoke the presence of God the Son. If the Lord's Supper is the event at which "every believer who was temporally removed from the first Easter could gain the assurance of the presence of the risen Lord," then the exposition of God's word is the event at which the presence of Christ is again assured to the believer as the divine voice is heard, a phenomenon that a believer far from the first Easter cannot experience audibly.[29] As it is with the ordinances, so it is with preaching. Both activities are closely related to the presence of Christ. Comparing the Lord's Supper with preaching, Donald Coggan writes: "The 'elements' are words, ordinary words, the words that we constantly use in the commerce of everyday life. But in preaching, the life-giving Spirit takes these words and makes them the vehicles of his grace. He fashions words into the Word. Who can doubt that, when such preaching takes place, there is the real presence of Christ?"[30] This corresponds to the elements of the Lord's Supper (ordinary things) being employed by the Spirit for the impartation of (extraordinary) grace in the presence of Christ. In other words, both preaching and the Lord's Supper are events that, in a powerful way, bring us into the real presence of the Savior.[31]

26. Hilber, "Theology of Worship," 182, 184.

27. In considering the "presence" of Christ in the Lord's Supper, I am not getting into Reformation debates—the "memorialism" of Zwingli, the "parallelism" of Bullinger, and the "instrumentalism" of Calvin. In any case, all these stalwarts affirmed some sort of presence of Christ at the Lord's Supper, which is really the point I wish to make. For more on those discussions of the sixteenth century, see Leanne Van Dyk, "The Reformed View," in *The Lord's Supper: Five Views*, ed. Gordon T. Smith (Downers Grove, IL: InterVarsity, 2008), 66–82.

28. *Institutes* 4.14.17 (3:315).

29. Hans-Josef Klauck, "Lord's Supper," *Anchor Bible Dictionary* (New York: Doubleday, 1992), 4:366.

30. Donald Coggan, *A New Day for Preaching: The Sacrament of the Word* (London: SPCK, 1996), 16.

31. Yet we must not forget, as Thomas G. Long declares, that "Christ is not present because we preach; we preach because Christ is present" (*The Witness of Preaching*, 2nd ed. [Louisville: Westminster John Knox, 2005], 17).

First, with regard to the Lord's Supper, the exhortation to "remembrance" (1 Cor. 11:24–25) does not signify mere cognitive reminiscence. In Semitic understanding, remembrance was a "re-presentation" of the thing remembered, which "comes alive to the person as a present and effective reality," a "re-experiencing the results of the basic event as something that is present and real now."[32] Thus the remembrance of Christ is not simply a cognitive exercise; it is actually an experience of Christ. Here is Calvin again: "If by the breaking of bread the Lord truly represents the partaking of his body, there ought to be no doubt whatever that he truly exhibits and performs it. The rule which the pious ought always to observe is, whenever they see the symbols instituted by the Lord, to think and feel surely persuaded that the truth of the thing signified is also present."[33] John Jefferson Davis reminds us that in 1 Corinthians 10:16–20 κοινωνία (koinōnia, "participation") occurs four times in the context of the Lord's Supper, underscoring this vital, active, and real concept of "remembrance": such "participation implies living communion and actual personal contact. . . . To participate in the body and blood of Christ involves, then, real-time, person-to-person, spirit-to-spirit contact with Christ."[34] H. C. G. Moule put it well:

> I believe that if our eyes . . . were opened to the unseen, we should indeed behold our Lord present at our Communions [Lord's Suppers]. . . . Such special presence, the promised congregational presence, is perfectly mysterious in mode, but absolutely true in fact; no creation of our imagination or emotion, but an object for our faith. I believe that our Lord, so present, not *on* the Holy Table, but *at* it, would be seen Himself, in our presence, to bless the Bread and the Wine for a holy use, and to distribute them to His disciples. . . . I believe that we should worship Him thus present in the midst of us in His living grace, with unspeakable reverence, thanksgiving, joy and love.[35]

Second, with regard to Scripture, Christian writers have always affirmed an equally intense sense of the immediacy of the voice of God—he speaks to his people in his word. All of God's words are personally addressed to those who open the Scriptures. Chrysostom declared that what was written in the Bible

---

32. Jerome Kodell, *The Eucharist in the New Testament* (Collegeville, MN: Liturgical Press, 1991), 80; and Helmer Ringgren, *Sacrifice in the Bible*, World Christian Books 2.42 (London: United Society for Christian Literature, 1962), 50.

33. *Institutes* 4.17.10 (3:399).

34. John Jefferson Davis, *Worship and the Reality of God: An Evangelical Theology of Real Presence* (Downers Grove, IL: InterVarsity, 2010), 139–40, 142.

35. H. C. G. Moule, "Statement by Professor Moule," in *The Doctrine of Holy Communion and Its Expression in Ritual: Report of a Conference Held at Fulham Palace in October 1900*, ed. Henry Wace (London: Longmans, Green, 1900), 91.

was "written for us" and therefore worthy of diligent attention. Gregory the Great asked rhetorically: "For what is sacred Scripture but a kind of epistle of Almighty God to His creature?"[36] It is God's voice addressing his people, made all the more potent by the presence of God the Son in the ecclesial gathering of the body of Christ, where God's word is exposited. The purpose (and result) of both preaching and the Lord's Supper is the communion of the church with Christ. "Christ—and indeed, not only his activity or his power, but the person of Christ himself, since a presence is always personal—is really present in the service of the Word and in the liturgical assembly of the faithful."[37] Such a view sees the presence of Christ as an integral part of the ontological (i.e., real and essential, not merely metaphorical or symbolical) union of the believer with Christ. And it is when preaching and the Lord's Supper are conducted in the context of the church's worship that this presence of Christ is enjoyed in a special way.

Far too often in church history, it is the mechanics of the event of the Lord's Supper that have been focused upon: What do the bread and cup signify? Should they be taken separately, or one dipped in the other? How often should the ordinance be celebrated? Et cetera. Correspondingly, with preaching the focus has historically been more on its mechanical aspects: How should a sermon be structured? What illustrations work well? What kind of introduction is necessary? Et cetera. Perhaps it is time we also carefully attended to what exactly is happening at such events, whether it be the celebration of the Supper or the occasion of the sermon. And what is happening at both these sacramental engagements is that Christ is there—he is really present! On the other hand, a blinkered focus on mechanics tends to disrupt the sacramentality of these activities. As a result, the presence of Christ in worship with those he redeemed is at best minimized or at worst neglected.

How does the location of Christ, who is exalted and seated in the heavenlies, comport with his "presence" in the earthly gathering of the faithful?

While it is perfectly true that Christ, after the ascension, is at the right hand of God until his return, and as such is bodily and visibly *absent* from the church,

---

36. Chrysostom, *Homilies on Genesis* 2:2; Gregory the Great, *Letter to Theodore the Physician*, in *The Nicene and Post-Nicene Fathers*, series 2, ed. Philip Schaff and Henry Wace (1886–1889; repr., Peabody, MA: Hendrickson, 1994), 12:156 (hereafter *NPNF*²). The Bible itself consistently affirms that the divine word directly addresses all future generations. See Deut. 6:6–25; 31:9–13; 2 Kgs. 22–23; Neh. 7:73b–8:18; Ps. 78:5–6; Matt. 28:19; Rom. 15:4; 1 Cor. 9:10; 10:6, 11; 2 Tim. 3:16–17; etc.

37. Edward Schillebeeckx, *The Eucharist*, trans. N. D. Smith (New York: Sheed and Ward, 1968), 103. This sacramental notion of preaching, from the perspective of a Roman Catholic theologian, reflects the fairly uniform understanding in Christendom of the ministry of word: it is ideally ecclesial and, at least functionally, sacramental.

this is not the whole story. He is still present with the church . . . [Matt. 18:20; 28:20; 1 Cor. 5:4; 14:25] in an invisible and spiritual and very real sense. The basic ontological axiom of New Testament theology applies here: The heavenly is as real or more real than the earthly; the spiritual and invisible is just as real or more enduringly real than the material and the visible. We need to see the full reality through the eyes of faith, not merely by the senses.[38]

In this connection, I am reminded of the conversation between the almost dying Harry Potter and the already dead Professor Albus Dumbledore, when they meet at a critical part of the story in the final volume of J. K. Rowling's fictional saga of Hogwarts.

> "Tell me one last thing," said Harry. "Is this real? Or has this been happening inside my head?"
> Dumbledore beamed at him, and his voice sounded loud and strong in Harry's ears even though the bright mist was descending again, obscuring his figure.
> "Of course it is happening inside your head, Harry, but why on earth should that mean it is not real?"[39]

There is more to reality than can be apprehended by sight, hearing, taste, smell, and touch. The *real* presence of Christ in the midst of his people—especially in the context of the preaching of the word and the celebration of the Lord's Supper—is a mysterious reality that can be grasped only by faith. Calvin's words are wise: "I will not be ashamed to confess that it is too high a mystery either for my mind to comprehend or my words to express; . . . I rather feel than understand it."[40] Perhaps Christians need to turn their attention once again to experiencing this core reality of the faith: Christ's presence, sustaining and inviting, graciously drawing each child of God into a closer relationship with the living Savior, all in the context of the worship gathering of those he gave himself for. And this presence is acutely experienced in the

---

38. Davis, *Worship*, 161.

39. J. K. Rowling, *Harry Potter and the Deathly Hallows* (New York: Scholastic, 2007), 723.

40. *Institutes* 4.17.32 (3:431). Nonetheless, in answer to how exactly divine presence is operating, Davis makes a helpful analogy with cyberspace. For instance, the location of Google's homepage might be on one's laptop as well as on the computers of millions of others in the world, though physically the code for that page is buried somewhere in some server on some server farm that comprises Google's vast mesh of networks. The ontological relation of this bit of code to all of its various representations (manifestations?) and to the material contexts of its expression (laptops, desktops, tablets, and a host of other devices) serves as a fair analogy of the relationship of the ascended Christ to his ubiquitous presence, particularly in the global, disparate gatherings of the faithful. However, it would be grossly inadequate to extend this analogy to label Christ's presence in each local gathering as "virtual"; rather, it is "real." See *Worship*, 162–63.

celebration of the Lord's Supper and in the preaching of God's word in that context of worship.

Summary

Preaching, the ministry of God's word, played an important liturgical role in both Old Testament and New Testament history. The early church carried on this tradition, at times giving this ministry the connotation of sacrifice. As with the Lord's Supper, Scripture and its exposition serve as the (visible) mode of imparting (invisible) divine grace. Therefore, the act of preaching may rightly be labeled "sacramental." Historically, throughout the life of the church, word and sacrament (i.e., the Lord's Supper) have been paired indivisibly. I submit that like the Lord's Supper, the preaching of Scripture is also marked by the real presence of the Lord Jesus Christ, in the hearing of the divine voice. That is to say, by the *written* word of God the Christian encounters the *living* Word of God. The ideal location for such an encounter is therefore the worship of the gathered body of Christ, where the presence of the Savior is felt most keenly. Barth concludes: "The place of preaching . . . is just not any place we fancy. It is the place which is defined by baptism, the Lord's Supper, and [S]cripture, and by what God does in this sphere. To this place and this place alone preaching must orient itself. Only then can we speak of its conformity to the church."[41] Thus the primary locus for the preaching of Scripture is the church, the assembly of God's people, a setting that provides the direction and thrust for its interpretation, in the presence of the Head of the church, the Lord Jesus Christ. The "rule," Fred Craddock affirms, is "preaching in the context of worship." All else is less than ideal.[42] *Preaching is ecclesial!*

Reflection

Mark 3:7–35—Christ's "Family"[43]

> For whoever does the will of God, he is My brother and sister and mother. (Mark 3:35)

A rather surprising description of the people of God is found in this pericope, Mark 3:7–35—the *family* of Jesus. Believers are family members of

41. Barth, *Homiletics*, 87.
42. Fred B. Craddock, *Preaching* (Nashville: Abingdon, 1985), 41.
43. For more details on this pericope, see Abraham Kuruvilla, *Mark: A Theological Commentary for Preachers* (Eugene, OR: Cascade, 2012), 62–74.

Jesus Christ! Not only does this label bind the body of Christ together; it is also symbolic of the intimate association of this body with its Head, the Lord Jesus Christ. And that makes the ecclesial presence of Christ in and with his people—his "brother and sister and mother" (3:35)—all the more profound and poignant. What a privilege for the children of God!

The mountaintop calling of the Twelve (3:13) is reminiscent of Moses's trip up Mount Sinai and the Israelites' covenanting with God (Exod. 19). This event in Mark 3 is almost a reenactment of that earlier scene: a new people of God is called and constituted (3:13–19). In a curious paradox, the disciples were appointed "to be with" Jesus *and* "to be sent out" by him (3:14). Indeed, one might say that only if one is *with* Jesus can one be sent *from/by* him. The first is a prerequisite for the second. The presence of Jesus Christ is essential for effectiveness in ministry.

In the subsequent "sandwich" episode, the answer is conclusively given as to what constitutes an "insider," a disciple, one who is for Jesus—with him and sent by him. Notice the play on "inside" and "outside" throughout the account.[44]

Narrative Summary: Large crowds; boat (3:7–12)	
A Those "with" Jesus—disciples (3:13–20) [ποιέω, *poieō*, "appoint," 3:14]	Insiders: Twelve
Narrative Foil: Crowd (3:20)	
B Those accusing Jesus of madness—family (3:21)	Outsiders: Family
C Those accusing Jesus of demonic control—scribes (3:22–30)	Outsiders: Scribes
B′ Those sending for and calling Jesus—family (3:31)	Outsiders: Family
Narrative Foil: Crowd (3:32)	
A′ Those "around" Jesus—"inner circle" (3:33–35) [ποιέω, *poieō*, "do," 3:35]	Insiders: Anyone
Narrative Summary: Large crowds; boat (4:1)	

The disciples are inside the house with Jesus (indicated by the plural: "*they* were not even able to eat," 3:20); they are *physically* inside the house. Because they are also with Jesus (3:14), they are *morally* insiders.

Jesus's family (3:21) goes "out" to seize him—so the genetic family is *physically* outside. And their accusation is that Jesus is "out" of his mind—Jesus

44. The "sandwich" story is a narrative style found at least six times in the Gospel of Mark. The author begins an outer story (here, 3:20–21), only to break it off in the middle to commence and conclude an inner story (here, 3:22–30), after which he returns to finish the outer story (here, 3:31–35): thus a "sandwich," with the two parts of an outer story enclosing an inner one.

is accused of being *morally* "outside." The irony is that these who are *genetically* "inside" are *physically* outside. And, accusing Jesus of being outside, it is they themselves who are *morally* "outside." Later, Jesus's family are said to be "standing outside" (3:31)—again, they are *physically* outside (3:32). They are not "with" Jesus, and they are certainly not being disciples. They do not enjoy the presence of Jesus Christ.

Then come the scribes, ostensibly insiders (from Jerusalem, 3:22)—*ecclesiastically* "inside."[45] They are likely to be within the house arguing with Jesus—so they are also *physically* inside. But, accusing Jesus of being in league with Satan, casting "out" demons by Satan (3:22, 23), they too imply that Jesus is *morally* "outside." Jesus counters, declaring forgiveness for them impossible because they reject the work of God; so they are the ones who are *morally* "outside"—cast out. Hardly disciples! They too do not experience the presence of Jesus.

Finally we get to the question of what exactly constitutes "insidership"—what it takes to be *with* Jesus: Who is the one who is present with Jesus? His true/new family, Jesus answers, is made up of those who do the will of God (3:35). These are the ones who are *morally* insiders with Jesus—the inner circle "around" Jesus (3:34). In contrast to outsiders, who fail to recognize Jesus's person and thus disregard his authority and lordship, insiders—those who do the will of God—are the true disciples, appointed by Jesus to be with him and then to be sent by him to extend Jesus's own mission in the world. And these are the "family members" of Jesus Christ!

Pastors/preachers are the leaders of a local "family" of Christ. May this chapter be a reminder to all in such positions of authority that Christ is intimately associated with his people and desires to be—nay, *is*—present with them, particularly in their gatherings of worship, where his presence is felt and his praises sung, where his word is preached and his Supper celebrated. Such assemblies are the prime loci for the hearing of his voice, as the word of God is faithfully expounded.

- The presence of Christ among us can be awe-/fear-inspiring (and I'm thinking of the apostle John's reaction in Rev. 1:17), but Mark 3:7–35 assures us Christ's presence is that of a "family member"! It should be a great comfort and encouragement for all believers—but especially for preachers—to recognize the presence of Christ in the midst of his body, his family. For us who preach, we can rest assured that God's voice in the Scriptures is accompanied by his *real* presence, strengthening,

---

45. An anachronous label, I admit.

assisting, and reinforcing our humble words as we exposit the divine word.

- Are we aware of the *real* presence of Jesus in our lives? Without being "with him," ministers cannot be sent "by him." Perhaps we should make it a point to reflect daily upon the presence of our Lord with us.
- How conscious are we of the special presence of Christ as his body gathers for worship? Is that a truth that has hit us hard? Is it something we make known to our fellow leaders in worship—the musicians, the readers, the drama team, the ushers? Is it something that is discussed at worship-planning meetings?
- Do our pastoral prayers reflect the presence of Christ in the corporate assembly? And do we comment on the presence of Christ as we lead the worship service of the ones he has redeemed?
- How aware is our congregation of the presence of Christ, particularly in the celebration of the Lord's Supper and, as this chapter has concluded, in the preaching of God's word? Are they conscious that the one who speaks to them is there with them? Are we mindful of his voice?

Preaching Is Ecclesial!

4

Preaching Is Communicational

―――――――――――――

May my tongue sing of Your word,
For all Your commandments are righteousness.
Psalm 119:172

Biblical preaching, by a leader of the church, in a gathering of
Christians for worship, is the *communication of the thrust of a
pericope of Scripture* discerned by theological exegesis, and of
its application to that specific body of believers, that they may be
conformed to the image of Christ, for the glory of God—all in the
power of the Holy Spirit.

Try reading what is shown below. Can you make sense of it?

തന്റെ ഏകജാതനായ പുത്രനിൽ വിശ്വസിക്കുന്ന ഏവനും
നശിച്ചുപോകാതെ നിത്യജീവൻ പ്രാപിക്കേണ്ടതിന്
ദൈവം അവനെ നല്ലവാൻ തക്കവണ്ണം
അത്രമാത്രം ലോകത്തെ സ്നേഹിച്ചു.

How will you read this text—assuming you recognize it as a text and not as a
random scribble? And even if you agree that it is a text, how do you know if

it is meaningful? Even if it is possible to make sense of this inscription, is it a writing that one needs to pay attention to and heed? Does it have any claim upon anyone? And, if it does, what exactly is its demand? A whole host of such questions swirls around the heads of interpreters of texts as they attempt to cross the gap in communication between author and reader(s).[1]

Preaching: Communication of Scripture

While the Torah in Hebrew may not have been as cryptic to an ancient Israelite audience as the text above is to many readers of this book, the reading of the Scriptures in Nehemiah 8 necessitated the bridging of a similar communication gap between an ancient text and a postexilic reader.

> And Jeshua, and Bani, and Sherebiah, Jamin, Akkub, Shabbethai, Hodiah, Maaseiah, Kelita, Azariah, Jozabad, Hanan, Pelaiah—the Levites—*explained* the law to the people as the people remained standing. And they read from the book, from the law of God, clarifying to give the sense so that they *understood* what was read. (Neh. 8:7–8)

The reading of the law in Nehemiah 7:73b–8:12 is considered one of the oldest descriptions of the formal, liturgical employment of Scripture in the gathering of the people of God, an event that took place sometime in the mid-fifth century BCE. This incident forms the climax of the Ezra-Nehemiah books, as the missions of the two protagonists, Ezra and Nehemiah, converge precisely within this enterprise: for the first time they are mentioned together in this section (8:9). Set in a liturgical context, the entire event described in Nehemiah 7:73b–8:12—the reading of Scripture, its subsequent exposition, and the response of the congregation—serves as a helpful device for reflecting upon preaching.[2]

The activity of the Levites described here is of particular interest to preachers. The task of these officers was to facilitate comprehension by the community of what God required of it in his word. Christians recognize that the content of the biblical canon is of immense significance for humans: it is abiding, weighty, and binding, its matter of great moment for the relationship between deity and humanity. Therefore, modern preachers, like the Levites of

1. By the way, this scrawl—indecipherable unless you read Malayalam, my mother tongue, a classical language in the Dravidian linguistic family, spoken by about forty million who hail from the southwestern coast of India—translates the sixteenth verse of the third chapter of the fourth Gospel of the New Testament.
2. This portion of Scripture has already been referred to in previous chapters of this book.

old, must ensure that its critical content is understood by God's people. The Levites' giving the sense of the reading in Nehemiah 8 involved an "explanation" (from the verb בִּין, *bin*), the outcome of which was "understanding" (also from בִּין). The root of the word shows up six times in the account (8:2, 3, 7, 8, 9, 12), emphasizing the importance of the Levites' act of mediating comprehension of the word of God to the people of God. If one does not understand, how can one obey?

> Give me understanding [also from בִּין], and I will observe Your law,
> And I will keep it wholeheartedly. (Ps. 119:34)

So preaching at its foundation must be *communicational*. "Communication" is derived from the Latin *communicâre*, which comes from *communis*, "common." Thus "communication" indicates having "meanings in common," between speaker and listeners, and between writer and readers. If preaching is to be communicational, what is in the preacher's mind must be duplicated—as far as is possible, given the signal-to-noise ratio in all utterances—in congregants' minds. However, in this chapter, we will not go into *how* the preacher is to communicate to the audience. Rather than dwell upon rhetorical techniques and communication strategies—the "how" (for which there is no end of resources, both sacred and secular)—I shall focus here primarily upon *what* the preacher needs to communicate to the audience.[3]

It all begins with a text, the Bible—preaching is biblical. Though the Bible is a text like no other, it remains a text, and its interpreters are called to treat it as one. Indeed, the very fact that preaching is an address founded upon a text makes it a unique kind of communication—a new form of rhetoric, in fact.

A New Form of Rhetoric

Though the exposition of the sacred text does occur in Old Testament history, it was in the practice of the synagogue and the early church that this act achieved prominence and developed into a new genre of communication. In the description of Paul's speech in Acts 13:15–41, labeled λόγος παρακλήσεως (*logos paraklēseōs*, "word of exhortation," 13:15), one detects a pattern:

---

3. Of course, the *what* and *how* of communication cannot be entirely separated; some of what is discussed in this chapter does deal with the latter. However, the constraints of space render it impossible to do justice to sermon composition and delivery, both important aspects of homiletics. Of the many resources that deal with these kinds of rhetorical issues, a recommended one is Chip Heath and Dan Heath, *Made to Stick: Why Some Ideas Survive and Others Die* (New York: Random House, 2007).

Scripture citations/references coupled with a concluding exhortation to action.[4] The utilization of a text—an *inspired* text—in this fashion to generate application is an unusual form of communication. "For texts [or speeches] that evidence the pattern of formal introduction, scriptural citation, exposition or thematic elaboration, and application, one might use the modern terms 'homily' or 'sermon.'" Indeed, it might well be that the traditional Aristotelian classification of rhetoric—that age-old demarcation of all public address into forensic, deliberative, and epideictic rhetoric—had, by the first century CE, "outlived its usefulness and that the Hellenistic synagogue provides a new social setting for what is effectively a new rhetorical occasion": *paraklēsis*, "a technical literary designation for a certain kind of oratorical performance."[5] While principles of rhetoric are certainly being followed even in this novel form of text-based communication, "there is no question that the Aristotelian division is breaking down."[6]

> The weekly confrontation with a revered text set the stage for a new rhetorical occasion, defined by the necessity of actualizing the significance of that sacred but often strange piece of literature for a community in, but not entirely of, the social world of the Hellenistic polis. Paraclesis [*paraklēsis*] . . . is the newly minted rhetorical form that actualizes traditional scripture for a community in a non-traditional environment. It certainly has affinities with the classical forms of oratory, and those who regularly practised it probably had some training in rhetorical art, but paraclesis is in fact a mutant on the evolutionary trail of ancient rhetoric.[7]

Almost every other sort of formal speech, categorized in the Aristotelian triplet, is essentially topical, dealing with a particular subject of importance and relevance, and all are conducted without recourse to a text. Preaching alone is unique in this regard. The use of a normative text on which to base

4. This pattern is also reflected in the letter to the Hebrews—Heb. 13:22 labels the entire epistle as a λόγος τῆς παρακλήσις (*logos tēs paraklēsis*, "word of exhortation")—as well as in other early Christian documents. See Alistair Stewart-Sykes, *From Prophecy to Preaching: A Search for the Origins of the Christian Homily*, Supplement to *Vigiliae christianae* 59 (Leiden: Brill, 2001), 31–33.

5. Harold W. Attridge, "Paraenesis in a Homily (λόγος παρακλήσεως): The Possible Location of, and Socialization in, the 'Epistle to the Hebrews,'" in *Paraenesis: Act and Form*, Semeia 50, ed. Leo G. Perdue and John G. Gammie (Atlanta: Scholars Press, 1990), 216–17. *Forensic* oratory was conducted in the realm of law courts to convince a jury of past events; *deliberative* oratory took place in legislative assemblies to persuade people of the appropriateness of future action; *epideictic* oratory happened at formal occasions of festivity or grief to praise the present value or character of a celebrated and/or mourned individual. See Aristotle, *Rhetoric* 1.3.1.

6. Stewart-Sykes, *From Prophecy to Preaching*, 37.

7. Attridge, "Paraenesis in a Homily," 217.

the sermon sets this form of oral communication apart from all other genres of address. And new forms of sacred rhetoric call for new approaches to homiletics.

Being unlike speech, in that the author of a text is far away in time and space from its readers, its interpretation has the potential for generating confusion: the signal of meaning tends to get lost in the noise that increases with distance between writing event and reading event. Take for instance this piece of Jewish folklore, in the form of a letter, that pictures the ever-present danger of such confusion[8]:

Dear Riwke,

Be good enough to send me your slippers. Of course, I mean "my slippers" and not "your slippers." But, if you read "my slippers," you will think I mean your slippers. Whereas, if I write: "send me your slippers," you will read your slippers and will understand that I want my slippers. So: send me your slippers.

Whose slippers are being asked for here? The distance in time and space between the writer and future reader, Riwke, necessitates the enterprise of interpretation: What is this communication all about? What is the author referring to, where and when, why and wherefore? In other words, if she is to respond to the writer with valid application, Riwke is going to have to figure out the thrust of the letter, what the author was trying to do—that is, whose slippers the author was referring to.

The same issues surface in the interpretation of Scripture: the human author is unavailable, and readers are far away from the origins of the text. Yet, unique discourse that the Bible is, it mandates its own application in times and spaces distant from the circumstances of its writing.[9] So if Scripture is to be employed in new locales of reading, the thrust of the text—what it is all about—must be recovered and communicated. This is the role of the preacher, the intermediary between God's word and God's people: to understand the thrust of the text, and to convey that thrust to listeners.[10] But, for most of Christian history, that has not been how the preacher's task has been conceived.

8. From Marina Yaguello, *Language through the Looking Glass: Exploring Language and Linguistics* (New York: Oxford University Press, 1998), 8.

9. See Deut. 4:10; 6:6–7, 20–25; 29:14–15; Matt. 28:19–20; Rom. 15:4; 1 Cor. 10:6, 11; 2 Tim. 3:16–17; etc.

10. Throughout this work, I will develop the thesis that the primary communicational role of the preacher is to lay out for listeners the *thrust* of the Scripture text that is handled in a sermon. There is, in addition, a secondary communicational task, that of providing valid *application* for listeners; this will be considered in "Preaching Is Applicational."

Looking Back: Arguments and Points

As far back as the fourteenth century CE, a "three-point sermon" was mentioned by Robert de Basevorn, writing tongue-in-cheek:

> Only three statements, or the equivalent of three, are used in the theme [i.e., exposition] either from respect to the Trinity, or because a threefold cord is not easily broken [Eccles. 4:12], or because this method is mostly followed by Bernard [of Clairvaux, a twelfth-century abbot], or, as I think more likely, because it is more convenient for the set time of the sermon.[11]

The use of points (and proofs and propositions) reflects the tendency to see preaching primarily as an argument, likely a vestige of early Christian preaching that saw its task as convincing listeners of the rightness of doctrine and the wrongness of heresy.[12] But it was during the Reformation that preaching as an argument became the rule, perfectly suited as it was for Reformers' polemics against Roman Catholicism. While the polemic has since abated, the employment of an outlined sermon with points has been the norm in Protestantism since the sixteenth century. The scientific advances of the Enlightenment in the late seventeenth and eighteenth centuries furthered this trajectory of homiletics. "Rational homiletics does seem to parody scientific procedure in which an object is isolated for study."[13] The preaching text gets analyzed, like a biological specimen, for information; it is dissected and diced to generate propositions and points for sermons—so much so that preaching became synonymous with argument, dependent on proofs and rules of evidence, as if in a courtroom. The influential American homiletics scholar John A. Broadus (1827–95) perpetuated that tradition: "Preaching and all public speaking ought to be largely composed of argument."[14] And that legacy of courtroom argumentation—the "old" homiletic—continues to burden the field of preaching.[15]

11. Robert of Basevorn, *The Form of Preaching*, trans. Leopold Krul, in James J. Murphy, ed., *Three Medieval Rhetorical Arts* (Berkeley: University of California Press, 1971), 138.

12. This style continued to be used through the Middle Ages and on into the age of Scholasticism (1100–1700): the defense of church dogma in an increasingly pluralistic world, characterized by reasoning and disputation—preaching as argument.

13. David G. Buttrick, "Preaching the Christian Faith," *Liturgy* 2 (1983): 54.

14. "Author's Preface to the First Edition," in *A Treatise on the Preparation and Delivery of Sermons*, rev. ed., ed. Edwin Charles Dargan (New York: Harper and Brothers, 1926), vii. Also see Lucy Lind Hogan and Robert Reid, *Connecting with the Congregation: Rhetoric and the Art of Preaching* (Nashville: Abingdon, 1999), 37–39.

15. For the terms "old" and "new" homiletic, see Richard L. Eslinger, *A New Hearing: Living Options in Homiletical Method* (Nashville: Abingdon, 1987), 11; and Lucy Atkinson Rose, *Sharing the Word: Preaching in the Roundtable Church* (Louisville: Westminster John Knox, 1996), 31.

How can such an approach work with Scripture that is mostly narrative and poetry? What distilled essence or proposition can one derive from a story or a psalm, or even a proverb or a prophecy?[16] Is that how the authors of Scripture are communicating, and, in turn, is that how preachers are to communicate to their listeners? The *modus operandi* of the "old" homiletic is to put the text through a grinder and then preach, in points, the pulverized propositional products that come out of the contraption. But with the blossoming of language philosophy in the late twentieth century, the understanding of how language works has matured considerably, moving away from the sterile model that saw biblical revelation essentially as propositional communication, with texts serving merely as husks for those propositional kernels. Instead, communication of any kind—sacred or secular, spoken or scripted—is now being increasingly recognized as a communicator *doing* something with what is communicated. Authors, including those of Scripture, *do* things with their words. "Texts are no longer viewed as inert containers, jars with theological ideas inside, but as poetic expressions displaying rhetorical and literary artistry," *doing* things, intending effects in readers.[17]

Take the case of the narrative in 1 Samuel 15. With the following words, the prophet Samuel passes on God's message to King Saul that he should annihilate the Amalekites: שְׁמַע לְקוֹל דִּבְרֵי יְהוָה (*shma' lqol divre yhwh*)— "Listen to the *voice* of the word of Yahweh" (15:1).[18] Saul, however, does not obey: rather than eliminate all the animals and humans, he saves the good ones of the former and the chief of the latter. Soon after, Samuel confronts Saul. The king declares he has done everything that God told him to do, whereupon Samuel says: "What then is this *voice* of the sheep in my ears, and the *voice* of oxen which I hear?" (15:14).[19] Did you catch the thrust of the text? The author is *doing* something here, telling readers that *the child of God listens to the* voice *of God, not the* voice *of worldly seductions.*[20] Rather

---

16. I submit that such courtroom techniques will not work even for didactic texts in the Bible.

17. Thomas G. Long, "The Use of Scripture in Contemporary Preaching," *Interpretation* 44 (1990): 350.

18. Surprisingly, such a literal translation of the Hebrew is found only in the KJV and the NKJV. The seeming redundancy of "voice" is swept under the rug in most major English translations, which essentially have: "Listen to the word of Yahweh." But read on for the significance of "voice" in this narrative.

19. Again, unfortunately, most English translations render "voice" in each case here as "bleating" and "lowing," respectively, and thus, combined with the omission of "voice" in translations of 15:1, the thrust of the text is almost completely negated! These translational missteps are a clear indication that Bible translators and scholars don't think in terms of what biblical authors are *doing* with what they are saying. More on this below.

20. Also see 15:19, 20, 22, 24, for other significant *voices* in the story. (Thankfully, these are translated accurately in English.)

than parse and slice and dice and atomize the text to extract propositions, and then preach a theological sermon on genocide, or a historical discourse on the egregious sins of the Amalekites, the preacher must communicate the thrust of the text, which is clearly the issue of listening/obedience to God: שְׁמַע (*shma'*) can be translated "listen" or "obey" (15:1, 4, 14, 19, 20, 22, 24). That is what the author is *doing* with what he is saying here. Such a thrust must be the interpretive goal that a preacher seeks from any text, and that thrust must be the communicational goal a preacher aims for in any sermon. This notion of authors' *doing* things with what they say falls into the field of language philosophy called pragmatics.

Looking Forward: Pragmatics and Authors' Doings

Pragmatics, studying communication as an event, deals with what authors/speakers *do* with what they write/say. In an event of communication, what is being conveyed by authors is the pragmatics of the utterance, the *thrust* of what they wrote—that is, what they are *doing* with what they are saying. To catch what communicators are doing takes more than just a dissection of the linguistic, grammatical, and syntactical aspects of an utterance, which is the operations of *semantics*. Semantics, though a necessary foundation of interpretation, does not by itself yield the thrust of the text, which is the function of *pragmatics*.

One sees this even in folktales. Take the old one by Aesop about the dog that found a bone. On its way home with its booty, the canine happened to cross a bridge over a stream, and as it looked into the water it spotted "another" dog with a bone. Well, greed took over: the real animal barked at the reflected one, and thereby lost the bone it had. While the story deals with dogs, bones, bridges, streams, and reflections, the thrust of the story is about being content (and the loss one incurs otherwise). This is what the text is all about, its thrust—the pragmatics of the text. That is what Aesop was *doing* with what he was saying, and that is what he would want readers to catch and respond to: *One practices the prudence of contentment rather than lusting for the ephemeral.* Indeed, only after grasping this thrust of the text can one ever move to valid application consonant with the author's purpose. In other words, it is not enough to comprehend what authors are saying (the semantics of the utterance); one must also arrive at what authors are *doing* with what they are saying (the pragmatics of the utterance)—the text's thrust. In the fable by Aesop, the semantics deals with the description of the specific events—the dog-and-bone theater; the pragmatics or the thrust of the text is an endorsement of contentment—that was what the whole story was about.

Without the pragmatic determination of utterances, spoken or written, an appropriate response (i.e., valid application) is impossible. If, for instance, *A* tells *B*, "The door is open," how *A* intends for *B* to respond is entirely dependent upon *B* catching the pragmatics of *A*'s utterance. The communication is an event, and its semantics—the linguistic-grammatical-syntactical analysis of *A*'s four-word utterance—though essential, is insufficient and will get *B* nowhere in terms of application.[21] For a proper response, the pragmatics of discourse (the thrust) must be grasped. If the two have just had a quarrel in *A*'s home, *B* is being told to leave. If they are leaving *B*'s home together on an outing, *B* is being reminded to shut the door. If *B* is about to reveal a juicy bit of company gossip to *A* when the former drops into the latter's office, *B* is being asked to refrain from saying anything, at least until the open-door situation is rectified. And so on. What *A* was *doing* with what he was saying is critical for *B* to grasp, in order that *B* may respond appropriately to *A*.[22] Communication, after all, is an event, not just pressure waves in the air impinging upon the eardrum, or black marks on paper registering on the retina. Speakers (and authors) are *doing* things with what they say.

For interpretation for preaching, too, the thrust of a text of Scripture—what the author is *doing* with what he or she is saying (pragmatics)—must be discerned. Only by catching the author's *doing* in and with that text can God's people discover valid application. In our earlier illustration using 1 Samuel 15, unless one catches what the author was *doing* with those word-plays on "voice," one will not be able to respond appropriately to the demand of that text. *Trust God's fairness without doubting* (from God's severe treatment of the Amalekites) or *Watch out for sin's serious consequences* (from the fate of those sinful people) is not at all what that text is recommending. Rather, it is something like *Listen to God's voice, not the voice of anyone else or anything else* (from the textual clues dealing with "voice").[23]

21. The necessity of semantic analysis—the study of the linguistic, grammatical, and syntactical elements of the utterance—is obvious: unless the interpreter understands what is meant by "door" and "open" and how those words are put together with the article "the" and the verb "is" connecting subject and predicate adjective, there can be no comprehension of what the author is *doing* or what the thrust of the text is. In other words, there can be no pragmatics without semantics, but semantics by itself is insufficient for one to catch the thrust of the utterance and to respond properly to it.

22. These open-door "conversations" were modified from Thomas G. Long, "The Preacher and the Beast: From Apocalyptic Text to Sermon," in *Intersections: Post-Critical Studies in Preaching*, ed. Richard L. Eslinger (Grand Rapids: Eerdmans, 2004), 7.

23. See "Preaching Is Applicational" for more on the applicational facet of the preaching vision.

Authors *do* things with what they say, and therefore preachers are obliged to discern what was being *done* with what was being said in the text, and to communicate that thrust to their audiences. This, according to David Buttrick, is "critical" for preaching and "may well mark the beginning of homiletical obedience."[24]

In sum, valid application of a text is possible only by discerning the thrust of the text—what the author is *doing* with what he is saying, its pragmatics. This is especially true when interpreting for preaching purposes. For the chunks of biblical text used in sermons, the text itself provides adequate clues as to what the author is *doing* with what he is saying, as we saw with the 1 Samuel 15 narrative. The thrust of a text is, thus, the unified force of a biblical passage, the sum of its textual elements, the integration of all of its pathos and potency, everything in one package, geared to change the lives of readers and listeners.[25]

"Old" and "New" Homiletics: Shaping Sermons

How should this understanding of what authors *do* with what they say influence how preachers shape their sermons? A comparison of sermon-shaping in "old" and "new" homiletics is revealing.

"Old" Homiletic: Sermon Constructing

The characteristic feature of argumentation in the "old" homiletic has been the *point*: "For years, preachers have talked of making *points* in sermons. The word 'point' is peculiar; it implies a rational, at-a-distance pointing at things, some kind of objectification."[26] Sermon preparation, it was taught (and still is), was the fitting together of an assortment of these points (or propositions) that are distilled from Scripture. Craddock's wry observation (noted earlier) in this regard is worth repeating: "The minister boils off all the water and then preaches the stain in the bottom of the cup."[27] Thereby, sermons turn out to be "didactic devices," more about arguments to persuade listeners to buy into

---

24. David G. Buttrick, "Interpretation and Preaching," *Interpretation* 35 (1981): 58.

25. I will later label the textual *thrust* as the "theology" of the text; see "Preaching Is Theological." The Reflection sections in each chapter of this work, dealing with a portion of Mark's Gospel, also serve as examples for how such thrusts of texts may be discerned.

26. David G. Buttrick, *Homiletic: Moves and Structures* (Philadelphia: Fortress, 1987), 23.

27. Fred B. Craddock, *Preaching* (Nashville: Abingdon, 1985), 123. As will be seen below, the typical "old" homiletic preacher is a "distiller." But unlike the "alchemist" (see Introduction for these labels), this one affirms that preaching ought to be biblical.

these propositions, and less about texts and what they (or their authors) are *doing*.[28] All this may even imply that once one has gotten the distillate of the text, that is, the reduction of the text into one or more propositions, one can abandon the text itself. That is a kind of preaching that offers "the illusion rather than the reality of listening to the text."[29]

Moreover, significant emphasis is given in preaching classes to sermon "structure." This construction metaphor is the natural result of the organization of propositions and points on paper, a spatial model that is "static, rationalistic, and discursive."[30] The preacher distills a main point/proposition out of the textual details, and then the sermon is structured/constructed/crafted, slicing that main point into subpoints that answer diagnostic questions ("What does it mean?" "Is it true?" "So what?"), or that create a problem–solution–application scaffolding, or that provide a convenient then–always–now outline, and so on. This veritable army of sub- and sub-sub-points, Roman and Arabic, all in neatly indented array, are then dispersed forthwith into the audience: distillation and dispersion (see fig. 4.1).[31]

Figure 4.1
Distillation and Dispersion

Such propositions and points, as seminary students are taught to create, are inherently stagnant, resulting in "static and turgid" sermons: the transitions between points are tenuous at best, making a three-point sermon "three sermonettes barely glued together," with no substantive single movement from

28. Thomas G. Long, *The Witness of Preaching*, 2nd ed. (Louisville: Westminster John Knox, 2005), 102.
29. Craddock, *Preaching*, 100. In this "boiling down" approach, there is the other implicit assumption that the various genres of Scripture were mistakes on God's part; he should, rather, have given his people a list of propositions for them to work from. Some have actually attempted to make such an addition to the Bible. The publisher of a recent work in this vein claims that their product "complements" the English text of the Bible "by elaborating on 1,500 principles in Scripture that are as relevant today as when the sixty-six books of the Bible were written. Distilling these truths into principles . . . helps the reader more easily remember and effectively apply the Bible's wisdom to everyday life." See "Life Essentials Study Bible," http://www.bh publishinggroup.com/books/products.asp?p=9781586400453.
30. Eslinger, *New Hearing*, 64.
31. Fred B. Craddock, *As One without Authority* (St. Louis: Chalice, 2001), 45–47.

start to finish that retains the thrust of the text, maintains the momentum of the sermon, and sustains the interest of the audience.[32]

Not only does such an approach to preaching turn out to be rather dull but it also becomes very one-sided, with the conclusions of the preacher being foisted on hapless listeners, who are not discovering anything for themselves. In other words, the traditional mode of preaching reduces the audience to a silent jury whose votes are being bought by the preacher with propositions and proofs and points. There is therefore the strong sense that the audience is not involved with the text at all; everything is handed to them in the sermon, like flowers all cut and dried—and, unfortunately, as dead as those blooms.

Thus, for the longest time, preaching has been conducted as a forensic argument that proves the putative proposition of the text for the congregation—an act of reasoning, a parceling of information, and an appeal to the cognitive faculties of listeners to bring them to a rational conviction about that proposition. This rather unnatural operation denudes the text of its power, for what is being conveyed is not the agenda of the author (the thrust/pragmatics of the text) but the agenda of the *preacher* that has only a tenuous link, if any at all, with the thrust/pragmatics of the text. Besides, there is more to spiritual development in Christian life than a cognitive apprehension of arguments. Transformation, rather than information, must be the end point of preaching. And "preaching, if it is to appeal to the whole person, must appeal to both the conscious and subconscious, to the emotive and intuitive as well as the rational."[33] For this, one has to discern the thrust of the text with all its power and potency and pathos. And without such an appeal to both reason and emotion, to both mind and heart, there can be no transformation of life. This was the reformation attempted by the "new" homiletic in the latter half of the twentieth century.

"New" Homiletic: Sermon Plotting

Rather than engage in a *space*-organizing maneuver of ideas (an outline) espoused by the "old" homiletic, Eugene Lowry argues that a "new" homiletic should relate more to *time* (a plot). Thus the sermon, with movement and direction, is in a way a story—"a narrative art form."[34] Sermons are to be seen

32. Ibid., 56; Long, *Witness of Preaching*, 123. Suspecting that the sterile orderliness of such sermons lacks audience interest, the enterprising preacher spices the sermon with dashes of anecdotes, clips of movies, snatches of songs, scraps of dramas, and other bits of entertainment. I have nothing against any of these . . . *if* they contribute to the demonstration of what the author is *doing*, the thrust of the text.

33. Eslinger, *New Hearing*, 40.

34. Eugene L. Lowry, *The Homiletical Plot: The Sermon as Narrative Art Form*, rev. ed. (Louisville: Westminster John Knox, 2001), 5–6.

less as argument than as art, less as static tableau than as dynamic story. With a plot, the sermon becomes narratival, or storylike, progressing in an organic development in time (a biological phenomenon) rather than petrifying as an ordered construction in space (an engineering phenomenon). Not that the sermon itself tells a story, but that it explains the "plot" (i.e., the thrust) of the biblical pericope, what the author was *doing*. The goal of the preacher is to facilitate comprehension of the thrust of the text preached, for only then can valid application be derived.

Craddock, therefore, challenges the preacher to reproduce in the pulpit the process that occurred in the study. This should be a sufficiently detailed reenactment of the "Aha!" moments that happened as the preacher prayerfully pored over the text and its details in concert with scholars from the past and present. What is discovered in the study is creatively rediscovered in the pulpit, for the benefit of listeners (see fig. 4.2).

Figure 4.2
Discovery and Rediscovery

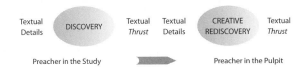

Rather than deliver a pre-chewed and digested meal, the goal is to guide listeners to experience the same momentum and excitement that came with the preacher's study of the text, enabling them to see the text in the same way as the preacher did, thus allowing them to catch the *thrust* of the text for themselves. "If *they* have made the trip, then it is *their* conclusion, and the implication for their own situations is not only clear but personally inescapable."[35] And as the burden of the text is now felt by the listeners, the application generated is also owned by them.

The word of God is for the people of God; they are the ones impelled by the thrust of the text to change their lives for the glory of God. The preacher is merely a facilitating intermediary who enables listeners to catch that thrust—what the author is *doing* with what he is saying in a particular pericope. Rather than argue one's way through the sermon, the preacher performs a creative, inductive exegesis of the text that develops and displays its thrust.[36] "The sermon, then, becomes not an essay, a lawyer's brief, a debater's rebuttal, or a piece of

35. Craddock, *As One without Authority*, 48–49 (italics original).
36. That this is a theological exegesis will be made clear in "Preaching Is Theological."

religious rhetoric; it becomes a journey . . . a journey which the preacher has taken once in the study and now guides for the congregation."[37] Thereby, the dullness of a dissertation is transformed into the delight of a discovery: "Aha! So that is what this passage is saying to us—that is the thrust of the text!"[38]

There is no reduction here of text; the thrust of the text is not a distillate of the passage into points and propositions (hence the cornerless circles in the figure above that illustrate the "new" homiletic, rather than triangles with points in the figure of the "old"). Instead, the preacher seeks to discover (and rediscover for listeners) the thrust of the irreducible text-as-a-whole, *in toto*, with the power and potency and pathos that is contributed indispensably by every part of the text. "Sermons should be faithful to the full range of a text's power, and those preachers who carry away only main ideas . . . are traveling too light."[39]

In his attempt to make preaching in the "new" homiletic storylike, But-trick calls for the sermon to comprise a series of "moves" (as opposed to the "points" of the "old" homiletic): paragraphs that open with a "statement of idea," proceed to a development thereof, and close with a "restatement of idea."[40] But that seems to be taking homiletics back to the "old" style, where each distilled "point" becomes a topic that is stated, developed (explained, proved, applied, etc.), and closed, before transitioning to the next "point." Thomas Long agrees, describing the "new" homiletic this way: "The preacher romps through the text, looking under rocks and peering into hidden caves in a stimulating exegetical hide-and-seek, but what is finally discovered, albeit with energy and excitement, is a main idea [aka 'proposition'] from the text."[41] In other words, even in the preaching propounded by the "new" homiletic, what is being carried over from text to audience via preacher seems to be a main idea of some sort, disguised for sure, but ultimately a distillate of the text that is then dispersed into "moves" in the sermon. Thus, in the final analysis, though the "new" homileticians are fine diagnosticians and have spotted the malaise

37. Thomas G. Long, "The Distance We Have Traveled: Changing Trends in Preaching," in *A Reader on Preaching: Making Connections*, ed. David Day, Jeff Astley, and Leslie J. Francis (Aldershot, UK: Ashgate, 2005), 16.

38. Long, *Witness of Preaching*, 103. Of course, with the preacher as the spiritual director and guide of the congregation (see "Preaching Is Pastoral"), it is incumbent upon such a one to also provide one or more concrete applications of the text. See "Preaching Is Applicational" for this second facet of communication in preaching.

39. Ibid., 101.

40. Buttrick, *Homiletic*, 35, 37.

41. Long, *Witness of Preaching*, 104. For Craddock, too, the goal became "the *point* the author sought to make," an unfortunate return to the "old" style (*As One Without Authority*, 85).

of the "old" homiletic, in their therapeutics they continue to prescribe bitter doses of "points," albeit somewhat sweetened by labeling them "moves."[42]

The "New" Homiletician: Curator and Witness

What, then, can be done to consolidate for preaching the concepts of the field of pragmatics and the understandings of the "new" homiletic, without lapsing back into the "old" style? For starters, we must reconceive the role of preachers. I propose the analogy of a curator or docent guiding visitors in an art museum through a series of paintings.[43] Each text is a picture, the preacher is the curator, and the sermon is a curating of the text-picture and its thrust for the congregants, gallery visitors.[44] A sermon is thus more a demonstration of the thrust of the text than an argument validating a proposition. A creative exegesis of the text is undertaken in the pulpit with a view to portraying for listeners what the author is *doing*. The sermon unveils the author's agenda. The distillation of the text into points and propositions is thereby obviated. Instead, as Long describes, the preacher is a "witness" of the text, to the text— equivalent to my analogy of the preacher being a curator of the text-picture.

The witness-preacher is "one who sees and experiences and tells the truth about what has been seen and experienced."[45] The preacher is trustworthy, not because of position, office, or status but because of what has been seen, heard, studied, and experienced, as this one "prayerfully goes to listen to the Bible on behalf of the people and then speaks on Christ's behalf what she or he hears there."[46] The verb "to witness" has the dual sense that corresponds to this twofold responsibility of the preacher. First, "to witness" means to see/ experience—to take something in. Second, "to witness" means to speak about what one has seen/experienced—to give something out. The preacher is thus a personal witness *of* the text and its *doings*, and then a public witness *to* the text and its *doings*. The first role is imperative for the second. "The move from

---

42. On the other hand, this work proposes a hermeneutic that discerns the thrust of a text by a close reading of the text itself, a *theological* exegesis (see "Preaching Is Theological"). A formal statement of this hermeneutic may be found in Abraham Kuruvilla, *Privilege the Text! A Theological Hermeneutic for Preaching* (Chicago: Moody, 2013).
43. Interestingly (and appropriately) enough, both "curator" (the museum officer) and "curate" (the church officer) are derived from the Latin *cura*, meaning "care": one cares for art, the other for souls.
44. As mentioned, how the thrust of a text is determined will be considered further in "Preaching Is Theological." It is also implicitly illustrated in the Reflection section of each chapter of this book—my efforts to curate for readers several text-pictures from the Gospel of Mark.
45. Long, "Distance We Have Traveled," 16.
46. Long, *Witness of Preaching*, 47, 52.

text to sermon is a move from beholding to attesting, from seeing to saying, from listening to telling, from perceiving to testifying, from *being* a witness to *bearing* witness."[47] In so witnessing, the *thrust* of the text will have been apprehended, first by the preacher, then by those to whom the sermon is preached.

Summary

This chapter focuses on the content of the biblical text that the preacher needs to communicate—the *what* of the text. The textuality of Scripture mandates that it is the *thrust* of the text that must be conveyed to God's people. For the longest time in church history, preaching has been governed by an "old" homiletic that distills propositions from texts and disperses them as points into the audience, without much synthesis or assessment of what authors *do* with what they say in the text—the thrust of the text. Such considerations fall in the domain of pragmatics, an integral part of communication of all kinds, written and spoken, sacred and secular. In keeping with this "new" homiletic—which has recognized the deficiencies of the "old" propositional approach—what is needed is to discover the pragmatics of the text and to creatively rediscover it in the pulpit for the audience's benefit. The preacher is a curator of the text-picture, or a witness to the text, whose essential task is to point out what is being *done* in the text and let its thrust impact listeners with all its power, potency, and pathos. *Preaching is communicational!*

Reflection

Mark 8:22–26 and 10:46–52—Two Blind Healings[48]

> "Do you still not see or understand? Do you have a hardened heart? Having eyes, do you not see? And having ears, do you not hear? And do you not remember?" (Mark 8:17–18)

> And Jesus said to him, "Go, your faith has healed you." And immediately he saw again and began following Him on the way. (Mark 10:52)

The Gospel of Mark is essentially a travelogue of Jesus and his disciples in three acts, set, respectively, in Galilee (1:1–8:21), "on the way" (8:22–10:52),

---

47. Ibid., 100.
48. For more details on these sections, see Abraham Kuruvilla, *Mark: A Theological Commentary for Preachers* (Eugene, OR: Cascade, 2012), 155–68, 226–37.

and in Jerusalem (11:1–16:8). An interesting feature—one of many in this Gospel—is the two healings of blind men that bracket Act II: a blind man is healed in 8:22–26, and another one, Bartimaeus, is cured in 10:46–52. What is Mark *doing* with these two blind healings?[49] Are they only about Jesus's power over the eyeball, optic nerve, and occipital cortex? If they are, one will likely end up with the same sermon from each of those passages: Jesus's power over human vision. Why would the depiction of this power need duplication? What exactly is Mark *doing* here?

The Healing of the Blind Man in Act I (Mark 8)

The continued lack of discernment of Jesus's person by his disciples is a constant theme in Act I (1:1–8:21): they were shown to be as uncomprehending as the crowds in their approach to Jesus in Mark 1:21–45; they were accused by Jesus of not understanding his parables in 4:1–34; they were fearful and faithless in 4:35–41; they were skeptical in 6:32–44, and fearful and faithless again in 6:45–56; and they continued to show no understanding in 7:1–23. Despite their having been with Jesus (3:14), having had access to the mystery of the kingdom (4:11) and to private instruction from him (4:10–20; 7:17–23), and having themselves been authorized to exorcise, heal, and preach (6:7, 12, 13), the disciples are "still" lacking discernment (8:21) here in this pericope, 8:1–21. Even after a miracle that fed five thousand, they are uncomprehending about Jesus's ability to provide for their daily needs. The crowds acclaim all these deeds of Jesus and respond positively, but the disciples neither *see* nor understand. And then comes the story of the healing of the blind man.

In the account of this healing of blindness (8:22–26), five different verbs are allotted to report the patient's restored sight in 8:24–25: ἀναβλέπω (*anablepō*, "look up"), βλέπω (*blepō*, "see"), ὁράω (*horaō*, "see"), διαβλέπω (*diablepō*, "look"), and ἐμβλέπω (*emblepō*, "see"). Coupled with the emphatic reminder that this man was blind (8:22, 23), this account, while true to fact, is to be understood theologically: Mark is *doing* something with the story.

This healing of the blind man is strategically placed at the end of Act I to contrast with the disciples who have eyes but do not see (8:17–18, 21), emphasizing the sorry state of their discernment of the person of Jesus. The specific note of having eyes and not seeing—the obtuseness of the disciples—links the episode of 8:1–21 precisely to the healing of blindness (8:22–26). This miracle

---

49. And, for that matter, what is Mark *doing* with two feeding miracles (in Mark 6 and Mark 8)? Are these simply repeated demonstrations of Jesus's power over matter? They are not; see ibid., 129–41 and 155–68.

signifies the lack of discernment of Jesus's *person* by the disciples (the thrust of Act I), but it also intimates, in the two-step process of healing, that something more is necessary if they are to see Jesus clearly. Act II (8:22–10:52) will emphasize the need for the disciple not only to discern the person of Jesus but also to accept his suffering *mission*—Jesus's passion is predicted three times in Act II. And at the conclusion of Act II we find another healing of a blind man (10:46–52; these are the only two healings of the blind in Mark), but this time the recovery of sight is immediate. A gradual understanding before has now become an instantaneous perception.

The Healing of the Blind Man in Act II (Mark 10)

Notably, the three passion predictions (Mark 8:31; 9:31; 10:33–34) occur in Act II, the "on the way" section of Mark (8:22–10:52). To be "on the way" of discipleship is to follow Jesus, not only discerning his person but also accepting his mission.

The story of Bartimaeus in 10:46–52 pictures a true disciple discerning Jesus's person and accepting his mission, ready to follow him to Jerusalem. Coming at the end of Act II and immediately prior to Jesus's entrance into Jerusalem in Act III (11:1–16:8), the account symbolizes the man's acceptance of Jesus's mission and his willingness to follow the Master on the way of suffering: Bartimaeus had become a disciple.

This is the last healing miracle in Mark; it is also the only one in which the healed one is named. By that token, this is a call to discipleship (three times the word "call" is used in 10:49), for in other similar summons in this Gospel, all the called characters are carefully named (1:16, 19; 2:14; 3:13–19). And what is striking is that only here in Mark is Jesus called Son of David by a human. So a blind man becomes the first to "see" Jesus as the messianic Savior, confessing him thus twice (10:47, 48)! And Bartimaeus follows up on his in*sight* by responding to Jesus without hesitation, leaving behind his (only?) possession, his cloak (10:50), to follow Jesus. The abandonment of the cloak may itself be a motif with symbolic value: all who were called to follow in this Gospel had to leave things behind, whether they be nets, boats, fathers, or livelihood (1:18, 20; 2:14; 10:28). The blind man had really seen Jesus!

These two blind healings frame Act II (Mark 8:22–10:52) at either end, effectively forming an introduction and conclusion to the act. The verbal similarities between the two miracles add to the effect: both narratives have Jesus and his disciples "come" to the particular location (8:22; 10:46), and both use ἀναβλέπω (*anablepō*, "look up/see again," 8:24; 10:51, 52). The importance of these bookends on either side of Act II—one a two-stage healing and the other an instantaneous one—is that they symbolize what happened between the two episodes, "on the way": the disciples are taught clearly ("plainly," 8:32) what the mission of Jesus is all about. Acceptance of Jesus's mission now becomes a possibility for all who follow him.

Those with eyes—the disciples—do not see; the blind man, Bartimaeus, in stark contrast, does. The account begins with Bartimaeus seated *"by the way"* (10:46), and ends with him following Jesus *"on the way,"* and he does so "immediately" after he is healed (10:52). Bartimaeus represents those disciples who have discerned Jesus's person and accepted his mission—they have seen, they have understood, and now they are ready to follow Jesus on the trip of discipleship. In other words, what Mark is *doing* is teaching his readers the importance of comprehending Jesus's person and accepting Jesus's mission—from dimly seeing to seeing clearly, and then following Jesus into Jerusalem (10:52) . . . to die (8:34): this is the thrust of the text.

- A disciple is to grow in the knowledge of Jesus's person and Jesus's mission. From blindness to sight is the motif of such growth. How are we growing in such sight? In the context of this chapter, how is our "sight" and insight into the biblical authors' *doings* improving? Are we catching the *thrust* of the text (its pragmatics) as we engage in interpretation?

- As our own hermeneutical "sight" is enhanced, are we preachers enabling the sight and enriching the understanding of our listeners? Are we, as curators and witnesses, opening to them the wonders of Scripture, what the human and divine authors are *doing* in the text?

- Enlightenment regarding the word of God, while contingent upon hard work on the part of the interpreter, is undoubtedly a divine initiative. Do we open our study of Scripture with a prayer for illumination, and conduct our examination of the text in an attitude of prayerful submission to this eye-opening ministry of the Holy Spirit?

- How about our prayers for the illumination of those who listen to our sermons? Are we privately and regularly praying for the ones we preach to? Are we—and others involved in leading worship—publicly praying for such illumination?

Preaching Is Communicational!

5

Preaching Is Theological

Open my eyes, that I may behold
Wondrous things from Your law.

Psalm 119:18

Biblical preaching, by a leader of the church, in a gathering of
Christians for worship, is the communication of the thrust of a
pericope of Scripture *discerned by theological exegesis*, and of
its application to that specific body of believers, that they may be
conformed to the image of Christ, for the glory of God—all in the
power of the Holy Spirit.

A few months ago, on an evening of heavy rain, I was turning into the
alley behind my home, ready to pull into my garage. That's when I
saw a utility truck parked right in front of my garage. I flashed my
headlamps. I honked. I waved. I pointed. All to no effect. In the downpour,
the driver couldn't make anything of my frantic gesticulations. And as for the
flashing and honking, he must have figured, "There's enough room in this alley
for another car to drive by. Why should I move? This dude can squeeze by."

I was stuck. Bereft of an umbrella and having no desire to be soaked to
the skin in the few moments it would take to get out of my car and approach
the truck, I really was stuck.

That's when I had a brainstorm. I punched that button under the rearview mirror that remotely operates my garage door. Said door opens. Said driver nods. Said truck reverses. And yours truly drives in, all safe and dry.

Now if I were to ask, "What did I do?" you might answer in a number of ways. You might say that the motor cortex of my brain initiated a signal that went down the spinal cord to the anterior horn cells at levels C4–C8 and T1, and thence to the muscles of my shoulder, arm, and hand, which, in response to those signals, contracted. Or you might say that I opened my garage door. Then again, you might say that I communicated to the truck driver that I wanted to get into the garage in front of which he was parked.

What did I do? From the point of view of accomplishing appropriate application, surely it was the last of those three options. It bore an implicit and expected response from the truck driver, and it succeeded in eliciting the response that I had intended. Riding upon my fundamental action (comprising of some muscle contractions) was a signal to the driver of the utility vehicle to move his truck. Yes, of course, I opened my garage door too, but the primary goal for my intended audience, the truck driver, was to get him to move his vehicle away from the entrance to my garage (the valid application I was seeking to provoke). From the point of view of the driver, the "reader," this is what I, the "author" of that communication, was *doing*.

The same distinctions operate in the analysis of biblical texts. One might interpret the Bible in many ways, for a variety of purposes. But when we interpret the text *for preaching* (and I stress that preaching is what we are dealing with here, not other legitimate uses of Scripture), we must focus upon what the author is *doing* with what he is saying in that particular text (i.e., the thrust of the text, its pragmatics) in order to elicit a particular (and valid) response from readers. The concept of authors' *doings*, introduced in the previous chapter, will be developed further here.

Pericopes and the World in Front of the Text

First, a word again about pericopes, or preaching texts. "Pericope" (περικοπή, *perikopē* = literally, "cutting around" or "sectioning"; thus a demarcated portion of text) refers to a segment of the biblical text that is of manageable size for homiletical use. Though the term is usually applied to portions of the Gospels, I use it in this work to indicate a slice of text in any genre that is utilized in Christian worship for preaching. In other words, a "pericope" is simply a preaching text, regardless of genre or even size. It is through pericopes, read and exposited in congregations as the basic units of Scripture, that God's people corporately encounter God's word.

Considered one at a time, pericopes allow a more intensive exploration of the thrust of the text, enabling its particularity and potency to impact the congregation, week by week. The goal of preaching, after all, is not merely to explicate the informational content of the chosen text, but to expound the text in such a way that its transformational implications are brought home to listeners.[1] Of course, life change is not a one-time phenomenon, accomplished instantaneously; rather, it involves a lifetime of gradual and progressive realignment to the will of God in Scripture. Such an incremental approach to the edification of God's people necessitates the sequential use of small portions of the biblical text—pericopes—in preaching.[2]

How does one discover the will of God in the chosen pericope, that one may align oneself to it? Here is where what authors *do*—pragmatics—comes in handy. In the previous chapter, "Preaching Is Communicational," we saw that authors *do* things with what they say—the thrust of the text. Let me carry the notion further here: what authors are *doing* is projecting *worlds in front of the text*.

A text is not an end in itself, but is the means to an end, a literary instrument of the author's action of projecting a transcending vision—what Paul Ricoeur called the *world in front of the text*.[3] Here is an example: In the previous chapter, I utilized the story of the dog and the bone. The folktale is projecting (or, if you wish, "painting") an ideal world for readers, a world in which inhabitants practice contentment: that's what Aesop wanted us to catch. Or in that 1 Samuel 15 narrative discussed earlier, the biblical author is projecting an ideal world in which inhabitants listen to/obey the voice of God, disregarding the seductions of all other voices. In essence, these worlds are the thrusts of those texts, and this is what their authors are *doing* with what they are saying; indeed, this is what these writers would want readers to respond to. And, in both cases, readers are being invited to dwell in such ideal worlds, abiding by the demands of those worlds. Here's Aesop: "Come, live in this ideal world by practicing contentment." And here's the author of 1 Samuel: "Come, abide in this ideal world by obeying only God's voice."

1. See "Preaching Is Applicational."

2. The demarcation of pericopes is a pragmatic decision to be made by the preacher. As has been mentioned before, choosing too small chunks of text may result in not very different ideas being preached from one week to another. Choosing too large sections would override the specific thrusts of smaller portions. Personally, I would employ the smallest sizes of texts that enable distinct ideas to be preached sequentially week to week. No doubt there is also the constraint of time allotted for a sermon that limits the size of the pericope that may be adequately exposited.

3. Paul Ricoeur, "Naming God," *Union Seminary Quarterly Review* 34 (1979): 217.

To live in those respective worlds projected is to abide by the values of those worlds—practicing contentment in one, obeying God in the other.

Thus a text not only tells the reader about the world *behind* the text, what actually happened (the story of the dog and its bone, or the story of a prophet, a king, some wicked people, and a bunch of animals); a text also projects an ideal world *in front of* the text that bids the reader inhabit it, a world characterized by certain precepts, priorities, and practices. With regard to our examples (Aesop's fable/1 Samuel 15), the projected world is one in which a critical *precept* is that such contentment/obedience to God's voice will prevent loss; it is a world in which contentment/obedience to God's voice is a key *priority*; and it is a world in which the *practice* of contentment/obedience to God's voice is the norm. Thus, in texts, a view of life is portrayed, projecting for the reader a world beyond the confines of the text. A world is portrayed, an invitation to that world is extended, and lives are changed as listeners respond to inhabit the world and live by its precepts, priorities, and practices.[4]

All literary texts function in this manner to project worlds in front of themselves; a text serves as an instrument or agent of that world-projecting action, and in this way, these texts have bearing upon the future. That is to say, a text's projected world enables application in the future. Because Scripture is intended for future application by God's people, its interpretation cannot cease with the elucidation of its linguistic, grammatical, and syntactical elements (its semantics), but must proceed further to discern the *world in front of the text*—the thrust of the text, its pragmatics: what the author is *doing*. This projected world forms the intermediary between text and application, and enables one to respond validly to the text (see fig. 5.1). When the text is rightly applied, its readers are, in effect, inhabiting the world it projects.[5]

Figure 5.1
Text to Application

Text   Pragmatics / Thrust / World   Application

Indeed, *all* communication functions this way. For instance, reverting to the same protagonists we encountered in "Preaching Is Communicational," if *A*

4. Needless to say, the fables of Aesop have nowhere near the authority or the transformational power of inspired Scripture.

5. For all practical purposes, these elements—*world in front of the text*, the thrust of the text, and the pragmatics of the text (i.e., what its author is *doing*)—may be considered equivalent, as indicated in the figure. Later, I will label this entity the "theology" of the pericope.

tells *B*, "Hey, you are standing on my foot!" the *semantic* meaning (what the author is saying) asserts the spatial location of *B* upon the lower limb of *A*, while the *pragmatic* meaning (what the author is *doing* with what he is saying— the thrust of the utterance) attempts to get *B* to relocate from that traumatic situation upon *A*'s anatomy. In fact, what *A* was *doing* with what *A* said was projecting a world in which no one is ever stationed upon *A*'s lower extremities to cause distress. *A*'s desire was for *B* to inhabit such an ideal "nobody-ever-standing-on-*A*'s-foot-to-cause-*A*-pain" kind of world. That inhabitation could be accomplished only by conforming to the requirement of that world—*B*'s removing the burden off *A*'s foot, thus alleviating the latter's agony, for in that projected world nobody ever stands on *A*'s foot to cause *A* pain.[6]

Unfortunately, that is not how biblical texts are looked at in the "old" homiletic style. For instance, if that statement by *A* to *B* ("Hey, you are standing on my foot!") were an inspired utterance in Scripture, a preacher in the traditional camp expositing that "text" on Sunday morning would conceivably expatiate on the derivation of the word "foot" from the Old English *fot* from the Latin *pes* from the Greek *pos*. The preacher might discourse upon the foot's kinesiology (twenty-six bones, thirty-three joints, over a hundred muscles, tendons, and ligaments), its hematology (blood vessels), and its neurology (nerve supply). This preacher would no doubt wax eloquent about the pathology of that extremity (the various abnormalities: club foot, flat foot, athlete's foot, skew foot, rheumatoid foot . . .), and so on, focusing on all the "-ologies" but completely missing the thrust of the utterance and its intended valid application: "*Get your foot off mine!*" In other words, unless one catches what *A* is *doing* with what he is saying (its pragmatics and thrust, i.e., the *world in front of the text*), valid application in response to *A*'s comment is impossible. Without a comprehension of the pragmatics, without grasping the ideal *world in front of the text* (in which no one stands on *A*'s foot to cause *A* pain), all this regurgitation of kinesiology, hematology, neurology, or pathology—or Christology, ecclesiology, or one's favorite "-ology" *du jour*—can never bring one to valid application.

So also for the biblical text. Look at it this way: The biblical canon as a whole projects a *world in front of the text*—God's ideal world, individual segments of which are portrayed by individual pericopes. Taken together, the integrated composite of all such segments makes up the canonical projection of God's ideal *world in front of the text*—the plenary canonical world (see fig. 5.2).

---

6. Likewise, by my opening my garage door, I was projecting a world in which no one obstructs the entrance to my garage. My intention for the utility-truck driver was that he inhabit this ideal world, abiding by its key requirement—that is, he needed to move his vehicle away from my garage door.

Figure 5.2
World in Front of the Text

Pericope	Segment of the World	Canonical World
Pericope 1	Segment 1 of Canonical World	
Pericope 2	Segment 2 of Canonical World	
Pericope 3	Segment 3 of Canonical World	
Pericope 4	Segment 4 of Canonical World	Plenary Canonical World
Pericope 5	Segment 5 of Canonical World	
. . .	. . .	
Pericope *n*	Segment *n* of Canonical World	

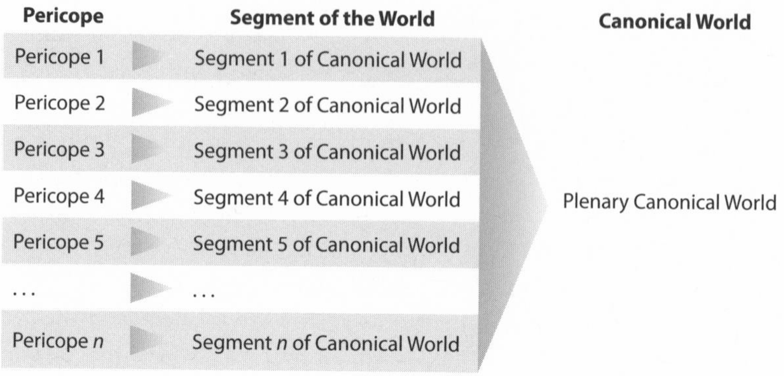

Thus each sermon on a particular pericope is God's gracious invitation to humankind to live in his ideal world by abiding by the thrust of that pericope—the requirements of God's ideal world (or divine demand) as called for in that pericope's world segment.[7] And as humankind accepts that divine invitation, week by week and pericope by pericope God's people are progressively and increasingly inhabiting his ideal world and abiding by the precepts, priorities, and practices of that world. One pericope at a time, the various aspects of Christian life, individual and corporate, are gradually being brought into alignment with the will of God for the glory of God—God's world is becoming reality. This is the goal of preaching.

Pericopal Theology

For each pericope, then, its particular world segment is what the author wants us to catch; this is what he would want us to respond to—this is the thrust of that text. The thrust of the text tells us how things should be in God's ideal world. It is a world in which his precepts regulate life, his priorities predominate for life, and his practices operate in life (precepts, i.e., why things occur in the *world in front of the text*; priorities, i.e., what things matter in the *world in front of the text*; and practices, i.e., how things function in the *world in front of the text*). In the 1 Samuel 15 narrative, a precept of that world it projects (why things occur) is that obedience

---

7. In similar fashion, my opening my garage door was an implicit invitation to the truck driver to come and live in the world I was projecting, a world in which my garage door remains always unobstructed.

yields blessing.[8] A major priority of that ideal world (what things matter) is, therefore, obedience to the voice of God. And so, obedience is the practice of that ideal world (how things function). One who wishes to abide in that ideal world of God must therefore adopt this world's precepts, priorities, and practices as proposed in that pericope, 1 Samuel 15.

Because this world speaks of God and how he relates to his creation, this projected world may rightly be called "theology." The segment of this ideal world that each pericope projects then becomes the theology of that pericope. Thus *pericopal theology is the theology specific to a particular pericope—representing a segment of the plenary world in front of the canonical text that portrays God in his relationship to his people—which functions as the crucial intermediary in the move from text to application.* Living by the theology of the pericope is to accept God's gracious invitation to inhabit his ideal world. By so doing, God's people align themselves to the precepts, priorities, and practices of that ideal world—that is, to the will of God, to divine demand.

In sum, each sermon must point out the theology of the pericope under consideration, elucidating what that specific text affirms about God and his relationship with humankind—the precepts, priorities, and practices of the *world in front of the text*. This "theological interpretation" is exegesis done with theological lenses: the preacher—the curator and witness of the text—essentially points out those elements of the text that serve as clues to the theology of the pericope (the repetitions of "voice" in 1 Samuel 15, for example), synthesizing these clues into the theological thrust of the pericope. What the pericope affirms in its theology forms the basis of the subsequent move to derive application. David Buttrick was right: "The odd idea that preachers can move from text to sermon without recourse to theology by some exegetical magic or a leap of homiletic imagination is obvious nonsense." He calls for "theo-*logic*" to grasp the thrust of the text.[9] Biblical interpretation that does not elucidate this crucial intermediary, pericopal theology, is *de facto* incomplete, for without discerning this entity, valid application can never be arrived at.

As a relatively new field in the past decade, "theological interpretation of Scripture" remains quite undefined, with a number of variant approaches to this hermeneutical operation. In this work, however, a unique strategy for theological interpretation is adopted, one operating from the vantage point of the pulpit of a preacher rather than from the desk of a Bible scholar or

---

8. Of course, in the narrative it was the negative image of this precept that was portrayed: disobedience leading to *un*blessing—King Saul's loss of throne (1 Sam. 15:26–28).

9. David G. Buttrick, "Interpretation and Preaching," *Interpretation* 35 (1981): 57.

from the lectern of an academic theologian. Specifically, the "theology" in the *"theological* hermeneutic" proposed here is *pericopal theology*, not biblical or systematic theology.

Here's how pericopal theology differs from systematic and biblical theology (as they are commonly defined). Systematic theology draws conclusions deductively from one text and integrates those with deductions from other texts, slotting them all into a variety of theological categories. D. A. Carson defines systematic theology as "the branch of theology that seeks to elaborate the whole and the parts of Scripture, demonstrating their . . . connections."[10] By virtue of this connecting and correlating activity, systematic theology operates at a level that is more general than does pericopal theology. The latter, on the other hand, is more inductively derived and is constrained by the particulars of a single pericope. It deals with matters pertaining to God and his relationship to his creation as proposed in *that* pericope; thus it is an expression of divine will in *that* text for God's people to abide by, if they are to inhabit God's ideal world.

The operation of biblical theology also tends to be more general than that of pericopal theology, for it develops broad biblical themes across the canon, with a strong emphasis on timelines. According to Sidney Greidanus, "biblical theology . . . helps us trace longitudinal themes from the Old Testament to the New."[11] Invariably, then, the preacher will find that several pericopes, especially adjoining ones, deal with the same general themes of biblical theology, potentially resulting in the same sermon week after week. Seeing a text in the wider historical context of the canon, for which biblical theology is certainly helpful, is not the same as seeing how a particular pericope makes a specific demand of its reader as it projects a segment of the ideal world of God. "Biblical theology involves the quest for the big picture, or the overview, of biblical revelation."[12] But big canonical pictures tend to miss the small pericopal miniatures. And it is these miniatures (i.e., the theology of

10. D. A. Carson, "Unity and Diversity in the New Testament: The Possibility of Systematic Theology," in *Hermeneutics, Authority, and Canon,* ed. D. A. Carson and John D. Woodbridge (Grand Rapids: Baker, 1995), 69–70. Also see Charles C. Ryrie, *Basic Theology: A Popular Systematic Guide to Understanding Biblical Truth* (Chicago: Moody, 1999), 15: "Systematic theology correlates the data of biblical revelation as a whole in order to exhibit systematically the total picture of God's self-revelation."
11. Sidney Greidanus, *Preaching Christ from the Old Testament: A Contemporary Hermeneutical Method* (Grand Rapids: Eerdmans, 1999), 267. Also see Edmund Clowney, *Preaching and Biblical Theology* (Nutley, NJ: P&R, 1977), 15–16: "Biblical theology formulates the character and content of the progress of revelation."
12. Graeme Goldsworthy, *Preaching the Whole Bible as Christian Scripture: The Application of Biblical Theology to Expository Preaching* (Grand Rapids: Eerdmans, 2000), 22.

the individual pericopes) that are essential for the week-by-week, life-changing transactions of preaching.[13]

So, on the one hand, with systematic or biblical theology as the basis of individual sermons, distinctions between the theological thrusts of successive pericopes are harder to maintain. Operating, as these species of theology do, at a level of generality somewhat removed from the specificity of the text and the intricacy of its details, sermons on contiguous pericopes will often have similar goals and applications. On the other hand, given the degree of specificity prescribed by pericopal theology, the sequential preaching of pericopes would not be impeded by this handicap. The particular theological thrust of each pericope would be heard clearly, without the weekly tedium caused by the repetition of the broad themes of biblical and systematic theology.

In sum, there is, in my conception, a twofold aspect to the sermonic transaction: the exposition of the theology of the pericope (i.e., the move from text to pericopal theology) and the discovery of how pericopal theology may be applied in real life (i.e., the move from pericopal theology to application) (see fig. 5.3).[14]

Figure 5.3
Pericopal Theology

Text → Pericopal Theology → Application

Pericopal theology thus helps bring that specific portion of the biblical text to bear upon the situation of the hearers, thereby aligning congregation to canon, God's people to God's word. Pericope by pericope, the community of God is increasingly oriented to the will of God as it progressively inhabits God's ideal world projected by the canon. William Willimon puts it well: "In preaching, we are moving people, little by little, Sunday by Sunday, toward new and otherwise unavailable descriptions of reality. . . . Christian preaching is not merely the skillful description of the world as it is but a bold, visionary, and demanding call to be part of a world that is to be."[15]

13. This is, of course, not to neglect the larger context in which a particular pericope is situated. The textual environs of that pericope will no doubt govern the interpretation of its specific theology. But it is that specific theology that is to be applied for the life change called for in preaching.
14. For this second move, see "Preaching Is Applicational."
15. William H. Willimon, *Conversations with Barth on Preaching* (Nashville: Abingdon, 2006), 115.

Theological Function of Pericopes: Covenant Renewal

As pericopes are sequentially preached from, and their theology exposited, the resulting transformation of lives reflects a gradual and increasing alignment to the precepts, priorities, and practices of God's kingdom (his ideal world). This is illustrated by the account of covenant renewal in Nehemiah 7:73b–8:12, a passage discussed in earlier chapters. Covenant renewal may be considered a prototype for how all future communities of God align themselves to the will of their divine Sovereign in his word.

The paradigmatic notion of God's people as purchased and delivered by him reflects all the acts of deliverance God performs for his people, especially the redemption wrought in Jesus Christ.[16] The redeemed of God of all time thus become citizens of his kingdom, their liberation by God making them subjects of a new King.[17] This extraordinary relationship between Redeemer and redeemed mandates that the maintenance of such an affiliation be given constant and careful attention in the corporate life of the people of God. Covenant renewal—the reaffirmation of the relationship between deity and humanity—provides the perfect occasion for God's people to focus upon their unique status under God and their resulting responsibilities to him.[18] Reminding itself of the status and responsibilities of its privileged position, the community, in covenant renewal, commits to aligning itself to the will of its divine Sovereign. Indeed, such communal acts were fairly standard in the milieu of Israel's neighbors, to preserve relationships between clients and overlords.[19] In the same fashion, regular and frequent readings of their foundational text, the Torah, played a critical role in preserving the Israelites' covenant relationship with Yahweh, the one to whom they owed ultimate allegiance. In pledging its loyalty to Yahweh, the nation placed itself under obligation to abide by the revealed will of God. Historically, therefore, the reading of Scripture was always intertwined with this principle of covenant renewal; it is particularly exemplified in Ezra's proclamation of the law in the mid-fifth century BCE.[20]

---

16. Moses's and Miriam's Song of the Sea (Exod. 15:1–21) clearly marked out the Israelites as having been bought and redeemed by Yahweh (Exod. 15:16). This theme is also reflected in the New Testament in 1 Cor. 6:20; 7:23; Titus 2:14; 1 Pet. 1:18–19; 2:9; Rev. 5:9; etc.

17. See Lev. 25:55; Isa. 43:1; and, in the New Testament, Rom. 6:17–23; 1 Cor. 7:22; Col. 4:7; etc.

18. I do not intend any particular biblical covenant when using the term "covenant renewal." It simply serves as a convenient template for the description of the alignment of God's people to their Sovereign in a formal and corporate context, in response to the preaching of God's Word.

19. See Robert H. Pfeiffer, *One Hundred New Selected Nuzi Texts*, trans. E. A. Speiser (New Haven: American Schools of Oriental Research, 1936), 103; and Gary Beckman, *Hittite Diplomatic Texts* (Atlanta: Scholars Press, 1996), 42, 47, 76, 86.

20. Deuteronomy 31:10–13 reports on a similar transaction under Moses.

The reading of the law in Nehemiah 7:73b–8:12 was the watershed phenomenon in the life of the postexilic community of Israel, and the climax of the Ezra-Nehemiah joint corpus. Within the larger body of the account (Neh. 6:1–12:47), the renewal of covenant forms the center of a chiasm.

6:1–7:4	A Completion of the city walls
7:5–73a	B List of ancestral inhabitants
7:73b–10:39	C Covenant renewal
11:1–12:26	B′ Repopulation of Jerusalem
12:27–47	A′ Dedication of the city walls

The interpolation of covenant renewal (C) within the broader undertaking that restored the Holy City (A and A′—its structure; B and B′—its people) made this transaction the critical event that reconstituted the children of Israel after decades of exile and reestablished their standing before God.[21] In this renewal of covenant, what is especially pertinent for preachers is the activity of the Levites in Nehemiah 8:7–8 (discussed in "Preaching Is Communicational"). Their task was to facilitate the community's comprehension of what God required of them, corresponding to the duty of preachers today. Comprehension by the congregation included application of Scripture to their lives (Neh. 8:9–12, 16–18). And this response is at the core of covenant renewal: the exposition of the biblical text in an ecclesial context culminates in application that realigns the congregation to God and his will, and restores them in proper relation to him.

What is being sought in the corresponding weekly homiletical undertakings of the church is also alignment with divine will. Pericopes of the biblical text are therefore the literary instruments of covenant renewal, performing this crucial function by portraying a segment of the larger canonical world projected by the full text of Scripture. It is to the theology of this pericope—the precepts, priorities, and practices of that projected world segment—that individuals are bidden to align themselves. Listeners are thus called to inhabit the pericopal segment of the projected world, abiding by the divine demand therein—covenant renewal in action. As this inhabitation takes place sermon by sermon and pericope by pericope, more and more facets of life are aligned to the will of God. Thus, gradually, God's ideal world comes to be: a world in which his precepts regulate life, his priorities predominate for life, and his practices operate in life. The facilitation of this alignment to divine will is

---

21. See Abraham Kuruvilla, *Text to Praxis: Hermeneutics and Homiletics in Dialogue*, Library of New Testament Studies 393 (London: T&T Clark, 2009), 151–55.

the responsibility of the preacher, the one ordained for the solemn task of interpreting and applying the text for the community of God, the chaperone for moving God's people from text to application: "I solemnly charge you in the presence of God and of Christ Jesus . . . preach the word" (2 Tim. 4:1–2).

Such a conception of covenant renewal and alignment to God's will as the model for preaching should not cause one to construe divine demand (and preaching) as merely a litany of dos and don'ts that a capricious God burdens his people with. Not at all! In fact, there is no compulsion to obey, although there are strong incentives to do so, both positive and negative. Instead, God's call to be aligned with his will is a gracious invitation to inhabit his ideal world, and to enjoy its fullness of blessing, in the presence of God. It is a divine offer that should capture our imaginations and set afire our affections for God's ideal world, for "our action emerges from how we *imagine* the world."[22] This vision of the good life captivates us not with propositions and points but with "a picture of what it looks like for us to flourish and live well" in every facet of our existence—a vision cast by the preacher from the word of God in the form of pericopal theology.[23] This is the vision of a *world in front of the text*, God's ideal world, painted by Scripture and portrayed in preaching—a glimpse of the divine kingdom. And as this world is gradually unveiled by faithful preaching, as the community of God inhabits this ideal world pericope by pericope, in faithful application,

> the goods and aspects of human flourishing painted by these alluring pictures of the good life begin to seep into the fiber of our . . . being (i.e., our hearts) and thus govern and shape our decisions, actions, and habits. . . . Attracted by it and moved toward it, we begin to live into this vision of the good life and start to look like citizens who inhabit the world that we picture as the good life. We become little microcosms of that envisioned world as we try to embody it in the here and now.[24]

It is the biblical canon, preached by the leader of the people of God in the context of their worship of God, that portrays what this divine world and kingdom looks like, how it functions, and how the community is to inhabit it. Pericope by pericope, the theological picture of the world is unveiled. This is the world God would have; and this is the kind of people God would have us be.

---

22. James K. A. Smith, *Imagining the Kingdom: How Worship Works*, Cultural Liturgies 2 (Grand Rapids: Baker Academic, 2013), 31–32.
23. James K. A. Smith, *Desiring the Kingdom: Worship, Worldview, and Cultural Formation*, Cultural Liturgies 1 (Grand Rapids: Baker Academic, 2009), 53.
24. Ibid., 54.

Theological vs. Traditional Exegesis

Such a conception of covenant renewal and the notion of pericopal theology call preachers to undertake a special kind of exegesis, a *theological* exegesis (pertaining to pericopal theology). But what has been taught and practiced over the centuries in the "old" homiletic is an indiscriminate excavation of the text, the exegetical turning over of whatever can be unearthed, whether it be earth, wood, bone, stone, potsherds, whatever.[25] These operations of traditional exegesis, integral to the "old" homiletic, involve a slicing and dicing of the text with word studies, sentence diagramming, linguistic analyses, historical investigations, geographical inquiries, and so on.[26] Much information is dug up; unfortunately, none of it very useful to the preacher to craft a sermon for changing lives with that particular text.

What is necessary is to grasp the thrust of the text, what the author is *doing* with what he is saying, to comprehend the projected world, the theology of the pericope. I therefore propose a *theological* exegesis that privileges the text, looking for clues to its theology—not a random dig but a directed one that searches specifically for those gold nuggets of pericopal theology. Within every text, there are literary and stylistic traces of authors' agendas, evidence pointing to the authors' *doings*, signs that lead to the discovery of pericopal theology. But only a privileging of the text by theological exegesis will discover that precious ore.

All texts, sacred and secular, and particularly those intended to influence behavior over a lengthy span of time (i.e., the classics), are agenda-driven creations of their authors. It is no different for the canonical classic that Scripture is. Its human authors, too, were writing with an agenda, and their literary productions were intended to convey that agenda—the theology of those texts.[27]

Take narrative, for example. These are not simply journalistic reports of what happened to whom, when, and where. Rather, they are carefully constructed theological treatises—of pericopal theology, that is—for the *primary* aim of these texts is to transform life, not impart information. To achieve this end, every part of the text is framed and fashioned precisely to create a discourse geared to further authors' theological goals. Consider the liberty they have just with regard to time—and I'll illustrate with examples from

---

25. In the introduction I called this a hermeneutic of excavation.

26. There is, of course, a place for all of these exercises. However, if they don't help the preacher discern the theology of the pericope—what the author is *doing*—all these exertions are futile.

27. As was noted earlier, for the purposes of these discussions, I will not make a distinction between the agendas of human and divine authors.

Mark's Gospel. Here's how Mark "plays" with time: flash forward (e.g., the foretelling of Jesus's passion, 8:31–32; 9:31–32; 10:33–34), flash back (e.g., the reviewing of the death of John the Baptist, 6:14–29), summary (e.g., the condensation of Jesus's forty days in the wilderness, 1:13), ellipsis (e.g., the silence with regard to the day following the crucifixion, 16:1), and pause (e.g., Mark's stopping of the story-clock to interpolate glossing remarks of his own, 7:3–4). The shackles of time are shed by means of the literary liberty exercised by the narrator—all purposefully done to accomplish his agenda. Or take Mark's shaping of his entire work as one linear journey of Jesus and his disciples, from Galilee to Jerusalem. That is surely an authorially imposed structure, for John's Gospel has those same characters going at least three times to Jerusalem, once a year as every good Jew should. You see, Mark is *doing* something with his storytelling: his theological agenda is to create a handbook of discipleship, what it means to go with Jesus from Galilee to Jerusalem . . . to die! So his text serves his agenda, as he creates a one-way trip of discipleship. Thereby, a worldview is portrayed, with each pericope projecting a segment of that world—pericopal theology. All authors exercise this same freedom to accomplish their goals—so much so that it is impossible to "narrativize *without* moralizing." Narratives in Scripture, too, are "primarily ideological [read: "theological"] in purpose," designed to change lives for the glory of God.[28]

A possible analogy is the difference between a portrait and a caricature of an individual: both represent the same person, but the portrait painter attempts to translate everything on the visage of the sitter to the image on the canvas, whereas the caricature artist "samples" a hooked nose, a beady eye, a cauliflower ear, a shaggy coiffure, or a gap-toothed grin. Likewise a text—say, a narrative—is more like a caricature than a portrait; not everything need be told, not everything need be marching forward in time in orderly detail. An agenda-driven storytelling emphasizes only those aspects that further that authorial agenda.[29] These emphases of the biblical author are critical to discover, for they are clues to what the author is *doing*; they help elucidate the pericopal theology, which in turn helps one discern valid application. So for preaching purposes, to discover what the author is *doing* with what he is saying—the theology of the text—one must pay close attention to the text

28. Hayden White, "The Value of Narrativity in the Representation of Reality," in *On Narrative*, ed. W. J. T. Mitchell (Chicago: University of Chicago Press, 1981), 23. This is not to imply that authors misrepresent facts. Rather, it is an admission that every narrative is an agenda-driven recounting of events, characteristic of *all* storytelling, inspired or otherwise.

29. In Scripture, this is true not only of narrative but also of any genre: all texts are written to further authorial agendas, to project worlds, to depict theologies.

itself for those all-important theological clues. Remember how, in the 1 Samuel 15 story of Samuel, Saul, and the Amalekites, the clue of "voice" played an important role in revealing the pericopal theology. Such clues can be discerned only by a careful reading of the text—theological exegesis.[30]

Unfortunately, rather than advocate close attention and a careful reading of the text, the "old" homiletic looks right through the text at the event itself that is described. In the narrative of 1 Samuel 15 the author's *doing* with what he was saying was significantly attenuated by translators with a misguided enthusiasm for what happened *behind* the text. In 1 Samuel 15:1 translators determined that what really happened was that the word of Yahweh came to Samuel, so they swept the redundant "voice" under the rug (remember that the Hebrew has "*voice* of the word of Yahweh"). Likewise, in 15:14 the Hebrew "voice" was translated into English as "bleating" and "lowing." After all, cattle and sheep don't have voices, do they? They bleat and they low, and that was what really happened—the event *behind* the text. But by focusing on the event *behind* the text rather than on the text itself, the theology of the pericope was completely negated! Instead, for preaching purposes, the interpreter must privilege the text; only in so doing can one discover what is projected *in front of* the text, pericopal theology.

In sum, it is the text that must be privileged, for it alone is inspired. Events *behind* the text are not inspired and therefore not expressly "profitable for teaching, for reproof, for correction, for training in righteousness" (2 Tim. 3:16). All this to say, for the goal of life transformation, it is not the events that must be attended to but the Holy Spirit's *accounts* of those events—the text must be privileged. Or to put it differently, the text is not a plain glass window that the reader looks *through* (to discern some event behind it—traditional exegesis in the "old" homiletic). Rather, the narrative is a stained-glass window that the reader looks *at* (theological exegesis in the "new" homiletic).[31] The glass, the stains, the lead, the copper, and everything else that goes into the production of the stained glass are meticulously planned for the appropriate effect, to tell a particular story. So too with narratives, textual or other-

---

30. Again, I have attempted to illustrate such readings in the Reflection sections of this work, a curating of selected text-pictures from the Gospel of Mark. For a working-out of all the pericopes of entire biblical books in this fashion, see Abraham Kuruvilla, *Mark: A Theological Commentary for Preachers* (Eugene, OR: Cascade, 2012); Abraham Kuruvilla, *Genesis: A Theological Commentary for Preachers* (Eugene, OR: Resource Publications, 2014); and Abraham Kuruvilla, *Ephesians: A Theological Commentary for Preachers* (Eugene, OR: Cascade, 2015).

31. The stained-glass metaphor is borrowed from Sidney Greidanus, *The Modern Preacher and the Ancient Text: Interpreting and Preaching Biblical Literature* (Grand Rapids: Eerdmans, 1989), 196.

wise. The preacher must, therefore, pay close attention to the text, not just to what is being said, but also to how it is being said and why, in order that the agenda of the author—that is, the thrust of the text, the theology of the pericope—may be discerned.[32]

Summary

Authors *do* things with texts, as the field of pragmatics explains. Scripture is no different. A pericope, a preaching text, is an instrument of the author's *doings*. Each pericope is projecting a segment of God's ideal world, and together, all the segments of all the biblical pericopes make up the transcending vision of the *world in front of the text*. God's ideal world is one in which his precepts regulate life, his priorities predominate in life, and his practices operate for life. Thus, as God's people abide by the precepts, priorities, and practices of this world, pericope by pericope and week by week they are progressively and increasingly inhabiting God's ideal world and aligning themselves to divine demand; covenant renewal is taking place. Each segment of this projected world, governing as it does the relationship of God to his people, is the theology of the pericope. The discernment of pericopal theology by theological exegesis is critical to preaching, for only through pericopal theology can one arrive at valid application—the inhabitation of God's world. Scripture, therefore, is God's gracious invitation to his people to live in his ideal world, with him, and in his presence, enjoying his blessings—a grand privilege indeed. *Preaching is theological!*

Reflection

Mark 11:1–25—Christ's Kingship[33]

> "Hosanna!
> Blessed is the one who comes in the name of the Lord!
> Blessed is the coming kingdom of our father David!
> Hosanna in the highest!"
>
> Mark 11:9–10

32. For sure, there is a place for the chronological organization and harmonization of events *behind* the text. However, the focus for preaching—our interest in this book—ought to be not on events *behind* the text but on the inspired text and its projected world *in front of* itself—pericopal theology. Only then can valid application, which is the goal of preaching, be arrived at.

33. For more details on this pericope, see Kuruvilla, *Mark*, 241–53.

Act III of Mark's Gospel (11:1–16:8) begins with this pericope, 11:1–25. Here, Jesus enters Jerusalem . . . to die. As one looks carefully, one notices that his entry into the city and into the temple precincts gets a lot of mention; in fact, in the larger section, 11:1–13:1, there are three such movements (A, A', and A″), separated by the two halves of the story describing the cursing of the fig tree (B and B'). The centerpiece (A') has the temple-cleansing episode.

A Jerusalem entry I: "came into," "Jerusalem," "temple" (11:11); "went out" (11:11)	11:1–11
B Fig tree cursed	11:12–14
A' Jerusalem entry II: "came," "Jerusalem," "temple" (11:15); "went out" (11:19)	11:15–19
B' Fig tree withered	11:20–25
A″ Jerusalem entry III: "came," "Jerusalem," "temple" (11:27); "went out" (13:1)	11:27–13:1

What's with all these entries into Jerusalem (and exits)? What exactly is happening, and what is Mark *doing* with what he is saying?

Jesus had just been identified as "Son of David" (10:47–48), and now he rides into Jerusalem on a colt, rather than walking as others did—likely a symbolic messianic claim. In his call for a colt (11:2–4), it is possible that Jesus was exercising a royal prerogative to requisition an animal for his own use. These elements of royalty subtly shade the narrative: the king has arrived! In fact, in this account all the elements of a victorious Roman emperor's triumphal entry into the capital are replicated.[34] The account includes a recognized status for the protagonist (Jesus's three passion predictions in Mark 8–10, and the authority symbols of the garments on the colt and on the road, 11:7–8), a formal and ceremonial entry (Jesus's colt and the crowd's leafy branches, 11:1–11), acclamations with invocations of God (the crowd's exclamations about Jesus, 11:9–10), entry to the city climaxed by entry into the temple (Jesus's temple entry, 11:11), and cultic activity within the temple (Jesus's temple cleansing, 11:15–18). Jesus is clearly being depicted as a king entering into his "capital" and his "palace." Both from Greco-Roman backgrounds and from Zechariah 14, one would have expected Jesus to enter Jerusalem and take up his abode there, inaugurating the new age of blessedness in his reign. Instead,

34. David R. Catchpole, "The 'Triumphal' Entry," in *Jesus and the Politics of His Day*, ed. Ernst Bammel and C. F. D. Moule (Cambridge: Cambridge University Press, 1984), 321. Also see Paul Brooks Duff, "The March of the Divine Warrior and the Advent of the Greco-Roman King: Mark's Account of Jesus' Entry into Jerusalem," *Journal of Biblical Literature* 111 (1992): 59–64.

there is an abrupt and anticlimactic end to this arrival—it takes only one verse (Mark 11:11): Jesus comes into the temple and then leaves both temple and city. His Jerusalem entry II (11:15) and Jerusalem entry III (11:27; see above) are equally jejune; no one in the capital or the palace of the king appears to have paid him any attention. In other words, this entry is the essence of irony. Rather than being appropriately received, Jesus is completely ignored. The king is rejected![35]

In sum, the remarkable thing about Jesus's entry into Jerusalem and into the temple is that *nothing* happens! For a king entering his capital and his palace, this was the ultimate insult. The failure, in antiquity, of cities to extend the customary greeting to entering dignitaries and military victors would have had dire consequences. "It seems that the evangelist himself . . . has carefully choreographed this 'street theater,'" provoking readers to ask themselves: How will *we* treat King Jesus?[36] How will the disciples themselves respond to the King? Will we receive Jesus appropriately? The accounts of the cursing of the fig tree (11:12–14, 20–25) and the cleansing of the temple (11:15–19), as well as the mention of the Temple Mount possibly being cast into the sea (11:23), carry an implicit threat of judgment for those who fail to recognize the divine King.

In light of our discussion earlier in this chapter of God's ideal world—his kingdom—as the vision projected in the canon of Scripture, the proper reception of the King takes on added significance. To recognize and respect the divine Regent involves, among other things, catching the vision of that Regent's realm, the kingdom of the King, a vision cast by the canon of Scripture. And with each pericope of Scripture, a portion of that vision of the kingdom is brought into prominence in pericopal theology. Preachers are the ones primarily responsible for the display of these segments of the divine kingdom to their congregations, pericope by pericope. Sermon by sermon, their imaginations kindled by the blessedness of God's reign and the magnificence of his kingdom, God's people are transformed according to the theology of the pericope. They "inhabit" God's ideal world more and more, week by week, until one day the kingdom will have come in its fullness, with Christ the King as its sovereign and believers his blissful subjects!

---

35. The only ones who seem to have recognized Jesus for who he was are the "they" of Mark 11:1, likely the "large crowd" of 10:46, of Galilean origin; these were the band of pilgrims accompanying Jesus and his disciples into Jerusalem. Their enthusiastic cheers are based on Ps. 118:25–26, which may well have been originally addressed to an ancient victorious Israelite king. But this acknowledgment comes from the crowd from Galilee, not from the mob in Jerusalem. The latter, apparently, could not care less for this king. No one in the big city deigns to pay attention to Jesus.

36. Duff, "March of the Divine Warrior," 55–56.

- Have we, as children of God ourselves, been attending to Scripture's depiction of the kingdom—God's ideal world? This is part of the proper reception of the divine King, Jesus Christ. Attention to the kingdom must, of course, lead to inhabitation of the kingdom; that is, we are to live by the precepts, priorities, and practices of that realm.

- Paying attention to the theology of the pericope, looking *at* the text (not *through* it), is a discipline we must cultivate, for it is an integral part of our responsibility as preachers, a responsibility that we have to discharge to God, to his word, and to his people. Let's commit to doing that, giving the careful study of the text and its theology our time, our energy, and our resources.

- An essential part of our preaching task is also helping God's people understand this theological hermeneutic, this way of reading Scripture and seeing God's ideal world, for only then will they fully grasp the underlying goal and rationale of preaching. This is probably best accomplished in a session or two, once or twice a year, in a venue away from the pulpit, say during a Sunday school class or a small group study.

- And let's not forget to pray, "Thy kingdom come!"

Preaching Is Theological!

6

Preaching Is Applicational

Give me understanding, and I will observe Your law,
And I will keep it wholeheartedly.

Psalm 119:34

Biblical preaching, by a leader of the church, in a gathering of Christians for worship, is the communication of the thrust of a pericope of Scripture discerned by theological exegesis, *and of its application to that specific body of believers*, that they may be conformed to the image of Christ, for the glory of God—all in the power of the Holy Spirit.

On June 27, 1976, Air France Flight 139, from Tel Aviv to Paris, was hijacked by a combination of Palestinian and German anti-Israel terrorists. The airplane was diverted via Benghazi, Libya, to Entebbe, Uganda, where the hijackers were aided by the pro-Palestinian forces of President Idi Amin. Though the hijackers freed their non-Israeli captives and offered to release the airplane personnel, the Jewish captain of the Air France flight and his entire crew (as well as a French nun) refused to leave, in solidarity with the Israeli hostages. Then the terrorists made their demand: fifty-odd Palestinian prisoners in Israel and elsewhere had to be released in four days, or else the hostages would be killed.

A week later, in what turned out to be a remarkable ninety-minute raid that freed all but three of the 105 hostages, Israeli forces landed in Entebbe covertly, and an assault team entered the terminal where the captives were being held. Through a megaphone, they yelled in both Hebrew and English, "Stay down! Stay down! We are Israeli soldiers!" Perhaps it was the military training all Israelis are familiar with, but without a murmur, all the hostages immediately sank to the floor. Except for one: Jean-Jacques Mimouni. He actually stood up when the disturbance began. As was planned, the raiding party opened fire on everyone standing, and Mimouni, along with the seven hijackers, was killed.[1]

It was not enough for Mimouni to hear and understand the demand of the Israeli commandos. For their command to profit him, he had to apply it. Unfortunately, he did not. So it is with divine demand in Scripture. Indeed, even more so for Scripture, for the words in this book—not the words of man but the abiding, weighty, binding words of God—have critical ramifications for the relationship between God and man, and that for all eternity. In the sixteenth century, the English Bible scholar (and martyr) William Tyndale pronounced eloquently on the necessity of applying Scripture:

> Though a man may have a precious and expensive jewel, if he knows not the value thereof, nor how to use it, he is neither the better nor richer even by a fraction. Likewise, though we read Scripture, and never stop babbling about it, if we know not its use, and why it was given, and what should be sought in it, it profits us nothing at all. It is not enough, therefore, to read and talk of it only, but we must also beseech God insistently, day and night, to make us understand why the Scriptures were given, that we may apply the medicine of Scripture, every man to his own wounds. If not, we remain idle disputers, and brawlers about vain words, ever gnawing upon the bitter bark outside, and never reaching the sweet pith inside.[2]

The Bible must not just be explained to bring out its theological thrust, but it must also be applied in preaching if the audience is to benefit from it. Therefore preaching, which exposits God's will in God's word to God's people, must be applicational.

1. As the assault team began their retreat with the hostages, they were attacked by Ugandan soldiers, and the Israeli commander Yonatan Netanyahu (brother of Likud politician Benjamin Netanyahu) was killed, the only casualty among the commandos. In his honor, the operation, originally code-named Thunderbolt, was retroactively renamed Operation Yonatan. Two other hostages were killed in the crossfire between Israeli and Ugandan troops.
2. William Tyndale, "A Prologue by William Tyndale Shewing the Use of the Scripture, Which He Wrote before the Five Books of Moses," in *The Works of the English Reformers: William Tyndale and John Frith*, 3 vols., ed. Thomas Russell (London: Ebenezer Palmer, 1831), 1:6 (Tyndale's archaic wording has been modernized).

The Demand of Application

The application of the text to the circumstances and contexts of those listening is the goal of all preaching. The Bible is a text that must be applied by those who acknowledge it as their Scripture. And it is by such application that the community of God is progressively and increasingly aligned to the will of God. This is true for the people of God in all times and in all places. It comes as no surprise, therefore, that the Bible itself consistently asserts the relevance of its message for subsequent generations, affirming that "whatever was written in former times was written for *our* instruction" (Rom. 15:4).[3] It is to achieve this goal of application and life change that pericopes are utilized in preaching; they play a crucial theological role as agents of a unique and momentous phenomenon, the alignment of God's people to divine demand, the will of their divine Sovereign:pericopes are instruments of covenant renewal (discussed in "Preaching Is Theological").

But how exactly "our instruction" (Rom. 15:4) may be achieved from this historical tome continues to tax preachers; the challenge of bridging the gap between ancient text and modern audience remains burdensome. Sandra Schneiders confesses that it is indeed a "baffling question" how these two come together, for separating them are time, space, culture, language, values, attitudes, and so on.[4] Stanley Porter agrees that this move from ancient text to modern audience "is one of the most demanding intellectual tasks imaginable"—a task that confronts preachers each time the Bible is expounded. He adds, "Anyone who proclaims how easy it is to do this is probably prevaricating, or is very bad at the task, or is so very experienced at it as to have forgotten the intellectual and spiritual task that it is."[5] Difficulties notwithstanding, there can be no denying the crucial nature of this facet of the sermonic enterprise: if God's people are to be aligned to God's will, this movement from text to praxis is a necessary responsibility preachers have to discharge. Therefore it is incumbent upon them to direct the traffic from the *then* of the Bible to the *now* of the audience. Words written in an earlier age are to be transposed across a great divide and applied in a later era. This lot of preachers is not easy: each week, these intrepid souls have to bridge the

3. Also see Deut. 4:10; 6:6–25; 29:14–15; 2 Kings 22–23; Neh. 7:73b–8:18; Matt. 28:19–20; 1 Cor. 10:6, 11; 2 Tim. 3:16–17.

4. Sandra M. Schneiders, "The Paschal Imagination: Objectivity and Subjectivity in New Testament Interpretation," *Theological Studies* 46 (1982): 65.

5. Stanley E. Porter, "Hermeneutics, Biblical Interpretation, and Theology: Hunch, Holy Spirit, or Hard Work?," in I. Howard Marshall, *Beyond the Bible: Moving from Scripture to Theology* (Grand Rapids: Baker Academic, 2004), 121.

chasm between ancient text and modern audience, to apply a specific biblical pericope to their listeners.[6]

Preaching is not only the explanation of the theological thrust of God's word but also its application to real people living real lives with a real need for that message. The authoritative text is to be extended to relevant practice, "to enable God's revealed truth to flow out of the Scriptures into the lives of the men and women of today"—that is, the text must be applied.[7] In other words, the biblical text, carefully attended to and privileged, is to be preached for the promotion of godliness among God's people, that the church would be "holy and blameless" (Eph. 1:4; 5:27), conformed to the image of Christ (Rom. 8:29), for the glory of God.[8] Such a concern for the application of Scripture dominated both Jewish and Christian communities from very early on. Expositional preaching for application was a fixture of synagogue worship, as Philo affirmed.

> On the seventh days [Sabbaths] there are opened before the people in every city innumerable schools of wisdom, and self-control, and courage, and righteousness, and other virtues. . . . Some of those who are experienced instruct [the assembly] in what is good and profitable, by which the whole of their lives may be dedicated to uprightness.[9]

This Jewish orientation of preaching with application was carried over into the practice of the church. In the early second century, Justin Martyr, describing a worship service in Rome, noted that after the reading of the Gospels, "the leader verbally instructs, and *exhorts the imitation of these good things*."[10] Later, the Christian apologist Tertullian wrote, "We assemble to read our sacred writings, . . . by inculcations of God's precepts *we confirm good habits*."[11] Augustine declared that the aim of an exposi-

---

6. James D. Smart, *The Strange Silence of the Bible in the Church: A Study in Hermeneutics* (London: SCM, 1970), 33–34, called this "a perilous road." While I am placing the issue of bridging this gap in the context of the preaching endeavor, the question is one that is pertinent to all biblical exposition intended to culminate in application, whether conducted in worship services, in Bible study groups, in Sunday school classes, or even in one's own reading of Scripture: *How do we/I move from ancient text to modern audience? How do I apply this text?*

7. John R. W. Stott, *Between Two Worlds: The Art of Preaching in the Twentieth Century* (Grand Rapids: Eerdmans, 1982), 138.

8. See "Preaching Is Conformational" for this notion of becoming transformed into the image of Christ and "Preaching Is Doxological" for the ultimate goal of preaching, the glory of God.

9. *On the Special Laws* 2.15.62.

10. *First Apology* 67.

11. *Apology* 39 (ANF 3:46).

tor of Scripture was "to be listened to with understanding, with pleasure, and *with obedience.*"[12] Thus, throughout church history the application of Scripture has consistently been considered the culmination of interpretation, though how exactly valid application may be derived from the particular text being handled in a sermon was never clearly explicated. With the preacher as the spiritual director and guide of the congregation (see "Preaching Is Pastoral"), it behooves such a one to provide concrete application of the text to the flock. Indeed, offering application distinguishes preaching from all other kinds of Christian discourse. As far back as the thirteenth century, in one of the earliest textbooks on preaching, Thomas of Chobham asserted:

> Preaching is the announcement of the divine Word for information in faith and morals. . . . Let other things be reserved for lecturing and debating.[13]

The impulse to change lives for the glory of God makes preaching a unique form of Christian communication. Needless to say, not only must preaching suggest application; listeners must take it on themselves to actually apply what they have learned from Scripture. James 1:22–25 emphasizes the importance of application: "Become doers of the word, and not merely hearers deluding yourselves," for "a doer who acts will be blessed in his or her doing." Only in personal application does the text ultimately accomplish its meaning. Therefore, Hans-Georg Gadamer could assert that application was an integral part of the hermeneutical process: interpretation must rightly involve application for the text to achieve its intended end.[14] A biblical pericope thus is more than informing; it is also transforming, for the application of its theological thrust (pericopal theology) aligns God's people to God's will, enabling them to inhabit the *world in front of the text* by adopting that world's precepts, priorities, and practices. In other words, application is the theology of the pericope put into practice.

12. *On Christian Doctrine* 4.26.56. And he decried the futility of persuading hearers of the truth, or delighting them with style, if the learning process did not result in action (*On Christian Doctrine* 4.13.29).

13. Thomas of Chobham, *Summa de arte praedicandi* ("Essence of the Art of Preaching"), Corpus Christianorum: Continuatio Mediaevalis 82, ed. Franco Morenzoni (Turnhout, Belgium: Brepols, 1988), 14 (lines 8–9, 16–17; my translation).

14. See Hans-Georg Gadamer, *Truth and Method*, 2nd rev. ed., trans. Joel Weinsheimer and Donald G. Marshall (London: Continuum, 2004), 307. So also Paul Ricoeur: "Interpretation actualizes the meaning of the text for the present reader" (*Hermeneutics and the Human Sciences: Essays on Language, Action and Interpretation*, ed. and trans. John B. Thompson [Cambridge: Cambridge University Press, 1981], 85, 159).

The Specification of Application

Application is therefore an indispensable component of preaching; indeed, it is its end point: preaching is incomplete without application. Without application, the field of homiletics lies fallow, preaching remains unfruitful, and the sermon barren. So it is not enough to elucidate the theology of a pericope; it is also incumbent upon the preacher to show, in each sermon, how that theology intersects real life, how exactly pericopal theology can be applied—that is, how God's people may undertake a specific response to that particular text. As was noted earlier, the preaching process therefore has two aspects: the exposition of the theology of the pericope (the *theological* move: text to pericopal theology) and the demonstration of how that theology may be applied in real life (the *applicational* move: pericopal theology to application) (see fig. 6.1).

Figure 6.1
Text to Application

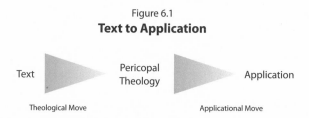

Text   Pericopal Theology   Application

Theological Move   Applicational Move

This is at the heart of preaching: divine demand from the biblical text is brought to bear upon the concrete circumstances of the community of God, to align it to the will of God for the glory of God; thus covenant renewal occurs.[15] By thus applying the theology of the pericope to the specific situations of believers, the values of the fallen world are gradually undermined, while the precepts, priorities, and practices of God's ideal world are increasingly established in the life of the community. This is part of what it means to acknowledge "Thy kingdom come!"

In this second step of preaching, theology to application, the thrust of the text is placed in the context and circumstances of the audience. This is how the biblical text maintains its relevance for readers in every generation, sustaining its value across time and space. The specifics features of 1 Samuel 15—prophet, king, voices, enemies, and failure—bore the theology of that

15. Again, "divine demand" is actually a gracious invitation on the part of God to human beings, offering us the possibility to live God's way in God's new world. I frequently use "demand" simply to remind myself that although it is an invitation that *can* be refused, repudiation of that gracious call comes with grave consequences. However one conceives of God's invitation, its prescriptive and normative nature should not be forgotten: hence, divine *demand*.

pericope with power, pathos, and potency (as did the specific aspects of Aesop's fable—dog, bone, bridge, reflection, and loss). Now, in application, it is not these elements but specific details of the audience—their circumstances, attitudes, inclinations, and spiritual maturity—that are to be considered when pericopal theology is brought home to listeners. The "voice" of the 1 Samuel 15 narrative would be muffled (pun intended!) if we were simply to view the whole episode as something that happened between the prophet Samuel and the king Saul in the eleventh century BCE, and completely irrelevant for us today. Instead, because 1 Samuel 15 is an integral part of the abiding, weighty, and binding canon of Scripture we hear this particular pericope as giving us guidelines for life here and now, dealing with something that transcends the transactions between an ancient Israelite seer and regent. Therefore, if the first task of the preacher is to convey the theology of the text to listeners, the preacher's second task of communication is to provide them with specific ways of adopting that theology into their lives. It is in providing application that spiritual (trans)formation takes place.

But it will not do, when one is preaching this narrative of 1 Samuel 15, simply to exhort listeners to "listen to the voice of God and not to the voices of the world!" Though accurately reflecting the theology of the pericope, this is an abstract imperative that leaves the burden for particular action entirely upon the audience, as they are left to figure out for themselves what this specifically means for their lives. Such a generalization fails to provide the specificity required for concrete responses on the part of God's people to God's word. How are my listeners (and I myself) going to put the theology of this pericope into practice on Monday, after listening to the sermon on 1 Samuel 15 the day before? What specifically can we do to listen more keenly to God's voice and to shut out the voices of the world? Listeners need help putting pericopal theology into shoe leather. This is why a preacher has been ordained: this is the one who walks with God and knows God, the one who pores over God's word and studies it, the one who loves the flock and prays for them, the one who seeks their spiritual growth and maturity. So it is up to this individual, wise and discerning in the ways of God and the ways of man, to help listeners with application, to be their guide through life and the director of their spiritual journeys.

Preachers must not only move from the text to pericopal theology but they must also advance from theology to the circumstances of the congregation's life, applying pericopal theology to the real lives of real people. If they have nothing to offer their congregations but a nonspecific abstraction like "Listen to the voice of God and not to the voices of the world," pastors are feeding their flocks only pious platitudes that will rarely get applied. That would be like a marriage counselor advising a couple with marital problems to "love one another!" Such generalities will never do. It is the responsibility of counselors to establish that truth, of course, but they must also proceed to the next step of showing how "Love one another!" can be put into concrete practice in the specific circumstances of that distressed marital situation. Likewise in preaching. The preacher, who is the spiritual director, the parent figure, the elder, the discipler, the shepherd and pastor, has the responsibility to guide the flock into *specific* application based on the theological thrust of the text that has just been preached. Specificity is the essence of application. If life change is being sought through a sermon, then specific application is absolutely essential.

As business writers Chip Heath and Dan Heath observe: "Any successful change [in life/behavior] requires a translation of ambiguous goals into concrete behaviors. In short, to make a switch, you need to *script the critical moves*."[16] This "scripting of critical moves" is the preacher's task—the move from theology to application. Karl Barth called this a "translation" of theology into "the language of the newspaper," into the vernacular and idiom of listeners, into the routines of their days and lives, into the specifics of practice and behavior.[17] If such translation into valid and concrete application does not occur in a sermon, the goal of aligning God's people with God's demand will not be achieved. Thus, this second step of preaching—from pericopal theology to application—is a crucial move in homiletics and, indeed, for the faith and practice of the church that is to be nourished by the preaching of God's word.

All this means that the preacher should know the audience well, for how can one tailor application to those one knows nothing about? Said Socrates:

> Since it is the function of speech to persuade souls, he who would be a rhetorician [or an orator] must know the differences between souls.[18]

In the sixteenth century, in one of the first books on preaching in the English language, the Puritan William Perkins called for application to be "appropriately fitted as the circumstance of place, time, and people require."[19] That

16. Chip Heath and Dan Heath, *Switch: How to Change Things When Change Is Hard* (New York: Broadway, 2010), 53–54.

17. Karl Barth, *Dogmatics in Outline* (London: SCM, 1966), 32–33.

18. Plato, *Phaedrus* 271. Jesus himself followed this principle: "With many parables like these he was speaking the word to them, to the degree they were able to hear" (Mark 4:33).

19. William Perkins, *The Arte of Prophecying; or, A Treatise concerning the Sacred and Onely True Manner and Methode of Preaching*, trans. Thomas Tuke (London: Felix Kyngston, 1607), 99 (I have modernized the archaic wording).

is another important reason that preaching should be *pastoral*, for it is the pastor-preacher who is responsible for and cares for the flock and is keenly aware of their spiritual state and growth. Such a person, with a burden for the people of God and a sensitivity for their specific situations, is well qualified to design application appropriate for listeners, suited for where they are in their walk with God.

This operation (theology to application) requires of the preacher attentiveness to new contexts of interpretation, as well as responsibility for and accountability to the particular community of God's people among whom one's sermons are preached. In a way, the preacher is like a person walking backward with eyes on the past, guided by where one has just been—that is, focusing on the pericope of Scripture and governed by its theology. Yet the preacher is also headed *away* from the past and toward the future—that is, moving toward the audience, translating the theology of the text into the lives of listeners with specific application.[20] Therefore, not only is preaching to be faithful to the text, but in application it needs to be faithful to the audience as well, relevant to them. The sixth-century Latin church father Gregory the Great stated:

> One and the same exhortation is not suited to all, because they are not compassed [united] by the same quality of character. . . . Wherefore, the discourse of a teacher should be adapted to the character of the hearers, so as to be suited to the individual in his respective needs.[21]

To arrive at valid application that is relevant to the listeners is the goal of preaching.[22] Returning to 1 Samuel 15, the obvious application, as noted earlier, is the rather abstract imperative "Listen to the voice of God and not to the

---

20. I borrow this metaphor from Keith Johnstone: "The improviser has to be like a man walking backwards" (*Impro: Improvisation and the Theatre* [London: Methuen, 1981], 116). In that sense the preacher, too, is improvising: creating fresh applications from an unchanging text. See Abraham Kuruvilla, *Text to Praxis: Hermeneutics and Homiletics in Dialogue*, Library of New Testament Studies 393 (London: T&T Clark, 2009), 176–80.

21. *The Pastoral Rule*, prologue to part 3, in St. Gregory the Great, *Pastoral Care*, trans. Henry Davis, Ancient Christian Writers 11 (Westminster, MD: Newman, 1950), 89.

22. Relevant application may be of different kinds. Classical rhetoric knows of three directions of audience responses sought by a speaker (and thus three kinds of oratory, as was mentioned in "Preaching Is Communicational"): a *forensic* assessment of an event (a change of mind), a *deliberative* resolve to act (a change of action), or an *epideictic* appreciation of particular beliefs or values (a change of feeling). See Quintilian, *Institutes of Oratory* 3.7–9; Anaximenes, *Rhetoric to Alexander* 1421b; Aristotle, *Rhetoric* 1.3.1. Sermonic application, in parallel to this threefold shape of rhetorical purpose, may also have one or more of these broad aims: a change of mind (a response of cognition), a change of action (a response of volition), or a change of feeling (a response of emotion).

voices of the world!" Clearly, providing such abstractions makes life easy for
the preacher; it does not require much effort to come up with counsel like this.
But it makes obedience quite difficult for the listener, who is left wondering,
*How am I to do this? Where do I start? What do I have to do to listen to God
and not to the world?* If specificity is the essence of application, the preacher
must offer specific ways to change lives—ways that are creative, concrete, and
compelling. The idea is to get listeners started on the lifelong journey of aligning
their lives with the theology of the pericope preached. The responsibility of the
preacher is therefore to get listeners moving, to get them to take the first step,
which hopefully will become a habit, which will become a disposition, which
will become part of their character. Application is spiritual formation begun
and continued. Needless to say, discovering application that is creative, concrete,
and compelling is hard work. It is not, as one scholar put it, "a relatively simple
matter . . . to move to the application."[23] Hardly! It takes all of one's pastoral
sensitivity, discernment, and wisdom—developed over a lifetime of Christian
maturity—not to mention a significant investment of time and energy, to come
up week after week with creative, concrete, and compelling application in one's
sermons. Here's a tip: frequently, if I am stuck searching for specific application, I find it very helpful to ask myself first, "What can *I* specifically do in
response to the theology of this pericope I am preaching? How is *my* life to
change concretely as a result of the demand of this text?" After all, preachers'
own lives must be impacted by the sermons they preach. And quite often, the
application I find with this self-examination is quite suitable for my listeners.[24]

Multiplicity of Applications

In the case of a sermon on 1 Samuel 15, perhaps the preacher might use this
occasion to introduce a church-wide Bible-reading or -memorizing program—a
way of listening more intently to the voice of God. Perhaps one might encour-
age the muting of worldly voices by recommending a more discriminating
consumption of media and the internet. Perhaps repentance for *not* having
listened to God's voice would be appropriate as well. And so on, whatever
one's creative mind can conjure (congruent with the theology of the pericope)
that is concrete and compelling. A multitude of application possibilities exist
for any given pericope.

23. Allen P. Ross, *Creation and Blessing: A Guide to the Study and Exposition of Genesis*
(Grand Rapids: Baker, 1997), 47.
24. Indeed, I have taken to doing this every time I prepare to preach, to force myself to apply
what I will call my listeners to do. See "Preaching Is Pastoral" and "Preaching Is Spiritual" for
the importance of the preacher's life being an example to the flock.

   This notion of multiple potential applications not only pertains to religious literature but has its analogy in the interpretation of legal literature as well, for preacher and jurist seek to apply their respective canonical texts (the Bible in one case, the Constitution in the other) to their particular hearers. The tasks of these practitioners in both fields are conceptually parallel. As in churches, so in courts: valid application must be made from the authoritative text in situations and circumstances distant and distinct from those of the original writing. Indeed, legal literature is replete with examples of the movement from text to "theology" to application. For instance, the United States Constitution empowers Congress "to raise and support armies," "to provide and maintain a navy," and "to make rules for the government and regulation of the land and naval forces" (Article I, ¶8, clauses 12 and 13). Written in 1789, this edict is understandably silent about any support for an air force. Yet, despite the absence of any explicit reference to this branch of the armed forces, the United States government continues to raise and support, provide and maintain, govern and regulate an air force. Presumably, then, the terms "army" and "navy" in that late eighteenth-century document projected a *world in front of the text* in which the federal government ideally regulates *all* manner of national defense undertakings. The pragmatic ("theological") thrust of the constitutional mandate clearly was to designate any conceivable military force as worthy of establishment and maintenance by the United States Congress. Such a "theology" would necessarily include an air force and, potentially, even a space force or, perhaps in the future, a robot force as valid applications, all congruent to and consistent with the *world in front of the text*, the "pericopal theology" of Article 1, ¶8.
   The rationale for this movement from text, via theology, to a multitude of possible applications in the future is obvious. No canonical work—whether it be the United States Constitution or Christian Scripture—can be expected to bear the burden of explicitly expressing all possible applications for all people in all times and in all places. The impossibility of even conceiving of that task is immediately evident. So these canons of court and church *inherently* bear a plurality of application. That is to say, the theology of the pericopes of Scripture may be applied in an unlimited number of ways. I might go with the Bible reading program for my congregation in a sermon on 1 Samuel 15; another preacher may opt to go with small group accountability for internet surfing; yet another might lead the congregation in a prayer of repentance. Indeed, the possibilities are endless, for the text carries "the richness of the ideal meaning which allows for a theoretically unlimited number of actualizations [applications], each being somewhat original and different from

others."[25] Such a conception of the multiplicity of potential applications is an essential property of Scripture; this enables the sacred text to cross the bounds of time and go beyond the needs of any one generation of its readers. And so the Bible's utility into the future is ensured, an abiding, weighty, and binding tome that is profitable for all God's children everywhere and always.

A Word about Significances

The theological thrust of 1 Samuel 15 portrays an ideal *world in front of the text* where God's people remain always attentive to his word, without being seduced by worldly noises. Now, if the congregation I am preaching to is prone to disobeying God because of a general addiction to internet pornography (a seducing "voice" of the world)—perhaps I am addressing a group of young men in the grip of this vice—I could, with my pastoral authority, suggest as an application that they install an internet-filtering software program, or that they permit a trusted friend to inspect their web browser's history folder at any time. Of course, "Install an internet filter!" and "Permit an accountability partner to inspect your browser's history folder!" and so on, are not mandates that arise directly from the theological thrust of 1 Samuel 15. The only direct application that can be drawn from the theology of that pericope is the abstract "Listen to the voice of God and not to the voices of the world!" However, my counsel regarding filters and accountability is certainly prudent and, if heeded, may help my listeners accomplish the direct application to listen to God's voice. Installation of filtering software and being accountable to others are applications that help move God's people toward fully inhabiting God's ideal world, helping them to live by the precepts, priorities, and practices of this world. That is to say, my specific suggestions could potentially help one "listen to the voice of God and not to the voices of the world!" Though not directly commanded by the text, these preemptive strikes (filter installation or becoming accountable) enable alignment to the obedience-to-God-without-succumbing-to-worldly-allures kind of world projected by 1 Samuel 15. Such applications—that do not emerge directly from the text and its theology but that help one move toward the demand of the text—are called "significances."[26]

25. Schneiders, "Paschal Imagination," 64.
26. E. D. Hirsch, "Meaning and Significance Reinterpreted," *Critical Inquiry* 11 (1984): 207, 210; also see Hirsch, *The Aims of Interpretation* (Chicago: University of Chicago Press, 1976), 80. Here's another idea for a "significance" when preaching 1 Sam. 15. For the longest time, I had an application-launching software on my laptop. I programmed this launcher to open my Bible software when I typed the letters *H*, *I*, and *A* in sequence—standing for "Here I Am!" (an allusion to 1 Sam. 3:4). Obviously, 1 Sam. 15 says nothing about application launchers, but this action helped me to attend more carefully to God's voice every time I opened my electronic

They are not "valid applications" in the strict sense of their arising directly from the thrust of the text, but they are nevertheless appropriate applications, for they help one arrive at the state (in this case, a state of obedience to God's voice) demanded by the text. Therefore, significances rightly belong in the preacher's quiver of homiletical arrows, and when designing application, one should always bear in mind the utility of significances. Again, it becomes obvious how important it is for the preacher to know the flock to whom the sermon is directed: therefore, preaching is never to be separated from shepherding, a point already made in "Preaching Is Pastoral."

In sum, the second step of preaching, from theology to application, is the culmination of the preacher's undertaking. Only by generating relevant and specific application (and/or significance) can the thrust of God's word impact listeners, giving them direction for life and godliness. This responsibility of the preacher to provide application is therefore one of great consequence for the community of God's people.

Relationship Precedes Responsibility

Lest there be confusion, let me clarify that preaching that calls for listeners' alignment to God's will in the text is not justification-oriented; that is, such obedience does not accumulate merit toward salvation. Rather it is sanctification-oriented, intended for those *already* in relationship with God. And, in Scripture, relationship with God is always followed by responsibility.[27] That is to say, when men and women come into relationship with God, God always places demands on how they should live—in accordance with the precepts, priorities, and practices of his ideal world, his kingdom. This has been true throughout biblical history, even in the Old Testament period. Indeed, such a theme resonates through the Pentateuch. God elected a people; *then* he required of them obedience to divine demand. Notice that the Ten Commandments (responsibility) were prefaced by an announcement of relationship: "I am Yahweh your God, who brought you out of the land of Egypt, out of the house of slavery" (Exod. 20:2). Then come the dos and don'ts of the Decalogue. Relationship always precedes responsibility. Being the Israelites' God—a relationship inaugurated prior to the giving of the Mosaic law—had significant bearing upon the subsequent responsibility of the people to be holy.

Bible. So this is a "significance" and may profitably be offered to listeners as application (at least for those who are somewhat technologically inclined).

27. See Abraham Kuruvilla, *Privilege the Text! A Theological Hermeneutic for Preaching* (Chicago: Moody, 2012), 151–209, for further discussion of this issue.

Yahweh had separated his people to himself as his possession; *therefore*, they were to be holy, as he was.[28]

> So you are to be holy to Me, because I, Yahweh, am holy; and I have set you apart from the peoples to be Mine. (Lev. 20:26)

Obedience, or even a willingness to obey God, was never a criterion for establishing a relationship between deity and his people. The initiation of the divine-human relationship was entirely a unilateral divine act of love and grace that was (and always is) apprehended from the human side by faith alone.[29] Thus, God's plan all along has been to direct, by his divine demand, the behavior of those who were already his children.[30] Relationship always precedes the responsibility of the people of God to meet his requirements and to be holy, as God was. In other words, obedience is the response of God's people to his prevenient operations of grace; relationship *precedes* responsibility. "First God redeems Israel from Egypt, *and then* he gives the law, so obedience to the law is a response to God's grace, not an attempt to gain righteousness by works."[31] Therefore, a loving relationship with God should result in the keeping of his commandments, as the New Testament is not hesitant to point out (see John 14:21; 1 John 2:3–5; 3:21–24; 5:3). It is the role of each pericope of Scripture to spell out what those commandments of God are—divine demand—so that the children of God might keep them and be holy, as God, their Father, is holy. Pericopal theology thus provides the text's direction for holiness, and the preacher's task, in the second step of preaching, is to help God's people apply this theology to the concrete circumstances of their lives. Their obedience would then be the discharging of their responsibility to reflect their relationship with God. And through this obedience God is glorified as his people manifest his holiness and represent him to the world.[32]

All that to say, obedience to divine demand is *not* a means to justification—that occurs solely by grace, through faith alone in Christ alone (Eph. 2:8–9).

---

28. Also see Lev. 19:2–3 ("You shall be holy, because I, Yahweh your God, am holy. . . . I am Yahweh your God") and the numerous echoes throughout the chapter (and book) of "I am Yahweh" (19:3, 4, 10, 12, 14, 16, 18, 25, 28, 29, 30, 31, 32, 34, 36, 37; etc.).

29. See, e.g., Deut. 4:37; 7:7–9; 10:15.

30. But with time, what God had intended as guidelines for sanctification were misconstrued as means of salvation: a self-glorifying, flesh-driven, merit-attempting, grace-rejecting, faith-negating obedience to law (divine demand)—the legalism Paul so often excoriated.

31. Thomas R. Schreiner, *Paul, Apostle of God's Glory in Christ: A Pauline Theology* (Downers Grove, IL: InterVarsity, 2001), 117–18.

32. See "Preaching Is Doxological."

Rather, obedience to God's will is an integral part of practical sanctification, the growth in holiness of those who are already children of God and have trusted Jesus Christ as their only God and Savior. Once a relationship with his people is thereby initiated, God intends for them to fulfill their responsibility to live by his requirements. Indeed, this obedience, too, is to be exercised by the agency of faith, because one can never on one's own fully obey God. Therefore, believers are called to accept, in faith, God's gracious empowerment through the Spirit for obedience. The Holy Spirit now indwells them, enabling them to overcome the flesh and meet God's "righteous requirement" (divine demand). Indeed, this was the purpose of God's redemptive intervention.

> . . . so that the righteous requirement of the law may be fulfilled in us, who do not walk according to the flesh but according to the Spirit. . . . For all who are led by the Spirit of God, these are the children of God. (Rom. 8:4, 14)

This empowerment for holiness is also part of the work of the Son, for it was he who sent the Spirit (John 14:16; 15:26; 16:7). This power of God through the Spirit is at work in the believer, enabling obedience and a life that pleases God (Eph. 2:10; 3:16; Phil. 4:13; Col. 1:9–11; 2 Pet. 1:3). In other words, it is God's grace through Jesus Christ and by the Holy Spirit that enables believers to obey divine demand, a fact that even the Old Testament affirmed.

> I will put My Spirit within you, and I will cause you to walk in My statutes, and you will keep and obey My ordinances. (Ezek. 36:27)

While there is no salvation-merit to be won by obedience, there is nonetheless immense value in obeying God.[33] Application of Scripture *is* profitable. God takes pleasure in the obedience of his children, and there are benefits that accrue from his pleasure even though, as we have seen, his people's obedience is a consequence of God's own gracious operation in them. Indeed, Colossians 1:10 encourages the believer to "walk worthy of the Lord, in everything pleasing [Him], bearing fruit in every good work." Jesus himself pronounced on the importance of obedience: the experience of divine blessing (here, God's love) is contingent upon such a walk with God.

> If you keep My commandments, you will remain in My love; just as I have kept My Father's commandments and remain in His love. (John 15:10)[34]

---

33. See Kuruvilla, *Privilege the Text!*, 252–58, for the benefits of abiding by divine will.
34. Also see 1 John 2:5; 4:12. And, of course, a reciprocal love for God remains a key motivation for obedience (John 14:15, 21; 1 John 5:2–3; 2 John 6).

The Bible is clear that the one who walks with God is blessed—and not just in eternity (Prov. 3:1–11). As with the experience of God's love, so also for the experience of God's peace. The promises of peace (in Rom. 8:6; 2 Cor. 13:11; Gal. 6:16; Phil. 4:6–7) are fulfilled when the child of God adopts certain kinds of behaviors. Indeed, any positive consequence from any divinely prescribed behavior is, in the end, God's gracious blessing.[35] Besides, there are eternal rewards for obedience (and loss thereof for disobedience).[36] All this to say, there is great value in application for the believer, not to mention that such obedience is God-glorifying.

> Now may the God of peace . . . equip you with every good thing to do His will, doing in us what is pleasing before Him, through Jesus Christ, to whom be glory forever. Amen! (Heb. 13:20–21)

Summary

The application of Scripture by the people of God is a mandate found in Scripture itself. This is the second part of the preaching movement: from theology to application. Once the thrust of the text has been discerned (i.e., the first move: text to pericopal theology), the responsibility of the preacher continues in the specification of application (i.e., the second move: pericopal theology to application) so that God's people are aligned to the precepts, priorities, and practices of God's ideal *world in front of the text*. Application is therefore indispensable to preaching, and such life change is the goal of preaching. This facet of the preacher's task calls for an intimate knowledge of the flock, its spiritual state and its growth, so that the theology of the text may be relevantly tailored to the lives of listeners in application. Thereby the people of God abide by divine demand, becoming holy, even as their God is holy.

Relationship demands responsibility. It is because God already is in relationship with his people that a divine demand is laid upon them—a gracious invitation from God to live in his ideal world, abiding by its precepts, priorities, and practices. The power for such obedience is the work of the indwelling

35. On the other hand, there are also consequences for the child of God who disobeys divine demand (though not loss of salvation; Rom. 8:1). This negative counterpart of blessing, God's discipline and chastisement of his children when they fail to walk with him, is also promised in Scripture: in the Old Testament, in Deut. 1:31–36; 4:23–28; 5:11; 6:14–15; 7:9–10; 8:19–20; 11:16–17, 26–32; 27:12–26; 28:15–68; 30:17–18; etc.; and in the New Testament, in 1 Cor. 5:1–13; Gal. 6:7; 1 Tim. 6:9–10; Titus 3:9; Heb. 12:5–11 (quoting Prov. 3:11–12; also see Prov. 15:5), 15–17; 13:17; 1 Pet. 4:17–19; Rev. 2:5; 3:19; etc.

36. Of the coming judgment of believers for rewards, the Bible is clear: Matt. 6:1–4; Rom. 14:10–12; 1 Cor. 3:13; 4:5; 9:24; 2 Cor. 5:10; Col. 3:22–25; 2 Tim. 2:5; James 5:7–11; 1 John 2:28.

Holy Spirit. Unlike legalism—an attempt to gain merit with God and glory for self by relying on one's own resources to obey—obedience is ultimately a matter of God's gracious empowerment of his children through his Spirit. And as God's people live lives pleasing him, God is glorified and they are blessed. Preaching is truly of great consequence. *Preaching is applicational!*

Reflection

Mark 4:1–34—Fruit Production[37]

> And He was saying to them, "Pay attention to what you hear. . . . For whoever has, to him it will be given; and whoever does not have, from him even what he has will be taken away. . . . By itself, the soil produces fruit." (Mark 4:24–25, 28)

There are essentially two sections to this pericope: Mark 4:1–25, dealing with the parable of the seeds/soils (and sayings about lamps and measures), and 4:26–34, dealing with the parable of the sower and that of the mustard seed. The pericope as a whole addresses the question: What does it take to produce fruit in the lives of disciples in response to God's word? The answer: Fruit production has a human element and a divine element.

The Human Element

In the first section, Jesus pictures three unsuccessful seeds (soils) and three successful ones (4:3–9). Though failure is not necessarily the predominant experience of the sower sowing the seed of the word (of God), the diversity of responses is unsettling. When the disciples ask Jesus for clarification, he explains that outsiders, with sightless eyes and soundless ears (4:12), do not grasp the life-changing significance of what they are hearing. And this failure to accept and apply truth is a function of willful human (ir)responsibility that culminates in fruitlessness.[38] Thus, Jesus here is encouraging his followers to have open ears and eyes to his teachings—to "hear the word" (4:16, 18, 20), "receive it with joy" (4:16), and "accept it" (4:20).[39] Receptivity to the word is demanded of the disciple, and such receptivity is the essential *human element*

---

37. For more details on this pericope, see Abraham Kuruvilla, *Mark: A Theological Commentary for Preachers* (Eugene, OR: Cascade, 2012), 75–91.

38. This is not to minimize God's sovereign role in the opening of eyes or hardening of hearts. Mark's focus, in this section of the pericope, is upon human responsibility.

39. Indeed, the verb "to hear" shows up thirteen times in 4:1–34 (4:3, 9 [2×],]; 12 [2×],]; 15, 16, 18, 20, 23 [2×], 24, 33). And "word" occurs nine times (4:14, 15 [2×], 16, 17, 18, 19, 20, 33).

for the subsequent bearing of fruit. This is, of course, more than mere cognition, and it includes commitment and obedience—that is, application is the right response to the hearing of the word, that one might bear fruit. And such fruit bearing represents normative discipleship (Matt. 3:8–10 [Luke 3:8–9]; 7:16–20 [Luke 6:43–44]; 12:33; John 15:1–17; Rom. 7:4–5; Gal. 5:22–23; Eph. 5:9; Phil. 1:11, 22; Col. 1:10; James 3:17–18).

Why only some respond positively to the word is not Mark's particular concern here; his interest is rather in seeing that the reader *should* respond. This is the factor of man's responsibility—the human element, the application of the word of God that leads to fruitfulness in life. God's kingdom (Mark 4:11, 26, 30) is thus being established not by military strategies and conquests but by the followers of Jesus participating in God's rule by applying his word and thereby bearing fruit.

The Divine Element

The first section leads to the next (4:26–34), which, with a final set of parables, pictures the sovereign work of God—the *divine element*—in disciples' growth and fruit bearing. In the parable of the ignorant sower, the work of God is not explicit but rather implicit in the sower's incomprehension about how the seed "sprouts and grows" (4:27). Indeed, the soil yields fruit "by itself " (αὐτόματος, *automatos*, 4:28). This is in contrast to the emphasized responsibility in the previous section (4:1–25) of the hearers to apply the word. There the contingency of the human element was stressed, but here fruit production occurs "automatically." Outside of the initial sowing and the final harvesting, the sower does nothing but wait (and sleep and wake up [4:27]!). Fruit production here is the inscrutable and sovereign work of God (see Eccles. 11:4–6 and 1 Cor. 3:6), underscoring the divine element in growth. In fact, this work of God yields incredible growth, as pictured in the abundant flourishing of the mustard plant (Mark 4:30–32). In other words, Christians are engaged in a grand program as they apply God's word, a project with tremendous ramifications for the future, when the kingdom of God will be consummated. Such a heightened sense of the whole should motivate the disciple to be faithful, receptive to the word of God and applying it diligently.

Thus, while the disciple is to persist in applying God's word (the human element), the child of God must not forget that there is an incomprehensible work of God in the production of fruit (the divine element). There is a balance between human responsibility and divine sovereignty, between work and trust. While trusting God's operations, the disciple must work hard to apply God's word, without allowing the distractions of Mark 4:14–19—Satan, affliction and persecution, the worries of the world, and the deceitfulness of riches—to sabotage one's sensitivity to God's word.

- The agencies and circumstances that cause the disciple to be unfruitful are worth reflecting upon: deception by Satan (4:4, 15), defection in tribulation (4:5–6, 16–17), and distractions of the world, its pains and pleasures (4:7, 18–19). Are any of these operating in our own lives keeping us from fully applying the Scripture that we preach from? Are they preventing application and fruit bearing in the lives of our congregations?
- In our personal and public pastoral prayers, do we petition God for empowerment through his Spirit to help us apply the truths of Scripture? We must be ever conscientious to lift up in private prayer those among the congregation struggling particularly hard against the diversions mentioned in this pericope.
- The responsibility of the disciple to apply Scripture is a magnificent one, viewed in the larger scheme of the consummation of God's kingdom. Application is not the whimsical fancy of a capricious God. How often do we reflect on this grand plan of God that, amazingly, co-opts believers into working with him? How often do we talk about it to the flock?
- While the pericope deals primarily with the importance of receiving and applying God's word, there is clearly a hint of encouragement here to those who proclaim God's word. If Jesus met with a diversity of responses to his preaching, then so will we—both positive and negative, perhaps more the latter. But we do well to remember that notwithstanding the human element in application, fruit bearing is ultimately in the safe hands of a trustworthy God. Take heart!

Preaching Is Applicational!

7

Preaching Is Conformational

How can a young man be pure in his way?
By guarding [it] according to Your word.
Psalm 119:9

Biblical preaching, by a leader of the church, in a gathering of
Christians for worship, is the communication of the thrust of a
pericope of Scripture discerned by theological exegesis, and of its
application to that specific body of believers, that they may be
conformed to the image of Christ, for the glory of God—all in
the power of the Holy Spirit.

Several years ago David Hajdu, a reporter for *Atlantic Monthly*, walked
into the famous jazz bar the Village Vanguard in Greenwich Village,
New York City.[1] He came in on a set in progress by a small combo, with
a trumpeter in an Italian-cut gray suit, a dark-blue shirt, and a muted blue tie.
Was it . . . ? No, it couldn't be. . . . Yes, it was: Wynton Marsalis!

The maestro got a solo on the fourth song. Unaccompanied. A ballad, a
1930s deeply melancholic piece called "I Don't Stand a Ghost of a Chance
with You." He performed the song in murmurs and sighs, at points nearly

1. David Hajdu, "Wynton's Blues," *Atlantic Monthly*, March 2003, 43–44.

speaking the words into his horn. It was a wrenching act of creative expression. When he reached the climax, Marsalis played the final phrase, the title statement, allowing each successive note to linger in the air a bit longer. Suddenly, at this most dramatic point, someone's cell phone went off, blaring a rapid sing-song melody in inane electronic bleeps. The spell was broken. People started giggling, glasses started clinking, some started leaving. The moment—the whole performance—unraveled.

Marsalis paused, motionless, his eyebrows arched. The cell-phone offender escaped into the hallway as the chatter grew louder. Still frozen at the microphone, Marsalis replayed the silly cell-phone melody note for note. Then he repeated it and began improvising variations on the tune, winding dexterously through several measures and modulations. After a few minutes of this—by now the audience was back with him, listening in rapt attention to the masterpiece Marsalis was creating—he resolved the improvisation, which had changed keys several times, and throttled back down to a ballad tempo. And . . . the maestro ended up exactly where he had been so rudely interrupted: "I don't stand . . . a ghost . . . of a . . . chance . . . with . . . you." The ovation was tremendous. Just then a friend of Mr. Hajdu came in, took her seat, leaned over to him, and asked, "What did I miss?"

If we don't let the Holy Spirit take our lives and make it into a masterpiece, we'll miss everything! Indeed, this is what preaching is all about: humanly facilitating the purpose and power of God to form his people into a masterpiece—something great from nothing much.

> Those He foreknew, He also predestined to be conformed to the image of His Son. (Rom. 8:29)

And that is God's ultimate intention, to conform his children to the image of Jesus Christ, his Son. All believers are headed in this direction in God's plan. Preaching facilitates this divine plan to conform believers to the image of the incarnate Word by the exposition of the written word, and so preaching is *conformational*. Christology thus plays a significant role in the intersection of Scripture and the church, and it is key to the broader goal of God with regard to humanity.

But how do Christology and preaching intersect? That spiritual growth and maturity are related to Christ is intuitively accepted by all Christians. That biblical exposition should lead to such spiritual growth and maturity also seems obvious. But how exactly a pericope of Scripture is to be preached to link it with Christ is a matter of some dispute. What sort of hermeneutical transaction is the interpreter to perform, for instance, on an Old Testament text to fit Christ into its exposition? The multitude of approaches to this issue (allegorical, typological, redemptive-historical, promise-fulfillment, etc.) render this operation of finding Christ in Scripture quite tricky. I propose a unique way of relating Christ to the preaching of any pericope—a *christiconic* mode of interpretation, a hermeneutic that may be applied consistently across the breadth of Scripture without violating the specific theological thrust of any given text.

Projected World and Christ's Image

In "Preaching Is Theological" we saw that each pericope projects a segment of the canonical *world in front of the text*. Each such world segment bears a divine demand, how God would have his ideal world function and how he desires his people to live in that ideal world—according to its precepts, priorities, and practices. I called this the theology of the text—*pericopal theology*. The goal of preaching is, therefore, to align God's people with God's will in Scripture, pericope by pericope, week by week, sermon by sermon, effecting covenant renewal. In other words, preaching is God's gracious invitation to his people to live with him in his ideal world, abiding by its requirements.

Since only one Man, the Lord Jesus Christ, perfectly met all of God's demands, being without sin (2 Cor. 5:21; Heb. 4:15; 7:26), one can say that this Person, and this Person alone, has perfectly inhabited the *world in front of the text*, living by all of its precepts, priorities, and practices.[2] Jesus Christ alone has fully met every divine requirement and comprehensively abided by the theology of every pericope of Scripture. In other words, each pericope of the Bible is actually portraying a characteristic of Christ. Each world segment is a facet of the image of Christ, showing us what it means to perfectly fulfill, as he did, the particular divine demand in that pericope. Thus, to be fully Christlike means to fulfill God's will in every pericope of Scripture. The Bible as a whole, the collection of all its pericopes, portrays what a perfect human looks like, exemplified by Jesus Christ, God incarnate, the perfect Man. By him alone is God's world perfectly inhabited, and by him alone are God's requirements perfectly met. If the world segment of a pericope is displaying a facet of Christ's image, then the composite *world in front of the text* (i.e., the

---

2. The impeccability of Jesus Christ is an established doctrine of Scripture. Satan failed to tempt Christ to sin (Matt. 4:1–11), and Jesus claimed that he always did what pleased the Father (John 8:29; 15:10). There was no response to Christ's challenge, "Who among you convicts Me of sin?" (John 8:46). Even Pilate assessed him not guilty (John 18:38). Mark 1:24; Luke 4:34; John 6:69; Acts 2:27; 3:14; and 13:35 refer to Christ as the "Holy One." Also see Rom. 8:3; 1 Pet. 1:19; 2:22; 1 John 2:1; 3:5.

integration of all the world segments projected by individual pericopes—or to put it another way, the integration of the theologies of all the pericopes of Scripture) is the complete, plenary image of Christ (see fig. 7.1). Thus the written word of God depicts the incarnate Word of God.

Figure 7.1
Image of Christ

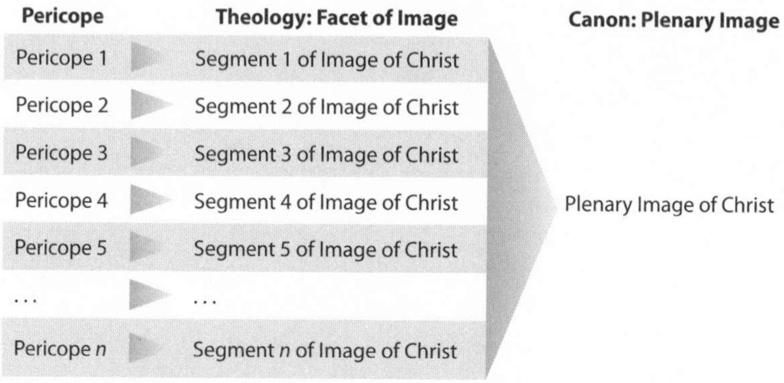

Pericope	Theology: Facet of Image	Canon: Plenary Image
Pericope 1	Segment 1 of Image of Christ	
Pericope 2	Segment 2 of Image of Christ	
Pericope 3	Segment 3 of Image of Christ	
Pericope 4	Segment 4 of Image of Christ	Plenary Image of Christ
Pericope 5	Segment 5 of Image of Christ	
...	...	
Pericope n	Segment n of Image of Christ	

It is by meeting divine demand, pericope by pericope and sermon by sermon, that the children of God become progressively more Christlike, as they align themselves to the image of Christ displayed in each pericope. Preaching is therefore conformational, for by expositing the demand of Scripture it facilitates the conformation of the children of God to the image of the Son of God. Clement of Alexandria, a second-century church father, declared:

> He [Christ] it is who is the spotless image. We must try, then, to resemble Him in spirit as far as we are able . . . to be as sinless as we can.[3]

After all, God's ultimate goal for his children is that they look like his Son, Jesus Christ, in his humanity—"conformed to the image [εἰκών, *eikōn*] of his Son" (Rom. 8:29; also see 2 Cor. 3:18; Eph. 3:19; 4:13–16; Col. 1:28). Even without the benefit of this christological truth, Philo was on the right track when he declared that "the proper end" of human existence was "attaining to the likeness of God."[4] This is a process that begins with conversion as one's trust is placed in Jesus Christ as God and Savior, that continues with increasing conformation to Christ as the believer is sanctified in practice, and that is

3. *Christ the Educator*, 1.2, trans. Simon P. Wood, The Fathers of the Church 23 (Washington, DC: Catholic University of America Press, 1954), 5.
4. *Creation of the World*, 144.

consummated in the last days when the child of God is glorified—transformed into the image of Christ (Phil. 3:21; 1 John 3:2; etc.).

God's goal in accomplishing this conformation to the image of Christ is to restore the *imago Dei*, the image of God, in human beings. That image was man's at creation but was defaced in the fall (Gen. 1:26–27; 9:6; Matt. 22:20 and parallels; 1 Cor. 11:7; James 3:9). But one day, in the plan of God, humankind will "share his holiness" (Heb. 12:10), fully conformed to the image of God (in Christ) again.[5] Philip Hughes notes that by faith, upon justification, the divine image is freely *imputed* to believers, by grace. Through the operation of the Holy Spirit, in sanctification, that image is increasingly *imparted* to them.[6] Therefore, as far as practical sanctification is concerned—that is, the impartation of the image of Christ to the believer—the New Testament has no hesitation in pointing to Jesus as a model (Matt. 9:9; 10:38; 11:29; 20:26–28; John 13:15; Rom. 15:1–3, 7; 1 Thess. 1:6; Eph. 5:2; Phil. 2:5; 1 Pet. 2:21–3:7; 1 John 2:6; 3:16; etc.).[7] Calvin agrees: "Christ, through whom we have returned to favor with God, is set before us as a model, the image of which our lives should express. The Lord adopts us for his sons on the condition that our life be a representation of Christ."[8]

A Christiconic Hermeneutic for Preaching

I submit that Scripture is geared for this glorious purpose of God, to restore the *imago Dei* in humankind, by offering a theological description of Christlikeness, pericope by pericope, to which God's people are to be aligned.

5. In fact, to be conformed to the image of Christ is a grand outcome that transcends the situation antecedent to the fall, for, in being like Christ, glorified humanity will be forever freed from the presence of sin and the possibility of sinning, unlike Adam and Eve in the garden of Eden before sin.

6. Philip Edgcumbe Hughes, *Paul's Second Epistle to the Corinthians*, New International Commentary on the New Testament (Grand Rapids: Eerdmans, 1962), 120. Extending Hughes's alliteration, I might add that finally, in glorification, the image of Jesus Christ is *impressed* upon Christians "in unobscured fulness, to the glory of God throughout eternity" (ibid.). This last process, though begun now, will be completed only when we see Christ face-to-face. All of these aspects of the believer's transformation occur by the grace of God. The imputation of the divine image (justification) is by grace; the impartation of the divine image (sanctification) is also by grace, for (as we have seen in "Preaching Is Applicational") God's power enables such sanctification. And, of course, the impression of the divine image (glorification), too, is an act of divine grace, for if everything else was accomplished by the initiative and power of God, what did human beings do to deserve this glorification?

7. This is not to state that Jesus Christ is *only* a model. It is because he is incarnate God and Savior of humankind that he can be, among other things, a model to this race.

8. *Institutes of the Christian Religion*, 3.6.3, trans. Henry Beveridge (Edinburgh: Calvin Translation Society, 1845), 2:255.

In this sense, the focal point of the Christian canon is the Lord Jesus Christ, the perfect Man and the paramount *imago Dei* himself (Col. 1:15; 2 Cor. 4:4; Heb. 1:3). Therefore, all interpretation of the Bible for preaching purposes must be consistent with this bedrock—the image of Christ portrayed by the canon. Since each biblical pericope portrays a facet of the canonical *image* (εἰκών; Rom. 8:29) of Christ to which human beings are to be conformed, I label this model of interpretation for preaching *christiconic* (from "Christ" and "icon"). Interpreting biblical pericopes in this fashion, to discern the divine demand that moves God's people closer to Christlikeness and to the image of God's Son, is the essence of christiconic interpretation. As Calvin says, "All the children of God are destined to be conformed to him."[9]

The process of gradual conformation to the image of Christ takes place through the textual agency of pericopes of Scripture, through the human agency of the preacher of Scripture, and through the divine agency of the Author of Scripture—a gradual, pericope-by-pericope and sermon-by-sermon conformation to Christlikeness.[10] Even in a verse such as Proverbs 25:16—which warns of consuming honey in excess and vomiting as a result: a call to eschew overindulgence and its deleterious consequences in favor of moderation—a facet of Christ is being depicted. Thus, part of what it means to be Christlike involves living a life that avoids greed and seeks moderation; such a life is a step closer to Christlikeness. Another facet of what it means to be Christlike is to listen exclusively to the voice of God, shunning all worldly voices (1 Sam. 15). And so on, pericope by pericope.

A recap is in order, since we have covered a lot of ground here. Each pericope, portraying a facet of God's ideal world, bears a divine demand (pericopal theology). Only the perfect Man, Jesus Christ, has comprehensively met all the demands of God in all of Scripture. Therefore, he is the prototype of the perfect human, and every pericope of Scripture is implicitly portraying a facet of the image of Christ. Since every pericope enjoins Christlikeness, preaching facilitates the growth of the believer into Christlikeness, more and more, week by week, sermon by sermon. This is why 2 Timothy 3:16–17 declares that "all Scripture is profitable" to render every person mature, that is, Christlike—to "the measure of the stature of the fullness of Christ" (Eph. 4:13). Believers thereby gradually become "partakers of the divine nature" (2 Pet. 1:4), a privilege that will be consummated on the day of glory. But even in this life, as one is increasingly aligned to divine will pericope by pericope, one is gradually being

9. *Institutes* 3.8.1 (2:274).

10. The role of the Holy Spirit in the entirety of the preaching enterprise is reflected in the vision for preaching; see "Preaching Is Spiritual."

conformed to the image of Christ. This is the purpose of preaching. That God has co-opted preachers to play a significant role in this monumental metamorphosis of believers into the image of his Son is nothing short of astounding!

> "We proclaim him, instructing every person and teaching every person with all wisdom, that we may present every person mature in Christ" (Col. 1:28).[11]

I liken preaching, then, to hypothetical weekly visits to a doctor. Say you are visiting me, a dermatologist, this week. I might tell you how to take care of your dry skin. Next week, if you return, I might advise you on how to take precautions in the sun. The week after that, I might give recommendations regarding your moles. After that, I'd offer tips on how to care for your hair. Then your nails, and so on. As you follow my recommendations, your dermatological status is being improved, week by week, and you are well on your way to developing perfect skin! After several weeks of this, you might decide to visit your cardiologist. The first week she might tell you all about controlling your blood pressure. The week after that, how to maintain an exercise regimen. Then, how to control your cholesterol with diet and a prescribed statin. And so on, week by week, till you attain to a perfect cardiovascular state. You might then move on to an endocrinologist, and after a few weeks of that, a gastroenterologist, nephrologist. . . . In short, slowly and steadily, you are being perfected in health.

So also for preaching. Week by week, pericope by pericope, sermon by sermon, as we align ourselves to the divine demand in these pericopes, to the precepts, priorities, and practices of their world segments (i.e., pericopal theology), we are being molded, slowly and steadily, into the image of Christ, the only one who fully kept divine demand and who perfectly inhabits the *world in front of the text*.[12] Thus in a christiconic hermeneutic, the image of Christ portrayed in Scripture is not exhausted by the Gospels or even by the rest of the New Testament. Rather, the entire canon is necessary to portray the plenary image of Christ. So it is through the entire corpus of Scripture that we learn what it means to be Christlike.[13] This, I submit, is the primary function of Scripture and, therefore, the primary purpose of preaching.

11. This behooves the preacher to select, each week, a portion of the biblical text that depicts a "bite-sized" facet of Christlikeness—a pericope—that can be applied to the congregation.

12. As with the clinic visits that assume sound medical advice from the doctor and diligent compliance from the patient, the success of preaching assumes faithful work on the part of the preacher and conscientious application on the part of the listener.

13. In this christiconic hermeneutic, each pericope of Scripture portrays a facet of the image of the perfect *Man*, Christ. That is not to deny Christ's deity, but one must remember that it is his *humanity* that God's people are called to emulate. It is to the image of his perfect *humanity*

In sum, the role of each pericope (and thus of preaching) is to demonstrate a facet of Christlikeness. To the extent that one lives in accordance with the divine requirement in that pericope, one has become more like the perfect Man, Jesus Christ. It is in aligning ourselves completely with this image, obeying God's will in every pericope, that God's purpose for his people is fulfilled—to be "conformed to the image [εἰκών, *eikōn*] of his Son" (Rom. 8:29): this is the heart of the christiconic hermeneutic.

Christiconic vs. Christocentric Interpretation

Christiconic interpretation is quite distinct from christocentric interpretation. The main difference between these two approaches is that the latter operation finds Christ *explicitly* in every passage, even in Old Testament pericopes, whereas the christiconic reading, in consonance with the canonical purpose of God (see Rom. 8:29), discerns an *implicit* depiction of Christlikeness in every pericope—the image of Christ.[14] And, on closer examination, the standard biblical passages offered in support of the christocentric hermeneutic—Luke 24:27, 44; 1 Corinthians 1:22–23; 2:2; and 2 Corinthians 4:5—do not support this mode of interpretation.

Indeed, Luke 24:27, 44 specifically notes that Jesus's lesson to the disciples at Emmaus was not intended to demonstrate how every text of Scripture points to him. Rather, Jesus only discussed *those* texts that *did* point to him. Let me give you an analogy: Some time ago, I discovered that my institution's 2013–2014 catalog referred to me, a member of the Dallas Seminary faculty, in six different places; two of these even had a photograph of me. Now if I point out to my students those six locations and my pictures, explaining how the catalog refers to me—"the things concerning himself in all the [catalog]"—I am in no way implying that the *entire* Dallas Theological Seminary Catalog for 2013–2014 speaks only of Abraham Kuruvilla! Instead, I'm only pointing out those places in the catalog that actually *do* refer to yours truly. Likewise, Jesus is not finding himself in *all* the texts of Scripture, but rather finding *just*

---

that mankind is being conformed, and it is that image that believers will one day bear (Rom. 8:29; Gal. 4:19; Phil. 3:21; 2 Thess. 2:14; 1 John 3:2).

14. Such an implicit christological approach respects Old Testament pericopes for what their authors are *doing* with what they are saying, without necessarily seeking immediate recourse to a New Testament text as is commonly undertaken by proponents of christocentric interpretation. See, for example, the interpretation of the pericopes of Genesis for preaching, in Abraham Kuruvilla, *Genesis: A Theological Commentary for Preachers* (Eugene, OR: Resource, 2014). Elsewhere I have shown how a christocentric interpretation in the redemptive-historical fashion is inadequate (Abraham Kuruvilla, *Privilege the Text! A Theological Hermeneutic for Preaching* [Chicago: Moody, 2013], 238–58).

those texts that concern himself in all the major divisions of Scripture. And what is equally striking is that it was not a christocentric lecture from the Old Testament delivered by the Son of God himself that sparked his recognition by the two Emmaus disciples with him. What opened their eyes was the sharing of a meal, perhaps at that very instant when Jesus identified himself as he broke bread, saying, "This is my body" (= "This is I, the Messiah," Luke 24:30–31)![15]

Proponents of christocentric preaching also point out that Paul preached only "Christ crucified" (1 Cor. 1:22–23; 2:2; 2 Cor. 4:5).[16] As a matter of fact, Paul himself did not preach Christ in *every* sermon of his that is recorded in Scripture. At least in the one delivered on Mars Hill (Acts 17:22–31), neither Jesus nor the cross is mentioned.[17] Moreover, on closer examination, one finds that the Corinthians proof texts are all firmly set in the context of Paul's *evangelistic* ministry (see especially 1 Cor. 1:21; 2:1; 2 Cor. 4:3–4): one would naturally expect Paul to preach only "Christ crucified" in evangelistic messages. Let me hasten to add that presenting the atoning work of the Lord Jesus Christ in sermons is an essential practice for preachers, one that I myself frequently follow. But this is not because I see every pericope as placing preachers under such a hermeneutical constraint.[18] Rather, it is because of a pragmatic constraint, because one can rarely be certain that every listener in one's audience is a believer. In other words, there is no hermeneutical imperative emerging from each pericope that compels one to sketch redemption history and narrate its glorious benefits in every sermon (unless, of course, the theology of a particular pericope actually demands it). On the other hand, the hermeneutical constraint of any pericope is the guidance it offers for godliness in a specific area of life—that is, how to meet divine demand and become more Christlike.

15. Elsewhere in the Synoptic Gospels, Jesus had done exactly that, broken bread with his disciples while claiming to be the Messiah: Matt. 26:26; Mark 14:22; Luke 22:19. In any case, Jesus's assertion that the Scriptures "testify about Me" (John 5:39) obviously could not mean that every pericope, paragraph, verse, sentence, and word (and even jot and tittle) was explicitly referring to himself. After all, explicit messianic promises and foreshadowings in the Old Testament are few and far between in relation to the totality of Scripture. At best, one might point to Gen. 3:15; 12:3; Num. 21:9; Deut. 18:15 (as Jesus claims in John 5:46, "He [Moses] wrote about Me"); and perhaps a finite assortment of other texts, such as Pss. 2; 16; 22; and Isa. 53.

16. This has, in fact, resulted not in christocentric preaching but in "crucicentric" (i.e., cross-centered) preaching, with sermons reciting details of the atoning work of Christ. The other facets of the life of the Lord seem to languish in relative obscurity.

17. Of course, one cannot say for certain that his entire sermon is recorded for us in Acts 17, but the gist of it surely is, and there is no indication Paul had any reference to Christ or the cross in that discourse—and this in an *evangelistic* proclamation!

18. After all, preaching—at least as conceived in this work as a text-based sermon—is for those already belonging to the family of God, as was emphasized in "Preaching Is Ecclesial."

In summary, the incarnated Word, the Lord Jesus Christ, portrayed in the inscripturated word, is the summit of revelation to whose image humankind is to be conformed. His life is the divine standard to which God's people are called to be aligned. Therefore, preaching Christ is, in this sense, the proper goal of preaching. The thrust of the entire canon is the plenary image of Jesus Christ—what it is to be Christlike—and it is the will of God to conform his people to that image of his Son (Rom. 8:29). Such a conception of Jesus Christ in Scripture superintends biblical interpretation for application and plays a critical role as the guardian of the hermeneutical process in homiletics, maintaining the focus of each pericope upon the image of Christ, incarnate God and perfect Man: thus, *christiconic* interpretation.[19]

Imitation and Following

In a sense, this week-by-week and sermon-by-sermon alignment to the divine demand in each pericope is an *imitation* of Christ, a movement toward increasing Christlikeness. Paul employs the concept of "imitation" frequently: of Christ/God (Eph. 5:1; Phil. 2:4–11; Rom. 15:1–3, 5), of himself and Christ (1 Thess. 1:6; 1 Cor. 10:32–11:1), of himself (1 Cor. 4:16; 11:1; Gal. 4:12; Phil. 3:17; 4:9; 1 Thess. 1:6; 2 Thess. 3:7, 9), and also of other churches and believers (1 Thess. 1:6, 7; 2:14; 2 Thess. 3:7–9). Elsewhere in the New Testament, the imitation of God is found in Matthew 5:44–48; Luke 6:36; John 17:11, 21; Colossians 3:13; and 1 Peter 1:15.[20] These New Testament exhortations were likely rooted in the Old Testament notion of "following Yahweh" (Num. 14:24; 32:11–12; Deut. 1:36; Josh. 14:8–9, 14; 1 Sam. 12:14; 1 Kings 11:6; 14:8; 2 Kings 23:3; also see Sir. 46:10). Perhaps reflecting this Old Testament

---

19. If the congregation is aware of God's larger goal of conforming his people to the image of his Son, the preacher may not need to rehearse these conceptual details of the christiconic purpose of Scripture in every sermon except to state, for instance when preaching 1 Sam. 15, that part of what it means to be Christlike is to be attentive to God's voice and to shut out those voices of the world. That's all that is necessary in most sermons. I would spend most of my pulpit time drawing out the pericopal theology from the text, substantiating it, illustrating it, and then applying it specifically to the lives of God's people. Perhaps a periodic exposition of the christiconic concept may be useful, say, in an adult Bible study, a small-group gathering, or a Sunday school class, or even in a one-off didactic sermon for that purpose. I for one keep ceaselessly talking about it in one-on-one conversations to all who will listen.

20. Also see 1 John 2:6; 3:16. From ancient days, in a variety of religious traditions, the imitation of deity was considered a valuable goal to be attained. In *Theaetetus* 25.176a–b Plato urges humans to flee from evil in this world to the place of the gods: "To flee is to become like God; and to become like [him] is to become righteous and holy and wise." Philo cites this passage approvingly in *On Flight and Finding* 12.63; elsewhere, this first-century Jewish philosopher denies there is any "greater good than for mortals to imitate the eternal God" (*On the Special Laws* 4.73); and God is to be imitated "as much as possible" (*On the Virtues* 31.168).

emphasis, rather than calling for an imitation of Jesus, the command in the Gospels, quite frequently, is to *follow* him (as in Matt. 8:22; 9:9; 10:38; 19:21; etc.). In either case, whether disciples are imitating or following, their model is the perfect Man, Jesus Christ.

> A man who could be seen was not to be followed; God was to be followed—but he couldn't be seen. So in order to present human beings both with one who could be seen by human beings and with one whom human beings might properly follow, God became a human being.[21]

Because children of God are called to imitate/follow Jesus Christ, preachers are called to discern the theology of the pericope—that is, the facet of Christlikeness depicted therein—and apply it to the widely diverse situations of believers across the globe, across millennia, and across cultures, to enable them to imitate/follow the perfect Man, their divine Master. In other words, while pericopal theology tells us *what* Christ looks like, application in sermons tells us *how* we can look more like him, in our own particular circumstances.

Preaching Is Trinitarian

Christiconic preaching is Trinitarian in concept and function. Each of the three entities that constitute the preaching process—text, pericopal theology, and application—relates to a person of the Trinity, making the whole endeavor Trinitarian (see fig. 7.2). The text inspired by the Holy Spirit (2 Pet. 1:21) depicts Jesus Christ, the Son, to whose image humankind is to conform (Rom. 8:29). In so being conformed, the will of God the Father is done and his kingdom comes (Matt. 6:10).

Figure 7.2
Trinitarian Preaching

21. Augustine, "Sermon 371: On the Lord's Nativity," in *The Works of Saint Augustine, Part 3: Sermons 341–400*, trans. Edmund Hill, ed. John E. Rotelle (New York: Augustinian Heritage Institute, 1995), 10:312. Augustine's statement was later cited by Aquinas, *Summa theologica* 3.1.2.

In other words, the agenda of God the Spirit in Scripture reveals the perfect, divine demand–fulfilling life of God the Son, so that when that life is imitated/followed (applied) by believers, the kingdom of God the Father is being established as his subjects are aligned with his will.[22] Thus, preaching is not for the information of minds but for the transformation of lives, that God's children may conform to the image of Christ, in the power of the Holy Spirit, through the instrumentality of Scripture, by the agency of the preacher. Week by week, sermon by sermon, pericope by pericope, habits are changed, dispositions are created, character is built, the image of Christ is formed, and humans become fully and completely what they were meant by God to be. "Men are [the] image of God in so far as they are like Christ. The image is fully realized only through obedience to Christ; this is how man . . . can become fully man, fully the image of God."[23]

Excursus: The Work of Christ

All of this discussion of practical, ongoing sanctification and alignment to Christ's image, and of the responsibility of God's people to apply Scripture and move closer to Christlikeness, should not be misconstrued as a sort of do-it-yourself lifting up of oneself by one's own theological bootstraps. Not at all! The gradual conformation to the image of Christ in this life (and ultimate conformation in the next) is wholly a matter of God's grace—notwithstanding the critical component of human responsibility of listeners to obey God's will.[24]

Without the grace extended to humankind in Christ, divine demand (which includes law in the earlier dispensation) in and of itself cannot do anything to justify the sinner, cannot make expiatory provision to wipe away sin, cannot exercise forgiving grace to effect reconciliation with God, and cannot empower obedience to its own requirements. But with Christ all things have been made new. Sinners have been justified, sin expiated, forgiveness extended, and reconciliation with God accomplished for those who believe in Jesus Christ as their only God and Savior. Eternal condemnation for disobedience to divine demand is no more, for Jesus has paid the price for sin (Rom. 8:1). Moreover, it is not just his atonement that is efficacious for believers' sanctification

---

22. Of course, the arrival of this kingdom in all its fullness and glory will have to await the second advent.

23. D. J. A. Clines, "The Image of God in Man," *Tyndale Bulletin* 19 (1968): 103.

24. See the section "Relationship Precedes Responsibility" in the previous chapter.

but also his ongoing ministry before the Father on behalf of the ones he redeemed: intercession (Rom. 8:34; Heb. 7:25) and advocacy (Heb. 9:24; 1 John 2:1).

But this newness of creation post-Christ does not nullify the divine demand in each pericope of Scripture. Sanctification is an ongoing process, and vital to this process is the obedience of the believer: *relationship with God demands responsibility toward God.*[25] And here we encounter yet another aspect of the work of Christ that is crucial to our sanctification: Christ's sending of the Holy Spirit (John 14:16; 15:26; 16:7). With the indwelling of the Holy Spirit, a new life is begun and the believer is enabled to fulfill the will of God in all of Scripture (Rom. 8:4, 12–16).[26] Indeed, as Romans 8:4 makes clear, Christ's work was accomplished *so that* God's divine will ("righteous requirement") may be fulfilled by his Spirit-indwelt and Spirit-empowered children, "who do not walk according to the flesh but according to the Spirit." That it is the Holy Spirit who gives the ability to obey divine demand is also established by the Old Testament (see Deut. 30:6; Jer. 31:31–34; Ezek. 36:26–28; 37:1–28; etc). Of course, Jesus also declares that "apart from Me you are not able to do anything" (John 15:5).[27]

All this to say, the child of God is never to attempt obedience in self-justification, with self-resources, for self-glory: that is legalism and devoid of grace, and entirely futile. Rather, with a faith-filled dependence upon the work of Christ and upon the Spirit, the flesh is defeated, obedience to divine will is achieved, and God is glorified.[28] In short, in everything pertaining to the sanctification of the Christian, Christ is the initiating and sustaining agent, directly or indirectly, from start to finish. And one day, when we see him face-to-face, "we shall be like Him," bearing the image of God in Christ (1 John 3:2). No wonder that in the end the angels and the multitudes in heaven will acclaim: "Worthy is the Lamb who was slain, to receive power and riches and wisdom and strength and honor and glory and blessing," a rousing cheer echoed by "every creature which is in heaven and on the earth and under the earth and on the sea and all that is in them" (Rev. 5:12–13).

---

25. See "Preaching Is Applicational" and also Kuruvilla, *Privilege the Text!*, 189–95.

26. Obedience to God's will is a consistent teaching of the New Testament, particularly in John's writings: see John 14:15, 21; 15:10, 12; 1 John 2:3–4; 3:22–24; 4:21; 5:2–3; and 2 John 6.

27. Also see 1 Cor. 4:7; 2 Cor. 3:5; 4:7; 8:1 with 8:7 (the grace of God becomes the Macedonians' own work of grace); 12:9–10; Gal. 6:3; 1 Thess. 5:24; Heb. 13:21; and 1 Pet. 4:10–11. All attest to the working of God in/with the work of his children.

28. See "Preaching Is Doxological" for this concept of faith-filled obedience—the "obedience of faith" (Rom. 1:5).

Summary

The canon of Scripture, we have seen, projects an ideal world of God, invit-ing believers to inhabit that world by abiding by its precepts, priorities, and practices—that is, by aligning themselves to the divine demand in each scrip-tural pericope (pericopal theology). It is obvious that there is only one Man, the Lord Jesus Christ, who has fully and perfectly aligned himself to divine demand; he is the only one to comprehensively inhabit God's ideal world. Thus, each pericope depicts a facet of Christlikeness, and the integration of all these facets in all biblical pericopes portrays the plenary image of Christ in Scripture. To that image of his Son, God's people are to conform, in the power of the Holy Spirit. As they do so pericope by pericope and sermon by sermon, they are being molded into the image of Christ. This is God's ultimate goal for his children—to conform them to the image (εἰκών, *eikōn*) of his Son, the Lord Jesus Christ (Rom. 8:29). When preached in this fashion, with this *christiconic* hermeneutic, the text inspired by the Holy Spirit that depicts Jesus Christ will have become life in the people of God, and the will of the Father will have been done, and his kingdom will have come! *Preach-ing is conformational!*

Reflection

Mark 14:51–52; 15:46; 16:5—The Great Exchange[29]

> And a certain young man was following Him, wearing a linen cloth upon [his] nakedness, and they seized him. But he abandoned the linen cloth and fled naked. (Mark 14:51–52)

The story of the naked runaway in Mark 14:51–52, found right after the account of Jesus's arrest, is one of the least understood narratives in the en-tire New Testament. Scholars have described the account as strange, bizarre, confusing, enigmatic, and whimsical. And if it is left out (which is apparently what Matthew and Luke did in their respective Gospels: Matt. 26:56–57; Luke 22:54), Mark 14:50 segues seamlessly into 14:53. But this two-verse vignette is firmly fixed in Mark's Gospel, and so we have to assume that Mark included it for a reason. Who was this strange "young man," and—more important—what was Mark *doing* with what he was saying about him?

29. For more details, see Abraham Kuruvilla, "The Naked Runaway and the Enrobed Reporter," *Journal of the Evangelical Theological Society* 54 (2011): 527–45.

Most scholars believe that, like an artist painting himself or herself in a corner of the canvas, Mark is including a cameo of himself here in his Gospel. The history of identifying this character with the writer began with a thirteenth-century Coptic manuscript in which a footnote identified the young man as Mark the Evangelist. But Papias, the early second-century bishop of Hierapolis, declared that "Mark neither heard the Lord nor followed him" during Jesus's lifetime.[30] Others have speculated that the naked runaway was Lazarus (the linen garment a leftover from his recent occupancy of a tomb), or Joseph of Arimathea (linking him with another Joseph who fled, shedding his garments), or James (who, it is thought, wore a linen cloak all his life; perhaps this was his penitence for having abandoned a linen cloak at the arrest of Jesus), or an idealized representation of Jesus himself in his death, burial, and resurrection. For some scholars, the fact that this misadventure was omitted by Matthew and Luke is proof enough that it lacks any obvious theological meaning and that it is irrelevant to the purpose of Mark's overall story.

Such hypotheses and evaluations tacitly assume that Mark was an inept writer, but that conclusion is completely unwarranted: of capricious editing, Mark knows nothing. His work is the product of a sophisticated theological mind, assisted by the Holy Spirit. In fact, with this minidrama, as with all the other scenes in his Gospel, Mark was *doing* something deliberate and purposeful, as narrators always do. Mark had a goal in telling this particular story. What was that goal?

The juxtaposition of the brief episode in question with that of the fleeing disciples is telling. Following the betrayal by Judas and the arrest of Jesus (Mark 14:43–49), all the disciples left him and "fled" (14:50). Immediately thereafter comes this account of a young man who "followed Jesus" and who, when seized, abandoned his garment and also "fled." It is significant that this youth is described as one who "followed" Jesus. To follow was what Jesus called the disciples to do, and following was what they had been doing (1:18; 2:14, 15; 6:1; 8:34; 10:21, 28, 52). "Following" is therefore a literary clue: Mark is labeling the young man a disciple. The disciples followed; the young man followed. The disciples fled; the young man fled. Here, then, in the picture of the naked runaway: followers have become "flee-ers." In Mark's narrative, the ignominious flight of this anonymous sympathizer serves to underline the complete failure of Jesus's disciples. At one time Jesus's disciples had left all to follow him. But now, in the abandonment of even the shirt off this young man's back, readers are shown that the disciples have left all to get

---

30. As cited by the Roman Christian historian Eusebius, of the second and third centuries, *Ecclesiastical History* 3.39.15 (*NPNF²* 1:172).

away from Jesus. Mark is portraying this naked runaway as symbolic of the total abandonment of Jesus by the band of disciples who fled to escape the baleful consequences of association with their Master.

But why include this little scene in 14:51–52? The only substantive fact added by this story is that the young man had an unfortunate wardrobe malfunction. His nakedness, mentioned twice, points to the shamefulness of the disciples' abandonment. Those who had been called to follow had failed, and disgracefully. They had chosen shame over fidelity to Jesus! At the Mount of Olives, on his way to Gethsemane, Jesus had warned his disciples that they would "all" fall away (14:27); Peter protested that even if "all" fell away, he would not (14:29); and the rest of the disciples—"all" of them—vehemently denied the possibility that they would be faithless (14:31). Yet, now, they "all" fled (14:50, 52). Naked failure—shame!

And who among us has not failed in our discipleship as we have followed Jesus? In one way or another, to some degree or another, at some time or another, we have all fallen in sin, failed in faithfulness, flagged in courage, and backslidden in commitment. And we continue to stumble in discipleship. Is there hope for us?

What is interesting in the cryptic account of 14:51–52 is that there is only one other instance of the single Greek word for "linen cloth" in all of Mark's Gospel—and that is in reference to the burial shroud of Jesus (15:46). There, as in the story of our naked runaway, the word for "linen cloth" occurs twice. In utterly discreditable circumstances, the disciple/follower is stripped of the "linen cloth" he wears (14:51–52), and following an equally degrading assassination, a "linen cloth" becomes Jesus's burial shroud. The former garment, which represents shame, buries Jesus in death. In other words, Jesus "gets" the garment of shame from the young man. That, of course, is not to assert that it was one and the same linen cloth. Rather, Mark uses the cloth as a literary device.[31]

The purpose for this device becomes evident when we read of the announcement of Jesus's resurrection (16:1–8). Another "coincidence": there we find the only other use in all of Mark of the term "young man," to describe the angelic reporter clad in white (16:5). The only reason for Mark's unique appellation, labeling as "young man" the one whom the other Gospel writers call "angel"—indeed, according to Luke 24:23 and John 20:12, there were more than one of these species—must have been to link the two incidents

---

31. Incidentally, just as "linen cloth" occurs twice in both instances (in Mark 14:15–52 and in 15:46), so also "nakedness" is found twice in 14:51–52. One also remembers that Jesus was himself stripped naked twice, once to dress him in purple and again as his own garments were replaced (15:17, 20).

with "young man" in them (Mark 14:51–52 and 16:5), thus connecting the naked runaway and the enrobed reporter.[32]

But this "young man" in Mark 16 is not wearing a "linen cloth"; he is wearing white (16:5). Another "coincidence": the only other instance of the word "white" in Mark's Gospel is in 9:3, where the garments of Jesus's transfiguration are so described. Aha! So that's where the "young man" in Mark 16 got his whites from: Jesus "donates" his garment of glory to the "young man."

It appears, then, that garments have been exchanged (in a literary sense, of course). The "linen cloth" the young man wore, which was stripped from him, rendering him naked (14:51–52), now covers Jesus's body in the tomb (15:46). In exchange, the "white" garment Jesus wore at his transfiguration now covers the young man who makes the announcement at the empty tomb (16:5). In other words, the runaway's garment of shame in Mark 14 becomes Jesus's garment of shame in Mark 15, and Jesus's garment of glory in Mark 9 becomes the reporter's garment of glory in Mark 16. The garment of shame of the "young man" buried Jesus; Jesus's garment of glory restores the "young man." This not-so-subtle literary sleight of hand points to the rehabilitation of the failed disciple: the naked, shamed one is clothed, and this with the clothing of glory of his Master, while the Master takes on the clothing of shame, the garb of his failed followers.

This artistic portrayal of the exchange of garments bears an implicit promise: for those disciples who have failed in discipleship, God offers hope. Yes, there is hope for all of us who follow Jesus, albeit stumbling and failing, clumsy and hesitant. The shame of our failures is exchanged for the brilliance of Jesus's glory, and we have hope indeed—because of what our Lord did for us! Amazing grace!

Indeed, even as we ponder the concept of being fully conformed to Christ's image in the future, we are humbled as we realize what Christ has already done for us: forgiveness free, full, and final. He has made us his own, and God has adopted us to sonship and wrapped us in the glorious and righteous garment of his Son. Our responsibility, now that we are in relationship to this God, is to live out the image of Christ, to be conformed to his likeness in our thoughts, words, and deeds, by the power of the Holy Spirit.

- Mark 14:51–52 reminds us that it is only because of what Christ has already wrought for us that we are able and empowered to move in the direction of Christlikeness in our lives. How often do we make it clear

32. The verb "clothe/wear" is another link between Mark 14:51–52 and 16:5; it occurs only in these two locations in the entire Gospel.

to our listeners that, unlike legalism, Christian responsibility to obey divine demand is a divinely empowered operation?

- With all the strategizing of sermon development and delivery, and being deluged in the minutiae of textual detail, both we and our listeners may need reminders of where all this is going, what God's goal is in and through preaching and spiritual formation: Romans 8:29 needs to be brought to mind—God's conformation of his people to the image of his Son, Jesus Christ.

- What a privilege it is to be part of God's guaranteed program of conformation to Christ's image! "The one who began a good work" in us "will complete it" at the day of the revelation of his Son (Phil. 1:6). Let us never fail to be grateful to God for his grace that is molding us daily, to glorify us in the image of his Son (1 John 3:2). Do we lead our congregations in developing hearts of gratitude for this great work God is doing in us?

- The fact that preaching is conformational also reminds us preachers of the greatness of our stewardship, our preaching of God's word. We're involved in something far greater than we can imagine or than we are capable of undertaking on our own—the conformation of God's people to the *imago Dei*. What a privilege, and a greatly humbling one at that! May God empower us to discharge our responsibilities faithfully, and may we handle carefully the lives entrusted to our leadership, as God employs us as his agents, in the power of the Spirit, to mold them into the image of Christ.

Preaching Is Conformational!

8

Preaching Is Doxological

Establish Your word to Your servant,
Which is for those who fear You.

Psalm 119:38

Biblical preaching, by a leader of the church, in a gathering of
Christians for worship, is the communication of the thrust of a
pericope of Scripture discerned by theological exegesis, and of its
application to that specific body of believers, that they may be
conformed to the image of Christ, *for the glory of God*—all in
the power of the Holy Spirit.

There is an old story, probably apocryphal, told about Oliver Wendell
Holmes, the legendary American Supreme Court justice of the early
part of the last century, who had the reputation of being absentminded.
One day on a train out of Washington, DC, Holmes was studying a pending
case when the conductor came by and asked for his ticket. The eminent jurist
searched each pocket nervously, but to no avail.

As the embarrassment mounted with each second, the conductor interrupted: "Don't be concerned, Mr. Justice Holmes, we know who you are. When
you return to Washington, you can send us the ticket at your convenience."

Holmes lowered his eyes and shook his head sadly. "Thank you, my good man, but you don't seem to understand the problem. It's not a question of whether I'll pay the fare. The problem is: Where am I going?"

Indeed, that is a question preachers could well ask of themselves: Where are *we* going? What are we in this for? What is the ultimate goal of the homiletic endeavors we engage in?

The Doxological End of All Things

The answer to that question of ultimate goal is not a mystery for the Christian, of course. All of life—indeed, all of creation—is doxological: for the glory of God.

> For from Him, and through Him, and to Him are all things. To Him be glory forever! Amen. (Rom. 11:36)

And, declared Jonathan Edwards, "All that is ever spoken of in the Scripture as an ultimate end of God's works, is included in that one phrase, the glory of God."[1] Everything undertaken by humankind is to be done for God's glory—"whether, then, you eat, whether you drink, whatever you do" (1 Cor. 10:31)—and this doxological focus has to be maintained even in preaching:

> Whoever speaks, [let it be] as [one speaking] the words of God . . . so that in everything God may be glorified through Jesus Christ, to whom be glory and power forever and ever. Amen! (1 Pet. 4:11)

What exactly is "glory" (כָּבֹד, *kabod*)? The related word, כָּבֵד (*kabed*), means "heavy" (1 Sam. 4:18; Isa. 32:2; it also designates what was thought to be the heaviest organ in the body, the liver [Exod. 29:13][2]); as a verb, it means "to make heavy" (Lam. 3:7). Figuratively, by extension, it indicated "heaviness" of eyes (Gen. 48:10) or heart (Exod. 9:7), and "wealth" (Gen. 31:1), that is, the substantial nature and significant character of something or someone. Theologically, then, כָּבֹד (*kabod*) indicates God's substantiality and significance, his splendor and preeminence, that is, his glory (Exod. 24:16–17; Ps. 19:1). "When the Bible uses the word 'glory' or 'glorious' with reference to the LORD, it is basically saying that *he is the most important or preeminent*

1. Jonathan Edwards, "The End for Which God Created the World," in John Piper, *God's Passion for His Glory: Living the Vision of Jonathan Edwards* (Wheaton: Crossway, 1998), 242 (¶264).
2. It is not. The skin is.

person in this or any other universe. And when the Bible refers to the 'glory of the LORD,' it is usually referring to all the evidence of God's preeminence," whether it be his creation, his deeds, or his nature and attributes.[3]

In the Shorter Catechism created by the Westminster Assembly in the seventeenth century, the first question and its answer relate to the glory of God and to humankind's ultimate purpose in light of this preeminence of deity:

Q. What is the chief end of man?

A. Man's chief end is to glorify God, and to enjoy him forever.[4]

The Puritan Thomas Watson (ca. 1620–86), expounding on the Westminster Shorter Catechism, detected a twofold "glory." First, there is God's *intrinsic* glory that is essential to the Godhead, "as Light is to the Sun"—God is the "God of glory" (Acts 7:2). "God's glory is such an essential part of his being, that he cannot be God without it; God's very life is in his glory. His glory can receive no addition, because it is infinite." Neither can there be a subtraction of this glory, for God does not share it with any other (Isa. 42:8). Second, there is God's *ascribed* glory, "which his creatures labour to bring to him" (1 Chron. 16:29; 1 Cor. 6:20). "The glory we give God is nothing else but our lifting up his name in the world, and magnifying him in the eyes of others." Watson saw this ascription of glory to God as "the yearly rent we pay to the crown of heaven."[5]

Thomas Boston (1676–1732), a Scottish Calvinist, also discussing the Shorter Catechism, noted that to glorify is either to *make* glorious or to *declare* to be glorious. Since the former is exclusively the work of God—human hands do not make him glorious (Job 35:7; Acts 17:25), he is intrinsically glorious—humanity's glorification of deity must indicate their declaration of God to be glorious (Watson's *ascribed* glory). While God's "creatures inanimate and irrational" may glorify him (Ps. 19:1; Rom. 1:20), humanity alone can do so intentionally in their thoughts, "thinking highly of him, and esteeming him above all other persons or things" (Ps. 73:25), with their tongues (Ps. 50:23), and by their lives (Matt. 5:16).[6]

3. Allen P. Ross, *Recalling the Hope of Glory: Biblical Worship from the Garden to the New Creation* (Grand Rapids: Kregel, 2006), 47.

4. The Westminster Shorter Catechism (1646–47), 1.

5. Thomas Watson, *A Body of Practical Divinity, Consisting of above One Hundred Seventy Six Sermons on the Lesser Catechism* (London: Thomas Parkhurst, 1692), 1 (archaic wordings have been modernized).

6. Thomas Boston, "Of Man's Chief End and Happiness," in *An Illustration of the Doctrines of the Christian Religion, with Respect to Faith and Practice* (London: William Baynes, 1812), 1:2–3.

And as with all of life, so also with preaching. Preaching, too, is intended for the glory of God, because *all* things are headed in that direction. In and through preaching, and by all that preaching intends to accomplish, glory must be *ascribed* to God; he must be *declared* glorious. Preaching, therefore, is "doxological speech."[7]

Preaching and the Glory of God

Preaching is an *act* of glorifying God in the three arenas defined by Boston—in the preacher's thought, with the preacher's tongue, and by the preacher's life. But not only is the act of preaching—conducted in the context of the worship service of the local church (see "Preaching Is Ecclesial") and directed to the congregation of God's people—doxological (with the preacher as the one acting to glorify God); the *goal* of preaching is also doxological (with listeners as the ones responding to glorify God). That is to say, preaching is also doxological from a vantage point on the other side of the pulpit, from the pews: listeners acknowledge the magnificence and preeminence of God through preaching in the context of worship (glorification in thought); they magnify God in response to preaching by worshiping (glorification with tongue[8]); and they live out, in the power of the Spirit, the divine demand preached from the text (glorification by life). The preacher's own glorification of God in thought, with tongue, and by life—preaching as an *act* of glorification—will be considered further in "Preaching Is Spiritual." Here we focus on listeners' glorification of God—glorification as the *goal* of preaching.

The Goal of Preaching: Glorification in Thought and with Tongue

Preaching construes the Bible as the word of God, the Father's message to his children, and upholds this word as the foundation of the faith and praxis

7. Michael Pasquarello, *Christian Preaching: A Trinitarian Theology of Proclamation* (Grand Rapids: Baker Academic, 2006), 57. As was seen in "Preaching Is Conformational," preaching itself is Trinitarian in concept and function: this activity is grounded upon the words of the Spirit that depict the image of the Son, to which God's people are to be conformed, so that the Father's will is done and his kingdom comes. In this way also, with the exaltation of the Trinity, preaching is inherently God-glorifying. One must also note that preaching by a christiconic interpretation of Scripture is itself a declaration, pericope by pericope, of the attributes of God the Son, Jesus Christ, who is the final revelation of God's *glory* as the New Testament attests: John 1:14, 18; Heb. 1:3; 2 Cor. 4:4, 6 (see "Preaching Is Conformational"). Thus, in this christiconic operation as well, preaching accomplishes the goal of glorifying God by exalting the Second Person of the Trinity.

8. Of course, this worshipful glorification "with tongue" involves the whole body and not just the vocal apparatus.

of the church. As this word of God is preached, and as the divine demand in a pericope is exposited and its *Christicon* (image of Christ) depicted, the Spirit who authored Scripture is active among the faithful: minds are illuminated and strengthened in commitment, emotions are moved, wills are strengthened, and voices are united and raised in worship, in thought, and with tongue.

Let's return to the Ezra-Nehemiah account of the reading and interpretation of Scripture, encountered earlier in this work. This passage serves as a useful paradigm to reflect on several aspects of preaching, including its doxological role. In the momentous event of covenant renewal in the fifth century BCE that is described in Nehemiah 7:73b–8:12, several aspects of the undertaking point to God being glorified in the preaching of Scripture. The location of the Torah reader uttering a liturgical blessing from a position of prominence and visibility (on a podium "above" the people), and the response of the people when the scrolls are opened and read—rising to their feet, lifting their hands and answering "Amen," bowing and prostrating, and subsequently confessing and worshiping—as well as the Levites' praise of God, all make the liturgical event of preaching a glorification of God in thought and with tongue.

> Ezra the scribe stood upon a podium [literally, "a tower"] of wood which they had made for the purpose. . . . And Ezra opened the book in the sight of all the people, for he was [standing] above all the people; and when he opened [it], all the people stood. Then Ezra blessed Yahweh the great God. And all the people responded, "Amen, Amen!" lifting their hands; and they bowed down and worshiped Yahweh, their faces to the ground. (Neh. 8:4–6)

> And they stood in their place, and they read from the book of the law of Yahweh their God for a fourth of the day; and for a fourth they confessed and *worshiped* Yahweh their God. . . . Then the Levites—Jeshua, Kadmiel, Bani, Hashabneiah, Sherebiah, Hodiah, Shebaniah, Pethahiah—said, "Arise, bless Yahweh your God forever and ever. And may Your glorious name be blessed and exalted above all blessing and praise! You alone are Yahweh. You made the heavens, the heaven of heavens and all their host, the earth and all that is on it, the seas and all that is in them. You gave life to all of them, and the host of the heavens worships You." (Neh. 9:3, 5–6)

Then follows an extended recital of the mighty deeds of Yahweh in 9:6–38, punctuated often by the mention of his attributes: righteousness, graciousness, mercifulness, slowness to anger, lovingkindness, goodness, faithfulness to covenant, justness (9:8, 17, 25, 28, 29, 32, 33, 35). The chapter then concludes with the people resolving to serve him, a declaration registered in writing, signed and sealed by the leaders of the community (9:38). We thus have, as has been noted in earlier chapters, a paradigm for modern-day preaching: the exposition of Scripture, accompanied by the glorification of God in thought (the worshipful attitude and posture of God's people, as well as their commitment to obey) and with tongue (the praising of God's deeds and attributes).[9]

All this to say, the *goal* of preaching is doxological, the direct glorification of God in thought and with tongue: as the word of God is expounded, God's people respond in worship with heart and voice. But preaching is doxological indirectly as well, in that the ultimate goal of preaching is to bring about transformation of the lives of God's people, aligning them to the will of God: glorification of God by life.

The Goal of Preaching: Glorification by Life

Preaching, in the context of the worship of God's people, has as its proximal and immediate goal the direct glorification of God in thought and with tongue, as we saw above. But, more distally, preaching also redounds to the glory of God because its final and long-term goal is to conform the children of God to the will of God in the "image" (εἰκών, *eikōn*, Rom. 8:29) of the Son of God—the christiconic transformation of the lives of God's people. Thus preaching glorifies God by life.

Preaching is the ministry that facilitates the transformation of lives into Christlikeness, through the Scriptures. It is this human activity that brings God's word to bear upon latter to change lives for God's glory. Why God condescended to use the human agency of preaching for his glory is beyond our comprehension. But this we know: "Among the many noble endowments with which God has adorned the human race, one of the most remarkable is, that he deigns to consecrate the mouths and tongues of men to his service, making his own voice to be heard in them."[10] A singular privilege, indeed, for preachers to participate in the glorification of God! That the very voice of God is being heard through the preacher, when Scripture is accurately expounded, was recognized by Paul, who applauded the Thessalonians:

> For this reason we, too, constantly thank God that, receiving the word of God which you heard from us, you accepted not the word of men, but what it truly is, the word of God. (1 Thess. 2:13)

9. This further strengthens the claim made in this work that preaching is rightly and properly ecclesial: it is in the context of the worship of the gathered people of God that preaching ought to be conducted, for it is in such an event that God is glorified in thought and with tongue. That praise glorifies God is obvious from the parallelism of Ps. 22:23: "Those who fear Yahweh, *praise* Him; All the descendants of Jacob, *glorify* Him!" Also see Isa. 42:8, 12; Eph. 1:6, 12, 14; Phil. 1:11.

10. Calvin, *Institutes of the Christian Religion*, 4.1.5, trans. Henry Beveridge (Edinburgh: Calvin Translation Society, 1845), 3:15–16.

In this sense, "the preaching of the word of God is the word of God" (Second Helvetic Confession [1562]), to the extent, of course, that the preaching is faithful to its source text. And by such faithful preaching, pericope by pericope, sermon by sermon, week by week, the various aspects of Christian life, individual and corporate, are progressively and gradually brought into alignment with the will of God for the glory of God: glorification of God by life.

Preaching, we have already noted in "Preaching Is Theological," is best conceived as having two moves. The first move, from text to pericopal theology, draws meaning *from* the passage of Scripture; the second, from pericopal theology to application, directs meaning *to* the situations of listeners. This latter move toward application is critical to the life of the church, for it is by such application and in the resulting conformation to the image of Christ that God is glorified by changed lives. And this happens through the agency of preaching, when the divine demand in each pericope of Scripture is applied to listeners, gradually molding them sermon by sermon, by the power of the Spirit, into the image of Christ.[11] This transformation of life is God glorifying, because changed, holy lives manifest God and his holiness.

> As obedient children, do not be conformed to former lusts of your ignorant days. But like the Holy One who called you, become holy yourselves also in all conduct, for it is written: "You shall be holy, because I am holy." (1 Pet. 1:14–16)

The parallelism of Psalm 29:2 closely links the glory of deity with the holiness of humanity: to ascribe glory to God, one must be holy oneself—a holy worshiper.

> Ascribe to Yahweh the glory of His name;
> Worship Yahweh in holy splendor.
>
> Ps. 29:2

In other words, the holiness of humanity is inextricably linked with the glory of deity.

This is the heart of the preaching endeavor—to bring to bear divine guidelines for life from the word of God upon the people of God, to align them to the will of God, by the power of God, into the image of the Son of God, *for the glory of God*. Preaching is therefore the God-ordained, Spirit-powered,

---

11. As has been mentioned before, "divine demand" is actually a gracious invitation from God to his people, bidding them to live in his ideal world, abiding by its precepts, priorities, and practices, to be as holy as God is. The word "demand" serves to remind us that God's word is abiding, weighty, and *binding*: both its acceptance and its rejection have consequences.

Scripture-based human activity that facilitates the conformation of God's people to the image of Jesus Christ, thereby glorifying God by life. Through the agency of preaching, believers adopt a new way of life, aligning themselves to the precepts, priorities, and practices of God's ideal world—that is, abiding by divine demand. And this voluntary adoption of God's will, with its manifestation in the changed lives of God's people, glorifies God, for his will is being done and his kingdom is being brought about. As humankind is aligned with divine demand, God's attributes and nature are manifested to the universe through the church (Eph. 3:10)—a doxological end, as Ephesians 3:21 makes clear:

> To Him [be] *the glory in the church* and in Christ Jesus to all generations, forever and ever. Amen.

Human Holiness and Divine Glory

As was considered in prior chapters, preaching is a means to remind the people of God of their responsibility toward their Sovereign, the One who redeemed them and brought them into a relationship with him—a call to covenant renewal. So a relationship with God is always antecedent to the responsibility of the people of God to comply with divine demand to be holy as God himself is holy. "The law was not given as a means of salvation, but as a gift of grace to those whom God had already redeemed."[12] In other words, obedience is the response of God's people to a prior operation of his grace that brings men and women into relationship with God: relationship *precedes* responsibility.[13] The ultimate purpose of it all is God's glory. And his plan, all along, has been to guide, by his divine demand, the behavior of those who *already* are his children so that they would manifest his holiness and thus glorify him.

God chooses his people for this purpose: that they would live in a certain manner, worthy of him, displaying his attributes, reflecting his holiness. As Ephesians 1 tells us, God's election of believers was made "before the

---

12. Christopher J. H. Wright, *Old Testament Ethics for the People of God* (Downers Grove, IL: InterVarsity, 2004), 316. From the very beginning, God has called his people to be aligned to his demand. The Torah contains many such imperatives, most of them based on the holy character of God: Lev. 19:2–3; 20:26; etc.

13. See "Preaching Is Applicational" for a discussion of this notion; also see Abraham Kuruvilla, *Privilege the Text! A Theological Hermeneutic for Preaching* (Chicago: Moody, 2013), 151–209. In this chapter I address the same issue but relate it to the doxological nature of preaching.

foundation of the world" so that they would be "holy and blameless before Him," a choice carried out not capriciously but deliberately "in love" (Eph. 1:4). Of course, the fact that divine election is dependent only on divine love, and not at all on human will or action, does not preclude the chosen ones' responsibility to be "holy and blameless," the purpose and consequence of the relationship now established between God and his people.[14] They were chosen *in order to be* "holy and blameless," to live in a manner commensurate with the holiness of God himself. Obedience unto holiness—alignment to divine demand—is therefore a reflection of the loving relationship that children of God already have with their Father. Indeed, such obedience is evidence of one's own reciprocal love toward God, as the New Testament clearly teaches:

> He who has My commandments and keeps them, he it is who loves Me; and he who loves Me will be loved by My Father, and I will love him and will reveal Myself to him. (John 14:21)

> For this is the love of God [i.e., love toward God], that we keep His commandments. (1 John 5:3)

But the key element, for our interest in this chapter, is the end point of God's choice of humankind to be holy: "the praise of the glory of His grace" (Eph. 1:6). That is to say, once again, that the "holy and blameless" lives of believers glorify God.[15] Thus, "glory is how God looks through me; holiness is how I look like God."[16] God is glorified through the lives of believers, by how they resemble God in his holiness. That is why Paul prays for the Philippians that they might be "sincere and blameless for the day of Christ; filled with the fruit of righteousness through Jesus Christ, to the glory and praise of God" (Phil. 1:10–11). It is the holiness of his people, "the fruit of righteousness,"

14. Obedience was never a criterion for the establishment of this divine-human relationship. That was entirely a unilateral act of grace from God's side, apprehended from the human side by faith alone and not by works. Once this relationship was established, not even disobedience could disrupt it, for Scripture itself provided for restoration: atonement could be made for falling short of the perfect standard of God. All of this was nothing but an expression of the character of God that he himself affirmed in Exod. 34:6–7: "Yahweh, Yahweh God, merciful and gracious, slow to anger, and abounding in lovingkindness and faithfulness, keeping lovingkindness for thousands, forgiving iniquity, and transgression, and sin." Thus, even in his forgiveness of sin and sinners, God is glorified.

15. On the other hand, sin "falls short of the glory of God" (Rom. 3:23), and sinners are those who, living lives of depravity, "do not glorify Him as God" (1:21). And Paul affirms in 1 Cor. 6:18–20 that being mired in immorality is to live in a way that does not "glorify God with your body."

16. Ramesh P. Richard, personal communication, June 29, 2014.

that brings God glory—glorification by life. This is also what 1 Peter 2:9 affirms, that believers are "a holy nation" chosen so *that* they may "proclaim the excellencies" of God (i.e., glorify him).

That was true even in the former dispensation of the Old Testament. It was God's loving choice that had established the relationship between him and his people, the Israelites, not the latter's obedience or even their willingness to obey (Deut. 4:37; 7:7–9; 10:15; etc.). Indeed, the Mosaic law itself was given to the Israelites *after* their redemption from Egypt, *after* God had established a relationship with the Israelites. Election to a relationship always came before calls to holiness. As was noted earlier, we see this even in the Ten Commandments, which are preceded by a declaration of relationship: "I am Yahweh your God, who brought you out of the land of Egypt, out of the house of slavery" (Exod. 20:2). A list of responsibilities then follows, *after* this announcement of relationship. So also Leviticus 18:1–5 ("I am Yahweh your God. You shall not do . . . I am Yahweh your God. So you shall keep My statutes and My judgments, by which a man may live if he does them; I am Yahweh") suggests that *because* their sovereign was Yahweh, the Israelites' covenantal God, *therefore* the Israelites were responsible to live in a certain fashion. Biblical examples of this kind are legion.

Such responsible obedience to divine will glorifies the God with whom his people are in relationship by exalting his actions and his attributes. Thus the ultimate consequence of such obedience is the glory of God, for it is in the holy lives of his people that a holy God is manifest.

> Let your light shine before people in such a way that they may see your good works, and glorify your Father who is in heaven. (Matt. 5:16)

Through believers' obedience, facilitated by preaching, God is glorified as his people display the attributes of their holy God and represent him to the world.

> Keep your conduct good among the Gentiles, so that . . . they, observing your good deeds, may glorify God at his appearance. (1 Pet. 2:12)

Thus relationship not only precedes but also *mandates* responsibility, as God places the responsibility of living in God-glorifying fashion upon the people with whom he has a relationship. Indeed, this is why God chose and appointed his people.

And one day, in the eternal state, this relationship of God to his people will be perfected: "Behold the dwelling of God is among men, and He will dwell among them, and they will be His people, and God Himself will be among them" (Rev. 21:3). Perfect obedience, perfect alignment with divine demand, perfect inhabitation of the *world in front of the text*, and final conformation to the image of Christ will then have been achieved. God will be glorified as, even in that eschatological age, God's people in the image of his Son continue to serve him, testifying to his magnificence, holiness, and splendor: every aspect of creation and life will fully reflect his glory (Rev. 21:11, 23, 24, 26).

Therefore, preaching plays a significant role in furthering the glorification of God by life, as it delineates the divine requirement of each pericope so that God's people may align themselves to it. In sum, relationship precedes and mandates responsibility, and the faithful discharge of this responsibility (i.e., life change) is God glorifying. It is through preaching that the various aspects of Christian life, individual and corporate, are gradually brought into alignment with the will of God for the glory of God, pericope by pericope, sermon by sermon. Preaching is doxological.

Excursus: "Obedience of Faith"

As was noted in "Preaching Is Conformational," this God-glorifying obedience—alignment to the divine standard of holiness—is not something Christians can accomplish by sheer dint of toil, utilizing their own meager resources. Rather, the obedience called for in Scripture is an "obedience of faith"—that is, obedience to divine demand *undertaken by faith* for the glory of God. That was Paul's commission, and that is the commission of every preacher coming after him.

> We have received grace and apostleship to bring about the *obedience of faith* among all the Gentiles for the sake of His name. (Rom. 1:5)

"Faith," in "obedience of *faith*," is thus a descriptor of obedience—that is, "faithful obedience" (or "faith-full" obedience): every act of obedience to God is to be conceived in faith, characterized by faith, and carried out through faith.

How is obedience *faithful*? And what would *faithless* obedience look like? Ultimately, faith is an utter dependence upon God, a total trust in his capacity as the "one who began a good work" in us to bring his saving work in believers to completion at the day of Jesus Christ (Phil. 1:6). In other words, this faith (from us toward God) involves dependence upon God, not only for our justification but for our sanctification and glorification as well, just as grace (from God toward us) is essential, not only for justification but also for sanctification and glorification.[17] Here, of course, our focus is upon the "obedience of faith" that indicates the current, ongoing, earthly phase of believers' sanctification, their increasingly holy lives of "faith-full" obedience bringing glory to God.[18] The inadequacies of our own resources to achieve obedience, and the futility of our own attempts to do so, call for faith in the power of God that enables his people to abide by the will of God. In fact, the purpose of the Savior's atoning work as he condemned sin (Rom. 8:3–4) was that God's divine demand (his "righteous requirement," 8:4) may be met in his Spirit-indwelt and Spirit-empowered people (8:4, 12–16).[19]

On the other hand, a misguided effort to keep divine demand by one's own resources and for one's own glory, under the faulty assumption that one can easily achieve God's standard, is at the root of legalism—faith-*less* "obedience." Such a misconception of divine demand, that it can be humanly met without divine aid, and for the purposes of exalting self, is what meets with God's extreme disfavor. Augustine put it incisively:

> As many, therefore, as are led by their own spirit, trusting in their own virtue, with the addition merely of the law's assistance, without the help of grace, are not the sons of God.[20]

Instead, Spirit-enabled obedience to God's law is the faith-filled response of God's children to his divine demand: they acknowledge their own incapacity to meet it, and by faith draw upon the Spirit's power to do so. Thus the obedience of faith is "faith-full" obedience.

All this declares that it is God's grace through Jesus Christ, and his power by the Holy Spirit, that enables believers to keep divine demand and thus bring glory to God. No wonder we are told that "our" works are in

---

17. See 1 Cor. 15:10; 2 Cor. 12:9; Eph. 4:7; and Titus 2:11–12 for grace from God in sanctification; and 1 Cor. 1:4–9; Eph. 2:6–7; and 1 Pet. 1:10, 13, for grace from God for glorification. All these extensions of God's grace call for a reciprocal acceptance of these divine gifts by human faith, just as in the transaction for justification: Eph. 2:8–9—divine grace operating by the instrumentality of human faith.

18. Again, what is emphasized here is the phase of *practical* sanctification of believers, not their *positional* sanctification in Christ. "By this is My Father glorified—that you bear much fruit" (John 15:8); i.e., God is glorified by an ongoing process of fruit production by believers in this life.

19. That it is divine empowerment that grants the ability to obey and to gain victory over the flesh is also established from the Old Testament: see Deut. 30:6; Jer. 31:31–34; Ezek. 36:26–28; 37:1–28; etc. (Ezek. 37 will be considered again in "Preaching Is Spiritual"). Also see Eph. 3:16; Phil. 4:13; Col. 1:9–11.

20. *Grace and Free Will* 24.12 (NPNF[1] 5:453).

fact *God's* works; after all, it is God's power working in us that enables the obedience of faith, as a number of verses in the New Testament testify: "For we are His workmanship, having been created in Christ Jesus for *good works that God prepared* beforehand, so that we may walk in them" (Eph. 2:10); and, "*The one who began a good work* in you will successfully complete it to the day of Christ Jesus" (Phil. 1:6); and yet again, "*God is the one who is at work* in you, both to will and to work for His good pleasure" (Phil. 2:13). And there is also the declaration of Jesus: "Apart from Me you are not able to do anything" (John 15:5).[21]

Without the power of God in Christ through the Spirit working in the believer, nothing can be accomplished for sanctification, for becoming Christlike, and for glorifying God. Therefore the author of Hebrews can say that God is the one equipping his children to *do* his will, even as God himself *does* it all in us—and that is how God is glorified: "Now the God of peace, who brought up from the dead the great Shepherd of the sheep . . . even Jesus our Lord, equip you in every good thing to *do* His will, *doing* in us that which is pleasing in His sight, through Jesus Christ, to whom be the glory forever and ever. Amen!" (Heb. 13:20–21).

In sum, it is the obedience of faith of God's people that glorifies God, for from beginning to end it is the work of God and his amazing grace. Thus, Christian life in its entirety is a function of divine grace, accepted by faith, all designed to bring glory to God: the Father's choice of men and women to become a holy people (justification), their empowerment by the Spirit that they might be holy (sanctification), and, one day, their final transformation into complete holiness in the image of Jesus Christ (glorification). All of these are gracious provisions from God, received in faith by the children of God, that God may be glorified.

And this is the goal of preaching, that by the exposition of the text, the will of God might be made known, and that by the power of the Spirit, God's people might align themselves to that divine demand, pericope by pericope, sermon by sermon: this is the obedience of faith that glorifies God by life. For this, preaching is crucial. The call of preachers is indeed a marvelous one, for the endpoint of their endeavor is doxological. In fact, it is this obedience of faith that was the goal of Paul's ministry and what he boasted about. Romans 15:18 has the apostle recollecting the fruit of his ministry—"the obedience [of faith] of the Gentiles."[22] He then claims

---

21. Also see 1 Cor. 4:7; 2 Cor. 3:5; 4:7; 8:1 with 8:7; 12:9–10; Gal. 6:3; Eph. 4:7; 1 Thess. 5:24; 1 Pet. 4:10–11.

22. Romans 15:13 makes it clear that this is the obedience *of faith*; it records Paul's ardent desire that God may continue to fill the gentile believers with "all joy and peace in exercising

with pride, "I have fulfilled the gospel of Christ" (15:19): a comprehensive lifelong undertaking had been discharged successfully. In short, "obedience of faith" epitomized the expansive and overarching goal of all Paul's undertakings for the cause of Christ in every place.[23] This must be the preacher's long-term goal and ambition as well: to accomplish, in the power of Christ and the Spirit, the obedience of faith of listeners, so that God is glorified by life.

> Now to Him who is able to strengthen you according to my gospel and the proclamation of Jesus Christ . . . *to bring about the obedience of faith*—to the only wise God, through Jesus Christ, be the *glory* forever! Amen. (Rom. 16:25–27)

God is glorified in his people's obedience of faith. And if this is the goal of preaching, then preaching cannot but be doxological!

Summary

The glorification of God is the ultimate end of preaching. In thought and with tongue, God is glorified as the image of Christ in each text is displayed in the gathering of God's people for worship and as they respond with heart and voice. By life, God is glorified in preaching as believers are transformed by the power of the Spirit and progressively conformed to the image of Christ. Such life change is God glorifying, for it aligns God's people with God's will, manifesting God's holiness. God's loving initiative to bring his people into relationship with him mandates their responsibility of obedience, a mark of their reciprocal love for the Father. This is believers' obedience of faith (or "faith-full" obedience, conceived in, characterized by, and carried out through faith), accomplished only by total dependence upon God for his gracious empowerment for sanctification. Such faith pleases God, and the obedience stemming from such faith glorifies God as his people look more and more like his Son. And that is to be the preacher's goal and lifelong passion: the obedience of faith of listeners, implemented in the power of the Spirit, so that God is glorified as they are conformed to the image of his Son. *Preaching is doxological!*

---

faith"—the ongoing faith of practical sanctification. Thus, the "obedience of the Gentiles" in 15:18 is equivalent to the "obedience of faith among all the Gentiles" noted in 1:5. See Kuruvilla, *Privilege the Text!*, 195–204.

23. Don B. Garlington, *Faith, Obedience and Perseverance*, Wissenschaftliche Untersuchungen zum Neuen Testament 79 (Tübingen: Mohr Siebeck, 1994), 11.

Reflection

Mark 8:27–9:8—Suffering before Glory[24]

> If anyone wishes to follow behind Me, let him deny himself and take up his cross and follow Me! For whoever wishes to save his life will lose it; but whoever will lose his life on account of Me and of the gospel, will save it. . . . For whoever is ashamed of Me and of My words in this adulterous and sinful generation, the Son of Man will also be ashamed of him, when He comes in the glory of His Father with the holy angels. (Mark 8:34–35, 38)

Allusions to who Jesus is have permeated Mark's Gospel up until this point (1:1, 24, 34; 4:41; 6:3, 14–16); the disciples have been impacted by Jesus's teaching and miracles (1:18, 20, 36–37; 2:14–15; 4:34, 41; 5:42; 6:7, 12–13, 51); the crowds, too, have often been amazed at Jesus's words and deeds (1:22, 27; 2:12; 5:20, 42; 6:14–16; 7:37); and they have congregated in large numbers before him (1:45; 2:2, 13; 3:7–8; 4:1; 6:54–56). But all of them—crowds *and* disciples—have failed to grasp the person of Jesus. Here, in this pericope (Mark 8:27–9:8), Jesus gives the first of his three passion predictions: his suffering mission is now made clear. But no one seems to be catching that either.

In answer to Jesus's question, Peter confesses that Jesus was "the Christ" (8:29). In Mark's passion account, "Christ" is a royal designation as, for instance, in the mocking of Jesus as "Christ, the King of Israel" (15:32). For Mark, calling Jesus "Christ" is to label him as king, which is exactly what Peter did in 8:29. The problem with this one-sided identification was the inevitable lack of enthusiasm on the part of Jesus's followers for anything less than the pomp and pageantry of royalty. Jesus's suffering mission, described in his passion predictions, they find utterly unappetizing; kings are supposed to wield power, not knuckle under it. In the context of Jesus's first passion prediction (8:31), Peter's exclusively regal designation of "Christ," which fails to take into account Jesus's suffering, is therefore a deficient understanding of Jesus's mission. It appears, then, that the ultimate doxological destination—God's glory—is reached only through the path of suffering. That is something all of us preachers must remember—we who are engaged in the God-glorifying enterprise called preaching have been warned: suffering ahead!

Glory will indeed be manifest at the second advent of the Son of Man (8:38), but not *before* suffering or *without* it. And what is even more striking is that this suffering is part of God's plan. The ominous foreshadowing of Jesus's death in 8:31 is notable for the absence of any fatalistic overtones

---

24. For more details on this pericope, see Abraham Kuruvilla, *Mark: A Theological Commentary for Preachers* (Eugene, OR: Cascade, 2012), 171–87.

whatsoever. It is the *necessary* trajectory ("the Son of Man *must* suffer," 8:31) for the fulfillment of the larger purpose of God to establish his kingdom. Therefore, it comes as no surprise that Peter's attempt to thwart this necessary aspect of Jesus's mission earns him one of the sternest rebukes from Jesus ever recorded (8:33).

Peter's problem was not incomprehension—after all, Jesus's word was spoken "plainly" (8:32). His problem was with that unpalatable idea of suffering. Not thinking the thoughts of God, but rather those of men (and, therefore, of Satan), Peter is not amenable to—indeed, he opposes—the necessary will of God (8:33). And the disciple dares to "rebuke" the Master (8:32). That verb is used elsewhere to indicate the silencing of demonic elements (1:25; 3:12; 4:39; 8:33; 9:25), so its use by Peter for Jesus is shocking. Did he consider Jesus's explanation of his suffering and death (8:31) to be demonic? What Peter said in his rebuke is unstated; however, 8:32 (Peter's drawing Jesus aside—why did he have to do that?) and 8:38 hint that Peter may have actually been ashamed of Jesus. Notice that in 8:38 Jesus denounces those who are "ashamed of Me and My *words* [from λόγος, *logos*]." In 8:32, Jesus was described as stating the "word [λόγος]" plainly, upon which Peter rebukes him. With that verbal connection, this interpretation appears valid: Peter had been ashamed of his Master and his words! In other words, he and the rest of the disciples were unwilling to accept Jesus's mission of suffering-before-glory; in fact, they were embarrassed to hear him talk of such an ignominious end.

So, after rebuking Peter, Jesus teaches the rest of those gathered a lesson (he includes the crowd in his somber pronouncement [8:34]): all who desire to follow Jesus must acquiesce to the self-denial and cross-bearing modeled by their Master. The repetition of "behind Me" (8:33, 34) underscores the proper position of the disciple in relation to Jesus—the posture of following ("behind" Jesus was also noted in 1:17–18, 20; 5:27). So also the repetition of "follow" in 8:34. Jesus's suffering mission was to be the disciples' mission; they were called to take it on themselves as they followed behind the Master. What Jesus calls for is not a denial *to* self (of things) but a denial *of* self. And this inner attitude of self-denial is to be manifest in the outward action of bearing one's cross—a call not merely to endure hardship with patience, but to be ready even for death. As Dietrich Bonhoeffer put it, "When Christ calls a man, He bids him come and die."[25] In other words, God's doxological goal comes at a cost—a high price to pay for those who would follow his Son.

25. Dietrich Bonhoeffer, *The Cost of Discipleship*, trans. R. H. Fuller, rev. Irmgard Booth (New York: Simon and Schuster, 1995), 89.

Then, as a preview of this glory to come, three of Jesus's disciples are treated to a glorious vision of his transfiguration (9:2–3). This snapshot of future glory, albeit brief and transient, served as a reassurance to disciples dismayed by the grave predictions of suffering and death (8:34–38). Suffering there might be, but glory was certainly coming one day! The transfiguration scene of glory was a precursor to what was sure to happen in the future. And glimpsing this snapshot of the future now, knowing the certainty of the consummation of the glory of God, followers of Jesus are enabled and encouraged to persevere through suffering.

Unfortunately, it appears that the disciples on the summit still did not get it. Peter seems to have completely forgotten the details of the suffering mission Jesus had just announced in 8:31. He is willing to abandon the entire project of self-denial and cross-bearing for a more sedate and tranquil mountaintop existence with heavenly beings (9:5). He apparently thinks that the kingdom has already come in power and that suffering has been successfully circumvented. The incomplete confession of Peter that attempted to bypass the cross (8:29, 32) was now being followed by an incomplete proposal from Peter that attempted to bypass suffering (9:5–6). In short, the disciples fail to accept Jesus's suffering mission (and their own).

So God issues a corrective in 9:7: "This is My beloved Son; listen to Him!"—something the disciples had not been doing much of (see 4:3, 9, 23, 24; 7:14, 16; 8:18). Jesus had "plainly" spoken to his disciples here (8:32), but they had not been paying attention. Therefore this divine recommendation was apropos: they (and all future followers of Jesus) must pay close attention to Jesus and to his call to follow him in suffering discipleship. For preachers, who are engaged in a doxological enterprise more directly than are others, this is a powerful lesson. The best is coming, but the worst may be expected now: this is part of following Jesus in discipleship.

Suffering must come before glory. There can be no shortcut to glory—the path to glory is one of suffering. In the transfiguration we are given assurance that that glory is surely coming; it is a snapshot to carry around that gives us hope. And with that hope, Christ followers, including preachers, press on, on the trip of discipleship: the glorification of God involves suffering, but that glory is soon coming!

- Suffering is an integral, nay *necessary*, part of the journey of discipleship as we work toward God's glory. Particularly as leaders and preachers, we will be high on Satan's target list. Recognizing that to suffer as a disciple is to follow the pattern set for us by the Savior is the essential first step in preparing for this inevitability.

- Self-denial and cross bearing are serious undertakings that Jesus calls us to. One way to "practice" these is to engage in one or more of the traditional spiritual disciplines of the Christian life, conveniently distinguished by Dallas Willard into two categories: the disciplines of abstinence (including solitude, silence, fasting, frugality, celibacy, secrecy, and sacrifice) and the disciplines of engagement (including study, worship, celebration, service, prayer, fellowship, confession, and submission).[26] These are worthwhile exercises one can engage in that will prepare the way for a suffering discipleship.

- The right attitudes are critical as one goes through suffering. Self-denial and cross bearing imply humility: *I don't deserve better.* This is always a tough character trait for leaders to develop, but develop it we must, as we surrender ourselves to God and beseech his strength for the hour of crisis.

- Pouring ourselves out for the glory of God, as we engage in preaching the word of God, is a gracious privilege. *God did not have to use me as an instrument for his glory.* Let us, then, accept that privilege with gratitude and with responsibility. Indeed, every leadership role in pastoral ministry is a privilege. May our contagious attitude of gratitude be caught by others on the various ministry teams in church as we exemplify thankfulness.

- And, of course, we should keep our eyes on the glory to come. May the vision of heaven and of the consummation of all things be ever before us, keeping us going and persevering through these brief days of suffering!

Preaching Is Doxological!

---

26. Dallas Willard, *The Spirit of the Disciplines: Understanding How God Changes Lives* (San Francisco: Harper & Row, 1988), 158. Also see "Preaching Is Spiritual."

9

Preaching Is Spiritual

With all my heart I seek You;
Let me not wander from Your commandments.

Psalm 119:10

Biblical preaching, by a leader of the church, in a gathering of Christians for worship, is the communication of the thrust of a pericope of Scripture discerned by theological exegesis, and of its application to that specific body of believers, that they may be conformed to the image of Christ, for the glory of God—*all in the power of the Holy Spirit.*

On February 10, 2013, an engine room fire on the *Triumph*, a ship operated by Carnival Cruise Lines, caused a loss of power on board. Propulsion was completely lost and the 900-foot ship was set adrift in the Gulf of Mexico, about 150 miles off the coast of the Yucatán Peninsula.

An emergency generator did provide some power, and other Carnival vessels arrived to transfer food and water for the 4,200 weary and fed-up passengers and crew on board the stranded ship. Few toilets were working. There was no running water. Air-conditioning was out of commission. Vomit and waste were all over the boat. It was a "fetid nightmare," as one news report put it.

Another labeled it "the cruise ship from hell." Carnival's advertising tagline is "All for fun, fun for all." Not on this trip. No power, no fun.

Finally, four days later, on February 14, the ship docked in Mobile, Alabama. Some travelers kissed the ground upon disembarking. Thankfully, no lives were lost, and no one was hurt.

Carnival Cruise Lines CEO Gerry Cahill issued several apologies and guaranteed that passengers would be reimbursed in full, plus given transportation expenses and future cruise credit as well as an extra $500 per person for the ordeal undergone. But the loss to Carnival may total hundreds of millions of dollars. All disembarking passengers from the crippled ship had to be put up in hotel rooms in Mobile or taken to New Orleans, Louisiana. From there, buses transported them back to Galveston, Texas, from where the fateful journey had commenced. Charter flights returned passengers who had flown in. Needless to say, the saga received extensive (negative) coverage on all United States television news channels, another public-relations disaster for Carnival Corporation, the world's largest cruise company, which had already been badly bruised with its *Costa Concordia* liner running aground off the coast of Italy in 2012, killing thirty-two.

But four months later, the Carnival *Triumph* returned to the seas from Galveston, now outfitted with new emergency power capabilities, for, you see, when the power goes out, the party is over!

When the vision for preaching provided in this work closes with "*all* in the power of the Holy Spirit," the "all" includes the discernment of the thrust of a pericope of Scripture by theological exegesis, and the communication of that thrust and its application to a specific body of believers, to conform them to the image of Christ. Every facet of the sermonic undertaking is to be empowered by God's Spirit. Without this spiritual empowerment, all preaching is in vain, abortive, and fruitless. After all, preaching is based upon a text authored by the Holy Spirit (2 Pet. 1:20–21), and the goal of preaching is life transformation that is energized by the same divine agent (Rom. 8:1–17; Gal. 5:16). So without the enabling of the Holy Spirit in the entirety of the transaction, preaching might well be adrift, powerless.

The issue of the Spirit's enablement of believers' obedience has been considered in earlier chapters and will be dealt with again briefly here, using Ezekiel 37 as a template for understanding the work of the Holy Spirit in empowering God's people for holy living. But there is another critical facet of this work of the Spirit in the preaching process, and that is in the lives of preachers themselves. The final chapter of this work, "Preaching Is Spiritual," will therefore focus primarily on this essential aspect of preaching, the spirituality of the preacher, also using Ezekiel 37 as a starting point for the discussion.

Of all the biblical texts that deal with the transformative power of the Holy Spirit upon humans, none is as powerful as Ezekiel 37 for its sheer drama and the astounding description of the dead coming to life. As we will see, not only does this Third Person of the Godhead work on humans in general; he also works on the *human agent of God's word*—our particular individual of interest—as portrayed in the interaction between the Spirit and the prophet Ezekiel himself. Thus in Ezekiel 37 we see God's Spirit working both on God's people and on God's spokesman.

God's Spirit, God's People, God's Spokesman

The Jewish exiles in Babylon in the sixth century BCE were Ezekiel's immediate audience for his prophecies. The people of Israel had been guilty of idolatry and acts of social crime and were now suffering the consequences. It was in these dire circumstances that Ezekiel prophesied. His name, Ezekiel, appropriately enough means "God strengthens" or "May God strengthen [you]." God's strengthening was something both God's people and God's spokesman certainly needed at this time—and, indeed, that is what God's people and his preachers need in every age if their lives and ministries are to be pleasing to God. How God's efficient and sufficient power enables his people to meet divine demand and his spokesman to accomplish a divine ministry is the thrust of Ezekiel 37, a paradigm for the transformation of all God's people and the empowerment of all God's spokespersons.

God's Spirit and God's People

The book of Ezekiel challenges the dominant anthropological paradigm that humans are inherently capable of making adequate moral choices and engaging in appropriate moral actions that please God and that approximate divine standards of morality.[1] While people may make a few moral changes in lifestyle for the better, the ideal state that God would have humankind reach, perfectly aligned to divine will and perfectly conformed to the image of Christ, can never be achieved by the designs of humanity without the power of deity.

Without divine intervention and help, all that had been accomplished by God's people in Ezekiel's time was disaster, disintegration, and destruction of the nation. Nothing good had been achieved by the old scheme of affairs

---

1. Jacqueline E. Lapsley, *Can These Bones Live? The Problem of the Moral Self in the Book of Ezekiel*, Beihefte zur Zeitschrift für die alttestamentliche Wissenschaft 301 (Berlin: Walter de Gruyter, 2000), 6.

coordinated by defective humans; theirs was a desperate situation. And the result? The three elements of Israel's lament in Ezekiel 37:11—bones dried, hope perished, and people completely cut off (introduced strikingly by "behold")—are synonymous, expressing the Israelites' impression that they, like the dead, were cut off from the blessings of God.[2] In other words, these were people outside the sphere of divine blessing, as are all of God's people who do not walk with him and abide by his requirements. Thus, the sinful state of the Israelites was hopeless, their capacity to meet divine demand and to please God nonexistent—resulting in a loss of blessing.[3]

Therefore, something new was called for, something beyond the resources of inherently sinful humanity: God's gift of his Spirit was absolutely essential. This gracious initiative of God to aid humankind is the lesson of Ezekiel 37: for all of God's people everywhere, transformation to godliness is guaranteed only by the sovereign and powerful working of the Holy Spirit. The tenfold repetition of רוּחַ (ruakh, "breath/spirit/wind") in this chapter (37:1, 5, 6, 8, 9 [4×], 10, 14) and the numerous iterations of the first-person pronoun referring to God (37:5, 6, 12, 13, 14, 19, 21, 23, 28) clinch the role of God in the process of moral transformation. To do what was impossible for humankind to do on its own, God takes the initiative, provides the enablement, and becomes the "cause" thereof: "*I will cause* you to walk in My statutes" (36:27).

The result of this divine action in 37:1–14 is depicted in the subsequent section, 37:15–28—an ideal state follows upon the giving and enablement of the Spirit. It is a picture of perfection: people's total and permanent obedience to a God who is dwelling among his people forever. The consummation of such a complete allegiance to God must, of course, await the end times. Yet, in this present dispensation, because of the atoning work of Jesus Christ, God's people are already indwelt by the Holy Spirit (Rom. 8:9; 1 Cor. 3:16; 6:19; Eph. 2:21–22; etc.)—the end has begun! And therefore it remains the responsibility of believers of all time, even in this age of partial fulfillment, to align themselves obediently to the will of God, *in the power of the Spirit*.[4]

2. Interestingly enough, the stunned "behold" of the Israelites lamenting the bad news of hopelessness (Ezek. 37:11) is balanced later by the "behold" of Yahweh announcing the good news of restoration and empowerment (37:12). Note that Yahweh's announcement is also tripartite (like the cry of Israel in 37:11): graves opened, people raised, land regained.

3. See Abraham Kuruvilla, *Privilege the Text! A Theological Hermeneutic for Preaching* (Chicago: Moody, 2013), 252–58, for more details on the concept of divine blessing for human obedience.

4. The presence in humans of that ethical entity, the "flesh" of Rom. 6–8, makes this an ongoing struggle that will continue until the day of glorification. On that day, with the removal of the sinful and incorrigible flesh, God's people will be whole, as he intended them to be, fully conformed to the image of his Son, Jesus Christ.

When they do so, God's demand is met, God's ideal world is established, and God's name is glorified—nothing short of a vision of a transformed people of God living in a flourishing relationship with their Creator.

God's Spirit and God's Spokesman

But it is not just the exiles that are the focus of Ezekiel 37, revived and restored by God's power. Divine initiative and causation are frequently depicted with Ezekiel, God's spokesman, himself becoming the object of the Spirit's transforming activity. Notice the parallels between prophet and exiles: the Spirit works on Ezekiel and he is "placed" in the valley (37:1), and the Spirit works on the exiles and they are "placed" in their own land (37:14). Earlier in the book Ezekiel is "set on [his] feet" by the "Spirit," who "enters" him (2:2; 3:24), and here in Ezekiel 37 the bones are set "on their feet" by the "Spirit," who "enters" them (37:10). Thus Ezekiel is a prototype for how the Holy Spirit transforms God's people. If the Spirit's work in the people of God in Ezekiel's time is typical of how God empowers his people of all time, then the Spirit's work in Ezekiel must also be typical of how God works in his spokespersons—preachers—of all time. Allowing the Holy Spirit to have his way in us is critical for power and effectiveness in our preaching and shepherding.

In fact, the overriding activity of God upon Ezekiel renders the involvement of the prophet in this revival of dry bones quite minimal. In Ezekiel 37 Ezekiel does prophesy as commanded, but then he looks at what happens and exclaims, "Behold!" (37:8)—he could hardly believe what he was seeing! A lengthy dialogue ensues, but between God and *bones*; Ezekiel is a mere eavesdropper, one passive prophet. The prophet's job description is merely to see and tell (37:4, 7, 9, 10, 12).[5] Ezekiel's role reflects that of preachers everywhere: both prophet and preachers are unable, without the empowerment of God's Spirit, to be effective spokespersons of God's word. No amount of careful theological exegesis, rhetorical flourishes, creative illustrating, flashy props, and pastoral nagging can accomplish what only the Holy Spirit can—life transformation and conformation to the image of Christ, for the glory of God. And so it is God who gets the credit for his working through preachers. The words of Scripture are the Spirit's, and the power for transformation is the Spirit's; therefore the praise goes to God as well. He is glorified!

Pointedly, Ezekiel attributes the making of his own prophecies to the power of the Spirit (2:2; 3:24; 11:5), a radically different sourcing of prophecy from that of false prophets (13:1–6), charlatans who walked after their "own spirit"

---

5. The corresponding notion of the preacher as a witness was considered in "Preaching Is Communicational."

(13:3). Ezekiel is thus the model for the preacher. Spiritual empowerment is essential not only for the enablement of God's people to live by divine demand but also for the preaching of that very demand by God's spokespersons appointed to the task. Without such divine working of this Spirit of power, all preaching is in vain.

In sum, Ezekiel 37 asserts dramatically that both God's people and God's spokesman—and thus both flock and shepherd, both congregation and preacher—need the powerful operation of the Holy Spirit to achieve God's goals: life transformation and God glorification. How can preachers position themselves so that the power of the Spirit may work in and through them?

The Spirit and the Preacher

Without question, it is God who gives success in ministry (1 Cor. 3:6; 2 Cor. 3:5; 4:7). So there can be no doubt about whose power it is that works in preaching: the power of the Holy Spirit, as was depicted in Ezekiel 37. Jesus's declaration, "Apart from Me you are not able to do anything" (John 15:5), should also put to rest any idea that preaching is an enterprise conducted by preachers on their own resources. It is only by the power of the Spirit that preaching—or any other ministry, for that matter—can and should be undertaken. The Westminster Larger Catechism (1648), 155, asserts: "The Spirit of God maketh the reading, but especially the preaching of the word, an effectual means of enlightening, convincing, and humbling sinners; of driving them out of themselves, and drawing them unto Christ; of conforming them to his image, and subduing them to his will." And so, Calvin asserts, preaching is of no benefit unless accompanied by the Holy Spirit.[6] Therefore, the spirituality of preaching includes, on the part of the preacher, a deep sense of dependence upon the work of the Holy Spirit for every aspect of the preaching endeavor. It stands to reason that if it is the power of the Holy Spirit that is the dynamo of preaching, then preachers must be keenly conscious of their own incapacities and must remain in conscious, deliberate dependence upon the capacity of the Spirit throughout, from preparation to delivery of the sermon. As Barth declares: "Our attitude, then, must be controlled from above: nothing from me, all things from God, no independent achievement, only dependence on God's grace and will."[7] Such a dependent lifestyle will be considered next, attending specifically to the preacher's work in preaching, devotion to Scripture, example to the flock,

6. *Institutes* 4.14.17.
7. Karl Barth, *Homiletics* (Louisville: Westminster John Knox, 1991), 90.

and discipline for the inner life—all key elements of the spirituality of the preacher, the spokesperson for God.

The Preacher's Work

While God, who is sovereign, does it all and produces results in the ministry of preaching, human responsibility is clearly involved—in preachers' living lives in accordance with divine demand, as well as in their diligent and faithful preaching of sermons. Even in Ezekiel's account, there is a strongly struck note of human responsibility to live life God's way. Notice how, in 36:24–28, Yahweh's first-person pronouns indicating his own work alternate with second-person pronouns pointing to his people's responsibilities—assertions of divine initiative interwoven with imperatives exhorting human action.[8]

Ezekiel 36:24–25a	I will "take," "gather," "bring," "sprinkle"
Ezekiel 36:25b	*You will "be clean"*
Ezekiel 36:25c–27b	I will "cleanse," "give," "put," "remove," "give," "put," "cause you to walk"
Ezekiel 36:27c–28b	*You will "be careful to observe," "live," "be My people"*
Ezekiel 36:28c	I will "be your God"

Indeed, 36:26 has God declaring, "*I will give* you a new heart and *I will give* a new spirit in you*," but in 18:31 God had said, "*Make for yourselves a new heart and a new spirit.*" So it is a both/and situation: *both* divine prerogative *and* human duty must be affirmed; both divine sovereignty and human responsibility must be allowed to coexist in tensive balance. In the same way, the preacher has a responsibility both to live life and to carry out ministry diligently and faithfully, even though it is God who is at work in and through the preacher.

> We proclaim Him [Christ], instructing all people and teaching all people with all wisdom, so that we may present all people mature in Christ. For this also I *labor, striving* according to His *working* that *works powerfully* in me. (Col. 1:28–29)

The responsibility of the preacher is considerable, as indicated by *labor* and *striving*. Yet here, too, there is that same balance between divine sovereignty and human responsibility, for Paul acknowledges that it is God's *working* that *works powerfully* in him. While the preacher must work hard, no amount

8. Henry Van Dyke Parunak, "Structural Studies in Ezekiel" (PhD diss., Harvard University, 1978), 476.

of hard work will amount to anything unless the Spirit of God is at work. There are *two* teachers in preaching, Calvin would say. "God has therefore two ways of teaching; for, first, he sounds in our ears by the mouth of men; and, secondly, he addresses us inwardly by his Spirit."[9] Yet God *does* deign to use "the mouth of men." In preaching, hard work must be done faithfully and in dependence upon God's own working. It is in and through our hard work that God works—"His working that works powerfully in me" (Col. 1:29).

The Preacher's Devotion

Psalm 119 is an appropriate chapter of Scripture through which to consider the preacher's devotion to Scripture. The divine word, particularly the law, takes center stage in Psalm 119. Eight different terms indicate law: "law" itself (תּוֹרָה, *torah*), "commandment," "judgment/ordinance," "testimony," "statute," "precept," "word," and "word/saying." Torah ("law") is the first term to be used—it shows up in the first verse of the psalm—and, unlike the others, it is always singular, indicating the wholeness and unity of divine demand, thus encompassing every other term employed. The acrostic that this psalm is, further portrays the comprehensiveness of divine demand: in the twenty-two sections of the psalm representing the twenty-two letters of the Hebrew alphabet, each of the eight verses in any given section begins with the particular Hebrew letter that that section represents. And, as noted, eight synonyms for "law" are employed in Psalm 119—again marking the comprehensiveness of the scheme: *all* of God's demands are encompassed.[10] That it is *divine* demand is also clear: every one of the 176 verses in this psalm either addresses or refers to Yahweh.

Psalm 119 contains numerous supplications to God for divine insight into his word: that the psalmist would be taught God's statutes and ordinances (119:12, 26, 33, 64, 68, 102, 108, 124, 135, 171); that the psalmist's eyes would be opened to God's law (119:18); that God's commandments would not be hidden (119:19); that the psalmist would be made to understand God's precepts, law, commandments, and testimonies (119:27, 34, 73, 125, 144, 169); that his heart would be inclined to God's testimonies (119:36); and that God's word would be confirmed (119:38). In other words, the study of Scripture is

9. John Calvin, *Commentary on the Gospel According to John*, trans. William Pringle (Grand Rapids: Baker, 1999), 2:100–101.

10. Kent A. Reynolds, *Torah as Teacher: The Exemplary Torah Student in Psalm 119* (Leiden: Brill, 2010), 14, 105. Perhaps that is why Ps. 119 makes no mention of the Israelite cult, the covenant, or Moses, any of which would have circumscribed the notion of Torah to a particular historical revelation, whereas in this psalm "Torah" generically includes every divine demand of every age and dispensation.

not conducted according to a formula that automatically produces results when appropriate actions are engaged in. The exemplary student, à la the psalmist, gains knowledge in/of/through Scripture only when God grants him or her such knowledge and access. The Holy Spirit's work is an absolute necessity if preachers are to be effective, even in their preparatory work of studying the text.

Interestingly enough, the psalmist never exhorts readers to obey divine demand; in fact, there is no statement in Psalm 119 of what specifically divine demand calls people to do. Instead, after declaring that the ones who obey are blessed (119:1–3), the writer simply models an attitude of devotion to Torah: he learns God's judgments (119:7), he treasures God's word (119:11), he delights in God's statutes (119:16), he tells of God's ordinances (119:13), he meditates on God's precepts (119:15), he sets God's judgments before himself (119:30), he clings to God's testimonies (119:31), he longs for God's precepts (119:40), he trusts in God's word (119:42), he waits for God's ordinances (119:43), he raises his hands to God's commandments (119:48), he remembers God's ordinances (119:52), he believes God's commandments (119:66), he seeks God's precepts and statutes (119:94, 155), he fears God's judgments (119:120), and he loves God's Torah, his commandments, his word, his precepts, and his testimonies (119:47, 48, 97, 113, 119, 127, 140, 159, 163, 167). The verbs "keep" and "observe" are repeated often in this Psalm (twenty-one times and ten times, respectively), and the psalmist's life forms the pattern for devotion to—keeping and observing—divine demand. This is also surely the pattern for the preacher to follow: passionate devotion to Scripture. And by such modeling, the psalmist (and the Scripture-devoted preacher) implicitly attempts to persuade readers of the psalm (and listeners of sermons) that they, too, should treat the Torah as he, the psalmist (and the preacher), treats it; the result will be blessing:

> Blessed are those who keep His testimonies,
> Who seek Him with all [their] heart.
>
> Ps. 119:2

This devotion to Scripture of the psalmist (and of the preacher) is not merely lip service but a matter of the "heart." Aligning oneself to God's testimonies and God's commandments is equated to seeking God with all of one's *heart* (119:2, 10); God's word is stored up in one's *heart* (119:11); the psalmist desires to keep God's Torah with all his *heart* (119:34); he would have his *heart* be inclined to God's testimonies and statutes (119:36, 112); he keeps God's precepts with all his *heart* (119:69); he asks that his *heart* would be blameless in God's statutes (119:80); God's testimonies are the joy of his *heart* (119:111); and his *heart* is awed by God's words (119:161). So also should the preacher engage Scripture with a *heart*felt devotion to God and his word. One's study is not just to find nuggets in Scripture to be served to others in a sermon. Rather, just as the psalmist involves himself deeply in the intake and assimilation of God's word in his own life, so must the preacher, to arrive at a "fear of God" that is thoroughgoing and intimate (119:38, 63, 74, 79): an exemplary devotion to Scripture is called for.

The Preacher's Example[11]

Ambrose, the bishop of Milan in the fourth century, exhorted:

> Such, then, ought he to be who gives counsel to another—offering himself a pattern in all good works, in teaching, in trueness of character, in seriousness. Thus his words will be wholesome and irreproachable, his counsel useful, his life virtuous, and his opinions seemly.[12]

But it is not only in *overall* lifestyle that preachers must demonstrate the work of the Spirit, as Ambrose recommends. They must also, week by week and sermon by sermon, put into practice what has just been preached. The divine demand of each pericope exposited must first be applied in the lives of those who preach. Thus, there is an extra burden of responsibility on preachers, those who deal with things of God, to live spiritual lives worthy of emulation, seeking to apply every text preached. Preachers must strive to align themselves with God's requirements in every pericope that they deal with, for they, too, are being addressed by the Holy Spirit in that passage, perhaps even more directly than listeners are. The one who preaches must therefore be the first one impacted by the word of God. Shepherd and flock are all on the same journey of discipleship; both are needy for God's word; both are called by God to align themselves to his demand, for his glory; and both find sustenance from the same Scripture and empowerment from the same Spirit for godly living.

Thus, an integral element of being spiritual is the deliberate incorporation of the demand of the preached pericope into the preacher's own life. In fact, as was suggested in an earlier chapter, if a preacher is searching for specific application for a text, what might actually help is to ask oneself first, "How is *my* life to change specifically as a result of the call of this text?"

---

11. Also see "Preaching Is Pastoral" for the exemplary character of the preacher.
12. *On the Duties of the Clergy* 2.17.86 (NPNF^2 10:57).

And quite often, that very application arrived at for oneself can be preached fruitfully to others. Athanasius, a church father in Alexandria, wrote in the third century:

> You cannot put straight in others what is warped in yourself.[13]

In other words, "Physician, heal thyself!"[14] The life of a spiritual preacher, applying what is preached, becomes quite compelling to the rest of the congregation, as a fourth-century Christian treatise affirms.

> If the pastor be unblameable as to any wickedness, he will compel his own disciples, and by his very mode of life press them to become worthy imitators of his own actions.[15]

On the other hand, a minister lacking devotion to Scripture, a pastor unconcerned about spirituality, and a preacher who cares not to apply what is preached can only wound parishioners, stunt disciples, and atrophy the church's vitality. No doubt the dangerous consequences of such a devotionless life are why preachers of Scripture, as leaders of churches, are held accountable to a greater standard (James 3:1).

> For the faults of ordinary men, being committed as it were in the dark, ruin only those who practice them: but the errors of a man in a conspicuous position, and known to many, inflict a common injury upon all, rendering those who have fallen more supine in their efforts for good, and driving to desperation those who wish to take heed to themselves. And apart from these things, the faults of insignificant men, even if they are exposed, inflict no injury worth speaking of upon any one: but they who occupy the highest seat of honor are in the first place plainly visible to all, and if they err in the smallest matters these trifles seem great to others: for all men measure the sin, not by the magnitude of the offense, but by the rank of the offender. Thus the priest [pastor] ought to be protected on all sides by a kind of *adamantine armor*, by intense earnestness, and perpetual watchfulness concerning his manner of life, lest some one discovering an exposed and neglected spot should inflict a deadly wound.[16]

13. St. Athanasius, *On the Incarnation*, 3.14, trans. A Religious of CSMV, rev. ed. (Crestwood, NY: St. Vladimir's Seminary Press, 1993), 42.
14. Uttered by Captain Kirk to Dr. McCoy in *Star Trek II: The Wrath of Khan*, written by Jack B. Sowards and Harve Bennett (Hollywood, CA: Paramount Pictures, 1982), http://www.imsdb.com/scripts/Star-Trek-II-The-Wrath-of-Khan.html. Of course, Jesus used it a long time ago (Luke 4:23)!
15. *Apostolic Constitutions* 2.2.6 (ANF 7:398).
16. John Chrysostom, *On the Priesthood* 3.14 (NPNF[1] 9:52).

"Adamantine armor," Chrysostom recommends. In ancient history, "adamant," meaning "hard," referred to diamond, the hardest nonsynthetic material known.[17] In other words, preachers are to be encased in impenetrable armor, that their lives might shine forth unsullied, unblemished. While there might be a number of practical applications of this armor—perhaps most directly the armor of God in Ephesians 6:10–17—I'd like to suggest another series of pragmatic, "adamantine" undertakings in preparation for this warfare that preachers are constantly engaged in: the spiritual disciplines.

The Pastor's Disciplines

The disciplines for the spiritual life are time-tested activities of mind and body purposefully undertaken by Christians to bring their embodied selves under greater control so that they may cooperate effectively and harmoniously with the divine order.[18] They are means to an end—to direct us to God's demand and to get us into a routine of aligning ourselves to that demand; that is, these are practices for *godliness*.

> But discipline yourself for godliness; for bodily discipline is profitable in a small way, but godliness is profitable in every way, holding promise for life now and the future. (1 Tim. 4:7–8)

A number of traditional spiritual disciplines have been practiced in the church over the millennia. As noted earlier, Dallas Willard distributes them into two categories: the disciplines of abstinence (including solitude, silence, fasting, frugality, celibacy, secrecy, and sacrifice) and the disciplines of engagement (including study, worship, celebration, service, prayer, fellowship, confession, and submission).[19] There is one among these that needs to be an integral part of the preacher's life (indeed, of *every* Christian's life) at all times: prayer. I will discuss this discipline of engagement briefly, along with a few related disciplines of abstinence that go with it.

Prayer, in essence, is the communion of the believer with God, a manifestation of an intimate relationship with the Father in heaven, one's Creator. Thus all of life is to be a moment of prayer, an act of communion with the divine—*habitual* prayer. In that sense, then, one can "pray without ceasing"

17. "Adamant" and "diamond" are derived from the same Greek root.
18. This definition is modified from Dallas Willard, *The Spirit of the Disciplines: Understanding How God Changes Lives* (San Francisco: Harper & Row, 1988), 68, 156. The notion of spiritual disciplines was also briefly touched upon in the Reflection section of the previous chapter.
19. Ibid., 158.

(1 Thess. 5:17).[20] Yet the discipline of prayer involves acts of specific, *actual* prayer undertaken at specific times, besides the attitude of habitual and incessant prayer. I will assume that every preacher is actively engaged in actual prayer, often and devotedly.[21] But habitual prayer is what I'd like to touch on here.

While habitual prayer ought to be the practice of every child of God, it is the particular responsibility of the pastor and preacher, the one who is called to center all of congregational life upon God in heaven. And habitual prayer cultivates this vision of God at center of all things, mundane and exceptional: sunshine, thunderstorm, celebration, tragedy, recreation, vocation, feast, famine, pain, pleasure. Everything falls into the realm of the sacred; nothing is secular, for God is at the center of it all. An important role of the pastor is to facilitate the recognition of this divine interconnectedness of all of life, and of God's preeminence in it all. The "firstness" of God tends to be forgotten, as we humans are rooted in our self-consciousness and in the delusions of our own centrality and primacy. Therefore the centrality and primacy of God is a mind-set that preachers must first develop themselves, and I submit that unceasing, habitual prayer is an important way of cultivating this critical disposition in those who would be spiritual. In conjunction with preaching, prayer is a significant work of the pastorate.

It is easy to be drowned in the deluge of daily tasks in ministry. It is even easier to be stifled in the stratagems and techniques of preaching, to be buried in grammars and commentaries, mired in illustrations and alliterations, trapped in handouts and outlines, and seduced by dazzling slides and movie clips. All these are, no doubt, useful. But in and through all this work, the attitude of habitual prayer must be developed and made to impinge upon every other activity and engagement, as Basil of Caesarea, a fourth-century church father, taught:

> Thus, in the midst of our work we can fulfill the duty of prayer, giving thanks to him who has granted strength to our hands to fulfill our tasks, and wisdom

20. Simon Chan, *Spiritual Theology: A Systematic Study of the Christian Life* (Downers Grove, IL: InterVarsity, 1998), 126–27. See, for "always" prayer, Phil. 1:4; Col. 1:3; 4:12; 2 Thess. 1:11; and for "incessant" prayer, Rom. 1:9, 10; 1 Thess. 5:17.

21. Even in the process of sermon preparation, which, on the surface, might appear to be a grinding chore far removed from the divine operation of the Spirit, prayer remains essential. Centuries ago, Chrysostom observed that "we have need of much wakefulness, and many prayers, that we may arrive at the interpretation of the passage now before us" (*Homilies on Matthew* 2:1–2 [NPNF[1] 10:34]). One might pile one's desk with resources galore, and load one's laptop with software aplenty, but all of that is of no avail if the preacher is not dependent in prayer on the work of Spirit throughout the preaching process, from preparation to delivery.

to our minds to acquire knowledge, and for having provided the materials, . . . praying that the work of our hands may be directed toward its goal, the good pleasure of God. Thus we acquire a recollected [remembering] spirit—when in every action we beg from God the success of our labors and satisfy our debt of gratitude to him who gave us the power to do the work, and when, as has been said, we keep before our minds the aim of pleasing him. If this is not the case, how can there be consistency in the words of the Apostle bidding us to "pray without ceasing," with those others: "we worked night and day"?[22]

This is to take seriously the divine imperative to "pray unceasingly" (1 Thess. 5:17). This is to develop an unceasing consciousness of the presence of God and an unceasing communion with the person of God amidst the work of preaching and pastoring—an unceasing awareness of, and orientation toward, God.

For six rather unusual weeks in late 2004, Udo Wächter had an unerring sense of direction. Every morning, Wächter, a systems administrator at the University of Osnabrück in Germany, put on a wide beige belt lined with thirteen vibrating pads—the kind that make a cell phone buzz. On the belt were also a power supply and a sensor that detected the earth's magnetic field. Once the apparatus was turned on, whichever buzzer was pointing north would go off. Constantly.

"It was slightly strange at first," Wächter confessed. He became more aware of the detours he had to make while trying to reach a destination. "I finally understood just how much roads actually wind." Deep into the experiment, Wächter recollected his discovery: "I suddenly realized that my perception had shifted. I had some kind of internal map of the city in my head. I could always find my way home. Eventually, I felt I couldn't get lost, even in a completely new place." Indeed, Wächter even felt the vibration in his dreams, moving around his waist, just as if he were awake. Always oriented to north.[23]

This is what the pastor-preacher needs—a constant orientation to divine "north," toward the Creator, toward the heavenly Father. While this is to be true of every child of God, it is the shepherd who models this discipline of constant God-orientation for the flock—the discipline of being unceasingly aware of God and in continuous communion with him, whether at work or at play, whether in the study or in the grocery, whether in solitude or in company. And habitual prayer is conducive to this purpose. "Prayer as a discipline has

22. Basil of Caesarea, *The Long Road*, in *Ascetical Works*, trans. M. Monica Wagner, The Fathers of the Church 9 (New York: Fathers of the Church, 1950), 308. Paul both worked "night and day" (1 Thess. 2:9; 2 Thess. 3:8) *and* prayed "night and day" (1 Thess. 3:10; 1 Tim. 5:5; 2 Tim. 1:3).

23. From Sunny Bains, "Mixed Feelings," *Wired*, March 2007, http://archive.wired.com /wired/archive/15.04/esp.html.

its greatest force in strengthening the spiritual life only as we learn to *pray without ceasing*. . . . We can train ourselves to invoke God's presence in every action we perform . . . and our whole lives will be bathed in the presence of God. Constant prayer will only 'burden' us as wings burden the bird in flight."[24] While this habitual prayer will never be burdensome, the cultivation of this attitude/work does require practice. Indeed, this constant orientation toward God is habituated only by engaging in actual prayer, along with the coordinated engagement in some of the spiritual disciplines of abstinence: silence, solitude, fasting, and celibacy—the abstention, for a period of time, from noise/speech, company, food, and sex, respectively. It is imperative that as preachers we discipline ourselves for habitual prayer by undertaking regular actual prayer while abstaining, at least temporarily, from some of these normal drives of body. Let me address those disciplines of abstinence briefly.

To make habitual prayer a practice that becomes disposition that, in turn, becomes character, solitude—and along with it, silence—must be engaged in frequently, for the purpose of actual prayer. Otherwise the presence of God, amidst the hustle and bustle and the twists and turns of life, will never be consciously acknowledged.

> But Jesus himself frequently withdrew to the wilderness and prayed.[25] (Luke 5:16)

If the Second Person of the Godhead needed to disengage distractions periodically so that he could pray, surely his followers need to do so as well. The tyranny of demands made upon us by others, and the incessant whirring, buzzing, and chirping of those innumerable contraptions in our lives—not to mention the constant chattering of voices, ours and others'—hinder a habitual centering of attention upon God. And developing that habit calls for alone time and quiet time. To find this solitude and silence, one might need to rise early or stay up late. And, especially for those besieged by the constant pressures of ministry (and family), a more extended season of solitude can also be helpful; periodically, a day or more spent in the "wilderness" will yield great dividends.

Indeed, the taming of these constant distractions should be put to work the other way. Purposefully scheduling interruptions in our busy day to focus upon God is a "good" distraction! I have found it helpful to set an alarm on

---

24. Willard, *Spirit of the Disciplines*, 185–86.

25. The iterative sense of the Greek imperfect verb translated "withdrew" is reproduced in translation with "frequently." Also see Matt. 14:23. For Jesus inviting his disciples to solitude, see Mark 6:31.

my smartphone that goes off twice in the daytime, reminding me to say a word or sentence to God in actual prayer, or at least direct a thought toward him, even if I'm beleaguered by the busyness of life and shackled by the tyranny of schedules. Of late, I've even gotten my phone to chime the hour and the half hour (the buzzer goes off silently if I'm in public), for no other reason but to remind me that God is here—an attempt to evoke a habitual attitude of prayer.

And not just silence and solitude, but also fasting and celibacy are helpful disciplines of abstinence that may be effectively combined with prayer. At the very least, fasting reminds us of how powerful and insidious our bodily desires and cravings are, often inclining us flesh-ward and away from a God-ward orientation. Fasting, then, is a deliberate subjection of the alimentary passions of our embodied state in favor of greater devotion to prayer, both actual and habitual.[26] Celibacy likely affects the psyche in the same fashion, for this is a temporary "fast" from sexual activity, another powerful impulse of the body, and a fast expressly recommended by Paul for the purpose of deeper engagement in prayer (1 Cor. 7:5).[27]

In and through these disciplines of abstinence (solitude, silence, fasting, and celibacy), the discipline of engagement, prayer, must be diligently practiced—both habitual and actual prayer: "Be devoted to prayer" (Col. 4:2). All of this cultivates a deep sense of dependence on God, for "apart from Me you are not able to do anything" (John 15:5).

Summary

All of the facets of preaching, from preparation to delivery, are to be undertaken in the power of the Holy Spirit. Ezekiel 37 forms a unique paradigm for the Spirit's transformation of the lives of God's people, and, pertinent to our interest, it also depicts the role of preachers, God's spokespersons, and their interaction with the Spirit. That humans cannot change on their own, but only by the power of God, is underscored in Ezekiel 37; indeed, the power of God working through his appointed preacher is what accomplishes life change. While there is clearly a place for the diligent discharge of one's responsibilities in preaching, ultimately it is the Author of Scripture who should be depended upon for the success of the entire endeavor. Such dependence is expressed in the preacher's devotion to the word—to learn it and to live by it—thus becoming

26. See Ezra 8:23; Neh. 1:4; Dan. 9:3; Luke 2:37; Acts 13:3. Hopefully fasting is a regular part of the preacher's life, if it is not medically contraindicated.

27. For some, this may be a discipline adopted as a way of life, what I call *ecclesiological singleness*—celibacy by choice, for life, unto Christ, in community (Matt. 19:12; 1 Cor. 7:7–8, 26).

an example to the flock. And the constancy of this dependence upon God, who is the center of it all, is cultivated by the preacher's engagement in the spiritual discipline of prayer—habitual prayer, with appropriate temporary abstentions: silence, solitude, fasting, and celibacy. Without divine power there is nothing! *Preaching is spiritual!*

Reflection

Mark 9:14–29—Divine Power[28]

> And when He [Jesus] came into the house, His disciples began asking Him privately, "Why were we not able to cast it out?" And He said to them, "This kind is not able to come out by anything except by prayer." (Mark 9:28–29)

A major theme in this episode in Mark's Gospel (9:14–29) is faith/belief: Jesus laments the lack of faith of this "unbelieving/faithless" generation (9:19), pointing at his disciples who were unable to drive out the demon wreaking havoc in the child. Then Jesus tells the child's father that all things are possible for the one with faith ("the one who believes," 9:23), and the father immediately confesses his need and beseeches Jesus for help with his own lack of faith ("unbelief," 9:24). Notice that this dialogue on faith between Jesus and the father (9:21–24) forms the central element of this narrative.

> A Disciples' failure at exorcism reported (9:14–18)
> B Jesus and the boy ("spirit," "convulse") (9:19–20)
> C Jesus and the father: belief (9:21–24)
> B' Jesus and the boy ("spirit," "convulse") (9:25–27)
> A' Disciples' failure at exorcism explained (9:28–29)

So on the one hand we have these disciples—an "unbelieving generation," faithlessly incapable of performing the exorcism (9:19). They were no better than the Pharisees who had themselves just been labeled a reprehensible "generation" (8:12). Indeed, the exclamation of Jesus in 9:19 indicates that he had *expected* his disciples to be capable of handling even such an advanced case of demon possession. After all, they had been deputized and empowered to do so (3:15; and 6:7 with 6:13). The disciples, however, did not succeed here, unbelieving as they were (9:19). On the other hand, there is the agonized

---

28. For more details on this pericope, see Abraham Kuruvilla, *Mark: A Theological Commentary for Preachers* (Eugene, OR: Cascade, 2012), 188–93.

father of the afflicted child—quite different from the disciples: "I believe; help my unbelief!" (9:24). There was something creditable about the man's confession; unlike the disciples, he was at least aware of his problem—lack of sufficient faith.

This story is recounted here by Mark to demonstrate *how* the disciples should have used the power they had already been granted by virtue of being followers of Christ (in 3:15 and 6:7 Jesus had given them authority over unclean spirits). Later, after the child is healed, upon being questioned by the disciples as to why they were not able to perform the exorcisms, Jesus gives an illuminating answer: "This kind [of demon] is not able to come out by anything except by prayer" (9:29). In other words, they were to depend on God for his help and for his power to work through them—not just for victory over powerful spirits of darkness, but for success in every facet of life and ministry. Particularly for preachers and pastors, this is a poignant lesson that we must take to heart.

It appears that the disciples had been so taken with their own authority and ability that they had attempted an exorcism *without seeking divine power through prayer*, as Jesus chided them. Their problem was a lack of dependence on God's power. They should have recognized that theirs was only a delegated authority and that true, intrinsic authority was Jesus's alone. Therefore, they needed to rely upon him, even when exercising their own empowerment. Perhaps in light of their earlier successes in driving out demons (6:13), Jesus's disciples had gotten used to this power they wielded and now considered themselves experts, capable of conducting such operations on their own strength. They had forgotten that the power exercised earlier was no autonomous or automatic possession but the result of divine commission—deputized power. And that power had to be tapped into again and again from its divine source, on each individual occasion, by prayer and in faith. There was to be no place for presumption and pride in the ministry engagements of Jesus's disciples. Their humiliation here was hopefully teaching them humility and faithful dependence upon God as evidenced by prayer.

So, too, for the preacher. Self-confidence in ministry must be abandoned in favor of God-dependence. The minister must engage in prayer, not as a special mantra or manipulative technique but as a humble seeking of God by faith in his power for the tasks the preacher is called to undertake. In fact, it is striking that the only one who prays in this pericope, and the only one whose prayer is answered by the casting out of the demon, is the father: "I believe; help my unbelief!" (9:24). This was the attitude the disciples should have had, an attitude of trustful dependence expressed in prayer. The father's exclamatory "prayer" simultaneously confesses confidence in the power of God in Jesus and a lack of confidence in his own ability, even to maintain faith. In sum, preaching—indeed, ministry of any kind—is never a technique or skill that works simply because a formula is followed or because one is ordained. God's power does not manifest itself at the beck and call of humans. Preachers have to rely upon God in faith and in prayer, constantly, unceasingly, habitually, over and over and over again.

- Are we acutely conscious of our own inabilities and incapacities to minister on our own strengths as we prepare and deliver our sermons? Are we therefore consciously depending on the power of God in every step of our preaching endeavors? It is easy to be on a ministry "roll," to be comfortable preaching, and to assume it will all come together automatically. It won't!

- A critical way of acknowledging and expressing this dependence upon God and his power is by prayer. What do our prayer lives look like? Are we disciplined enough to engage in *actual* prayer—at set times each day, formally tackling a prayer list, deliberately focusing our attention on God in worship, confession, intercession, and thanksgiving?

- How about the discipline of *habitual* prayer, the unceasing prayer that the Bible calls for from God's children? As ministers, we have the responsibility of centering everything and everyone and every moment upon God, and an attitude of habitual prayer is key to remembering God's primacy and centrality. Perhaps we could create cues at odd times of the day to remind us to turn to God, thus cultivating an attitude of habitual prayer.

- We also have the responsibility of teaching and demonstrating this dependence upon God in habitual and actual prayer, perhaps starting with the team that enables and facilitates worship of the corporate body, and involving the leaders of the church, such as elders and deacons.

Preaching Is Spiritual!

Conclusion

". . . Giveth Light"

The entrance of Thy words giveth light.
Psalm 119:130 KJV

There is an old story of the prolific inventor Thomas Edison (1847–1931) first recounted by Walter S. Mallory, his longtime associate. Edison, of course, was the man who created the lightbulb and paved the way for the establishment of power utility industries. Once, upon learning that Edison had conducted over nine thousand failed experiments for a particular device, Mallory sympathized with the inventor: "Isn't it a shame that with the tremendous amount of work you have done you haven't been able to get any results?"

Edison turned to Mallory with a smile and replied: "Results? Why, man, I have gotten a lot of results! I know several thousand things that won't work."[1]

Light production is hard work! While the psalmist asserts that "the entrance of Thy words giveth light" (Ps. 119:130 KJV), this enlightenment is not necessarily as simple or as inevitable a result as it appears in that verse. Clearly

---

1. Frank Lewis Dyer and Thomas Commerford Marin, *Edison: His Life and Inventions* (New York: Harper and Brothers, 1910), 2:615–16. Apparently Edison was working on a storage battery when this interchange occurred. In another account, Edison describes his work with the lightbulb: "I speak without exaggeration when I say that I have constructed *three thousand* different theories in connection with the electric light, each one of them reasonable and apparently likely to be true. Yet only in two cases did my experiments prove the truth of my theory" (George Parsons Lathrop, "Talks with Edison," *Harper's New Monthly Magazine* 80 [1890]: 434).

the agent of enlightenment is the Holy Spirit, the Author of Scripture, the "Spirit of wisdom and revelation" who sovereignly "enlightens the eyes of the heart" (Eph. 1:17–18; also see 1 Cor. 2:10–16). But as we have seen all along in this work, human responsibility is also involved in this process of bringing Scripture's light to people's hearts: this is the role of preaching. Notice the duality of divine and human work in the ministry of the word:

> We proclaim Him [Christ], instructing all people and teaching all people with all wisdom, so that we may present all people mature in Christ. For this also I labor, striving according to His working that works powerfully in me. (Col. 1:28–29)

Preachers strive, but it is God's "working" that "works" (the words are related—ἐνεργεία, *energeia*, and ἐνεργέω, *energeō*). God's working and Paul's labor are a joint force. Elsewhere Paul exhorts:

> Do your best to present yourself approved to God, a worker [ἐργάτης, *ergatēs*] who has no cause for shame, accurately handling the word of truth. (2 Tim. 2:15)

In other words, notwithstanding divine operation, the preacher has a responsibility to work hard. To do otherwise, Calvin observed, would be tempting God:

> That would be like my stepping into the pulpit without deigning to look upon any book, and naïvely imagining to myself: "Oh, well, when I come here, God will give me enough to speak," while I scorn to read or study beforehand what I have to speak, and come here without thinking through how to apply the Holy Scripture for the edification of the people. Then I will be playing a presumptuous fool, and God will put me to shame for my overboldness.[2]

Yes, preaching is hard work. To understand the author's agenda in Scripture and to present that relevantly to God's people requires painstaking labor but is well worth the effort for a number of reasons implied in the vision for preaching.

Laboring for the Vision

Biblical preaching, by a leader of the church, in a gathering of Christians for worship, is the communication of the thrust of a pericope of Scripture discerned

---

2. *Sermons on Deuteronomy* 49, in *The Sermons of M. John Calvin upon the Fifth Book of Moses Called Deuteronomy*, trans. Arthur Golding (London: Henry Middleton, 1583), 292. The archaic wording of Golding's translation has been modernized.

by theological exegesis, and of its application to that specific body of believers, that they may be conformed to the image of Christ, for the glory of God—all in the power of the Holy Spirit.

The Bible is the authority and basis for the faith and practice of the church, and the preaching of Scripture is essential for the growth and well-being of the body of Christ, the local church. Therefore, preaching has to be exclusively focused on this source text, the Bible: *preaching is biblical*. This is why preaching is a solemn task, for it deals with the word of God to humankind. And it is through preaching that the community of God encounters the voice of God. Preaching that is biblical thus places preachers as intermediaries of God's word to God's people, binding them to an august responsibility.

Preaching forms the basis of spiritual formation in the body of Christ. Conducted in the worship gathering of the church, it is the most visible and public of pastoral ministries, as it seeks to impact the life of the congregation in a powerful way: *preaching is ecclesial*. It is at this event in the weekly cycle of church life that God's people meet him in corporate worship; here they encounter Christ in the celebration of the Lord's Supper and hear him (and see him—the image of Christ) in the preaching of God's word. And so, here, in this unique way, Christ is really present with his people, and his voice is really heard by them—the divine groom in a rendezvous with the human bride he has loved, espoused, and died for. All of this is facilitated by preaching.

It is the grave duty of the human leader(s) of the church to spiritually form this body, that is, to align its members to the will of God in every pericope of Scripture. This is the burden of the minister, the role of the pastor, and the task of elders. It is the fundamental reason for the appointment and ordination of qualified leaders into pastoral ministry. Therefore, *preaching is pastoral*. While such spiritual direction and formation occur even outside the pulpit, there is no doubt that, of all other ministries, preaching possesses the greatest impact for spiritual growth in the congregation, by the public, corporate, and vision-casting nature of this transaction conducted in the context of worship.

This formative influence of preaching upon believers is conveyed by the communication of the thrust of the particular text of Scripture chosen for that sermon. That thrust—that is, the agenda of the author, what the author is *doing* with what he is saying in that text—forms the crucial content of the sermon. This is what God's people must catch from God's word. And this is the primary reason for the interposition of the preacher between God's people and God's word: to convey the thrust of the word of God to the people of God. Thus, *preaching is communicational*, a wonderful privilege for preachers!

The thrust of the pericope is the theology of the text. Pericopes of Scripture project facets of God's ideal world, how such a world should be, and what God's will would be in his ideal world—that is, its precepts, priorities, and practices. Each sermon delivered by God's spokesperson, the preacher, is a gracious invitation from God to his people to inhabit this ideal world by abiding by the theological demand of the pericope that is preached: *preaching is theological*. Preaching thus is the means by which God extends this invitation to humankind to dwell with him in his kingdom. What a grand partnership with God we preachers enjoy!

In so conveying the theology of a particular pericope, preachers also provide relevant application for the congregation so that they might specifically respond to the requirement of that text. After all, the ultimate goal of preaching is life transformation according to the demand of God, so that God's people may fully inhabit his ideal world. For this to happen, incremental and concrete life change must occur, pericope by pericope, and week by week, as directed by preaching. Therefore, *preaching is applicational* and advances the arrival of the divine realm.

The only one who has met all of God's demands, comprehensively and impeccably inhabiting that ideal world of God, is Jesus Christ, God incarnate and perfect Man. He alone is perfectly aligned to the will of God. Therefore, the theology of each pericope—the divine demand in each text—is in effect a facet of Christlikeness. Thus, pericope by pericope and sermon by sermon, the incremental life change effected by preaching is actually a gradual and increasing conformation of God's people to Christ's image, the divine goal—a *glorious* goal!—for every believer (Rom. 8:29): *preaching is conformational*. And so it is no less glorious a ministry for the preacher.

As the people of God are conformed to the image of God's Son, God is glorified as his purposes for humanity, and indeed for the cosmos, are realized. His attributes are being manifest, his ideal world is becoming reality, and his eternal purposes are being fulfilled, all redounding to divine glory, as God's will is done and his kingdom comes to pass. Preaching plays a crucial role in this process, for God has deigned to accomplish his goals through this activity: the resulting change of lives, commensurate with God's own holiness, is an important means of glorifying God: *preaching is doxological*.

Needless to say, all sermonic undertakings are to be conducted by the power of the Spirit, the divine Author of Scripture. Such control by the Spirit will be manifested in the lives of preachers themselves, as the Spirit-inspired word first accomplishes life change in those who preach. In sum, the ministry of preaching is an act of God the Holy Spirit achieving his purposes both in the preacher and in the church, conforming the body of Christ to the image of Christ, making it the blemishless bride of Christ, "holy and blameless" (Eph. 1:4; 5:25): *preaching is spiritual.*

Vision for Preaching	Preaching Is . . .
Biblical preaching,	*Biblical*
by a leader of the church,	*Pastoral*
in a gathering of Christians for worship,	*Ecclesial*
is the communication of the thrust of a pericope of Scripture	*Communicational*
discerned by theological exegesis,	*Theological*
and of its application to that specific body of believers,	*Applicational*
that they may be conformed to the image of Christ,	*Conformational*
for the glory of God	*Doxological*
—all in the power of the Holy Spirit.	*Spiritual*

No wonder this is hard work! But it is ordained and empowered by God himself to conform his children to the image of his Son as his word is preached for his glory. Indeed, this is what a congregation wants their pastor to do—to direct them spiritually to be all that God wants them to be. Eugene Peterson imagines a church extending this charge to the preacher:

> We need help in keeping our beliefs sharp and accurate and intact. We don't trust ourselves—our emotions seduce us into infidelities. We know we are launched on a difficult and dangerous act of faith, and there are strong influences intent on diluting or destroying it. We want you to help us: be our pastor, a minister of word and sacrament in the middle of this world's life. Minister with word and sacrament to us in all the different parts and stages of our lives—in our work and play, with our children and our parents, at birth and death, in our celebrations and sorrows, on those days when morning breaks over us in a wash of sunshine, and those other days that are all drizzle. This isn't the only task in the life of faith, but it is your task. We will find someone else to do the other important and essential tasks. *This* is yours: word and sacrament. . . . There are a lot of other things to be done in this wrecked world, and we are going to be doing at least some of them, but if we don't know the foundational realities with which we are dealing—God, kingdom, gospel—we are going to end up living futile, fantasy lives. Your task is to keep telling the basic story, representing the presence of the Spirit, insisting on the priority of God, speaking the biblical words of command and promise and invitation.[3]

3. Eugene H. Peterson, *Working the Angles: The Shape of Pastoral Integrity* (Grand Rapids: Eerdmans, 1987), 24–25.

What a task! What could be grander than the calling of a preacher? Cotton Mather (1663–1728), the New England Puritan, was right:

> The office of the Christian ministry, rightly understood, is the most honourable, and important, that any man in the whole world can ever sustain; and it will be one of the wonders and employments of eternity to consider the reasons why the wisdom and goodness of God assigned this office to imperfect and guilty man! . . . It is a work which an angel might wish for, as an honour to his character; yea, an office which every angel in heaven might covet to be employed in for a thousand years to come. It is such an honourable, important and useful office, that if a man be put into it by God, and made faithful and successful through life, he may look down with disdain upon a crown, and shed a tear of pity on the brightest monarch on earth.[4]

Thomas Aquinas felt the same way in the Middle Ages:

> Preaching is the noblest of all the activities of the church.[5]

Despite the glory of the task, it must be acknowledged again that the burden is heavy and the work is hard. Indeed, two millennia ago Jesus warned about the dangers of preaching.

A Dangerous "Sandwich"

> And the apostles gathered together with Jesus. . . . And He said to them, "Come away yourselves privately to a wilderness place and rest a little." (Mark 6:30–31)

This pericope, Mark 6:7–32, is one of those Markan "sandwiches": he starts a story (Mark 6:7–13) and stops it midstream, then begins and ends a second story (6:14–29), and finally returns to the first story in order to finish it (6:30–32). So you have an outer story, the two halves of which sandwich an inner story.[6]

The outer story (Mark 6:7–13, 30–32) is the fulfillment of the earlier appointment of the Twelve in Mark 3; here they actually depart, to undertake the mission that had been entrusted to them: the terms "summon," "send," "preach," and "authority" all occur in both Mark 3 and 6 (3:13–15; 6:7, 12).[7]

---

4. Cotton Mather, *Student and Preacher* (London: Hindmarsh, 1789), iii–v.

5. *Against Those Who Assail the Worship of God and Religion* 2.6.

6. For more details on this pericope, see Abraham Kuruvilla, *Mark: A Theological Commentary for Preachers* (Eugene, OR: Cascade, 2012), 117–28.

7. Προσκαλέω (*proskaleō*, "summon") occurs in the present indicative only in 3:13 and 6:7 in Mark.

This was an official, authoritative commissioning. The dress code noted in 6:8–9 was the garb of the exodus generation (Exod. 12:11), the footwear symbolizing preparedness, and the staff serving as a token of authority and divine calling (Exod. 4:2–3; Num. 17:1–10; etc.).[8] Also, Deuteronomy 8:4 and 29:5 tell us about the durability of these accoutrements throughout the wanderings of the Israelites in the wilderness: God provides abundantly! And preachers need exactly that: God's abundant provision.

The message of the disciples (Mark 6:12) is intended to sound like the continuation of Jesus's own proclamation (1:14–15). In doing what Jesus did—three undertakings: preaching, exorcising, and healing—the apostles extend the scope of their Master's ministry. Indeed, his powers are seemingly eclipsed by them: they heal "many" (6:13); Jesus, in his own backyard, could heal only a "few," as noted right before this pericope (6:5).[9] But what is curious is that in this first half of the outer story (6:7–13), we are given the results for only the last two of their ministry activities—exorcising and healing: they cast out many demons and healed many sick (6:13): success! But how did their *preaching* go? What was the result of their ministry?[10]

Disciples preach (6:12)—result?
Disciples exorcise many (6:13a)—result: "they were casting out."
Disciples anoint many (6:13b)—result: "they were healing."

At this juncture in the outer story, Mark—the director of this movie/narrative— suddenly yells, "Cut!" and the scene changes. Now the inner story is recounted as a flashback (6:14–29) about how John the Baptist was decapitated at the behest of Herod. Notice the comparison between the disciples in the outer story and John in the inner. Mark is *doing* something with this "sandwich"—clearly the parties in its outer and inner stories are being held up for examination.

8. The staff "repeatedly mediates, through authorized leaders, God's demonstrable provision for God's people" (Suzanne Watts Henderson, *Discipleship and Christology in the Gospel of Mark*, Society for New Testament Studies Monograph Series 135 [Cambridge: Cambridge University Press, 2006], 155).

9. Of course, the disciples' was a deputized authority, their operations simply being extensions of Jesus's unique direct and divine activity.

10. There is already some anticipation of a less-than-enthusiastic welcome for the disciples: Jesus instructs them on what to do if they are not received or heard: they are to leave and "shake off the dust from their feet" (6:11). Besides, each of the earlier "calls" of the disciples was immediately followed by a controversy story or a negative response to the ministry of Jesus: 1:16–20 was followed by 1:21–28, an exorcism; 2:14 was followed by 2:15–17, opposition; 3:7–19 was followed by 3:20–35, accusations against Jesus; and 6:7–13 is followed here by 6:14–32, the execution of John the Baptist. In other words, the commissioning and sending of disciples here doesn't bode well.

Disciples (Outer Story)	John the Baptist (Inner Story)
Free	Imprisoned
"Sent" by a moral king (6:7)[a]	"Sent" for by an immoral "king"[b] (6:17, 27)
Preached repentance (6:11, 12)	Preached repentance (1:4; [6:18])
"Hearing" the disciples (6:11)	"Hearing" John (6:14, 16, 20 [2×])
Presence in the wilderness (6:32)	Presence in the wilderness (1:3, 4)
"*Opportune* moment" (6:31)	"*Opportune* day" (6:21)
[Result of their ministry?]	Loss of life (6:27)

a. And the disciples return as "sent ones," i.e., "apostles," derived from the same Greek verb (6:30). Jesus is doing to them what God did to him; "send" is used of Jesus's own commissioning by God in 9:37; 12:6.
b. Herod's title is itself striking. The designation "king" was explicitly refused to Herod Antipas by Augustus Caesar; he was simply a tetrarch, ruler of a fourth of the kingdom of his father, Herod the Great. Clearly Mark seems to be intent on contrasting one "king" with another, the real King, hence his use of the label.

And now we discover the result of their ministry, in a circuitous and indirect way. Rather than being told what happened to the disciples and their preaching endeavors, we are pointedly directed to the story of John's gruesome demise, at the hand of an immoral king. If the disciples and John were engaged in similar activities, then this "sandwich" tells us that their fates are linked too. Thus, the inner story bespeaks danger for the followers of Jesus, and that is the primary theological thrust of this pericope. This narrative serves as a forewarning to all who would follow their Lord "on the way," but particularly those sent to preach. It is dangerous business!

Preaching *is* dangerous business. John preached, he was rejected, and he was killed. Jesus preached, he was rejected, and he would soon be killed. The disciples preached, and what would happen to them is now implied. Dangerous business, indeed!

The outer story then resumes, and concludes, in 6:30–32, with the disciples returning to Jesus after their mission and reporting on their activities. Both this account and the earlier commissioning in Mark 3 had these dual thrusts: being sent by Jesus (3:14 and 6:7) *and* remaining with/returning to Jesus (3:14 and 6:30). This is not a contradiction: one must be *with* Jesus in order to be sent *by* Jesus. Even as one is sent, one remains with him: "Apart from Me you are not able to do anything" (John 15:5). Appropriately, then, the pericope closes with a moment of tenderness as Jesus bids his disciples, freshly returned—and scarred?—to come away and rest (6:31). No, they are not called to retire from their arduous mission when oppressed and rejected, but encouraged by Jesus, they are to keep on going, as are all of Jesus's subsequent followers, and even his preachers. As the first half of the outer story had already touched on, here we are again subtly reminded of the sufficiency of divine provision. And so, like the disciples, preachers, too, are to continue on their mission, faithfully, courageously, diligently, and conscientiously, resting on the abundant provision of God, even in dire circumstances, even when the going is hard and laborious . . . and dangerous.

> Now may the God of peace, who brought back from the dead the great shepherd of sheep, our Lord Jesus, equip you with every good thing to do His will, doing in us what is pleasing before Him, through Jesus Christ, to whom be glory forever and ever. Amen! (Heb. 13:20–21)

May God bless our preaching and enable it to bear abundant fruit for his glory!

Bibliography

Adams, John Quincy. *Lectures on Rhetoric and Oratory*. Cambridge, MA: Hilliard and Metcalf, 1810.

Aichele, George. *The Control of Biblical Meaning: Canon as Semiotic Mechanism*. Harrisburg, PA: Trinity, 2001.

Alan of Lille. *De arte praedicatoria*. Patrologia Latina 210, cols. 111–98. Edited by J.-P. Migne. Paris, 1855.

The Ante-Nicene Fathers. Edited by Alexander Roberts and James Donaldson. 10 vols. 1885–1887. Repr., Peabody, MA: Hendrickson, 1994.

Athanasius. *On the Incarnation*. Translated by A Religious of CSMV, rev. ed. Crestwood, NY: St. Vladimir's Seminary Press, 1993.

Attridge, Harold W. "Paraenesis in a Homily (λόγος παρακλήσεως): The Possible Location of, and Socialization in, the 'Epistle to the Hebrews.'" In *Paraenesis: Act and Form*. Semeia 50, edited by Leo G. Perdue and John G. Gammie, 211–26. Atlanta: Scholars Press, 1990.

Augustine. "Sermon 371: On the Lord's Nativity." In *The Works of Saint Augustine*, vol. 10, *Part III: Sermons 341–400*, translated by Edmund Hill, edited by John E. Rotelle, 312–15. New York: Augustinian Heritage Institute, 1995.

Bains, Sunny. "Mixed Feelings." *Wired*, March 2007. http://archive.wired.com/wired/archive/15.04/esp.html.

Barth, Karl. *Dogmatics in Outline*. London: SCM, 1966.

———. *Homiletics*. Louisville: Westminster John Knox, 1991.

Baxter, Richard. *The Practical Works of The Rev. Richard Baxter*. 23 vols. London: James Duncan, 1830.

Beach, J. Mark. "The Real Presence of Christ in the Preaching of the Gospel: Luther and Calvin on the Nature of Preaching." *Mid-America Journal of Theology* 10 (1999): 77–134.

Beckman, Gary. *Hittite Diplomatic Texts*. Atlanta: Scholars Press, 1996.

Bonhoeffer, Dietrich. *The Cost of Discipleship*. Translated by R. H. Fuller. Revised by Irmgard Booth. New York: Simon and Schuster, 1995.

Booth, Wayne C. *The Rhetoric of Rhetoric: The Quest for Effective Communication*. Malden, MA: Blackwell, 2004.

Boston, Thomas. "Of Man's Chief End and Happiness." In vol. 1 of *An Illustration of the Doctrines of the Christian Religion, with Respect to Faith and Practice*, 1–12. London: William Baynes, 1812.

Broadus, John A. "Author's Preface to the First Edition." In *A Treatise on the Preparation and Delivery of Sermons*, by John A. Broadus, edited by Edwin Charles Dargan, v–xi. New York: Harper and Brothers, 1926.

Brooks, Phillips. *Lectures on Preaching: Delivered before the Divinity School of Yale College in January and February 1877*. New York: E. P. Dutton, 1877.

Buttrick, David G. *A Captive Voice: The Liberation of Preaching*. Louisville: Westminster John Knox, 1994.

―――. *Homiletic: Moves and Structures*. Philadelphia: Fortress, 1987.

―――. "Interpretation and Preaching." *Interpretation* 35 (1981): 46–58.

―――. "Preaching the Christian Faith." *Liturgy* 2 (1983): 51–56.

Calvin, John. *Commentary upon the Acts of the Apostles,* vol. 2. Translated by Henry Beveridge. Edinburgh: Calvin Translation Society, 1844.

―――. *Institutes of the Christian Religion*. Translated by Henry Beveridge. Edinburgh: Calvin Translation Society, 1845.

―――. *Theological Treatises*. Edited by J. K. S. Reid. Library of Christian Classics 22. Philadelphia: Westminster, 1954.

Carson, D. A. "Unity and Diversity in the New Testament: The Possibility of Systematic Theology." In *Hermeneutics, Authority, and Canon*, edited by D. A. Carson and John D. Woodbridge, 65–95. Grand Rapids: Baker, 1995.

Catchpole, David R. "The 'Triumphal' Entry." In *Jesus and the Politics of His Day*, edited by Ernst Bammel and C. F. D. Moule, 319–34. Cambridge: Cambridge University Press, 1984.

The Catechism of the Catholic Church. 2nd ed. New York: Doubleday, 2003.

Chan, Simon. *Spiritual Theology: A Systematic Study of the Christian Life*. Downers Grove, IL: InterVarsity, 1998.

Chemnitz, Martin. *Ministry of Word and Sacrament: An Enchiridion*. St. Louis: Concordia, 1981.

Cicero. *On Invention, Best Kind of Orator, Topics*. Translated by H. M. Hubbell. Loeb Classical Library 386. Cambridge: Harvard University Press, 1970.

Clement of Alexandria. *Christ the Educator*. Translated by Simon P. Wood. The Fathers of the Church 23. Washington, DC: Catholic University of America Press, 1954.

Clines, D. J. A. "The Image of God in Man." *Tyndale Bulletin* 19 (1968): 53–103.

Clowney, Edmund. *Preaching and Biblical Theology*. Nutley, NJ: P&R, 1977.

Coggan, Donald. *A New Day for Preaching: The Sacrament of the Word*. London: SPCK, 1996.

Collins, Adela Yarbro. *Mark: A Commentary*. Hermeneia. Minneapolis: Fortress, 2007.

Craddock, Fred B. *As One Without Authority*. 4th rev. ed. St. Louis: Chalice, 2001.

———. *Preaching*. Nashville: Abingdon, 1985.

Craig, William Lane. "'Men Moved by the Holy Spirit Spoke from God' (2 Peter 1:21): A Middle Knowledge Perspective on Biblical Inspiration." In *Oxford Readings in Philosophical Theology*, vol. 2, *Providence, Scripture, and Resurrection*, edited by Michael Rea, 157–91. Oxford: Oxford University Press, 2009.

Crouzel, Henri. *Origen*. Translated by A. S. Worrall. Edinburgh: T&T Clark, 1989.

Cullman, Oscar. *The Early Church*. London: SCM, 1956.

Davis, John Jefferson. *Worship and the Reality of God: An Evangelical Theology of Real Presence*. Downers Grove, IL: InterVarsity, 2010.

Duff, Paul Brooks. "The March of the Divine Warrior and the Advent of the Greco-Roman King: Mark's Account of Jesus' Entry into Jerusalem." *Journal of Biblical Literature* 111 (1992): 55–71.

Dyer, Frank Lewis, and Thomas Commerford Marin. *Edison: His Life and Inventions*, vol. 2. New York: Harper and Brothers, 1910.

Edwards, Jonathan. *The End for Which God Created the World*. In John Piper, *God's Passion for His Glory: Living the Vision of Jonathan Edwards*, 125–251. Wheaton: Crossway, 1988.

Eslinger, Richard L. *A New Hearing: Living Options in Homiletical Method*. Nashville: Abingdon, 1987.

Feynman, Richard P. "Testimony of Lawrence B. Mulloy, Project Manager, Solid Rocket Boosters, Marshall Space Flight Center, NASA." In *Report to the President, by the Presidential Commission on the Space Shuttle Challenger Accident, June 6th, 1986, Washington, DC, Volume 4: February 11, 1986 Session*, 617–80. http://history.nasa.gov/rogersrep/genindex.htm.

Forde, Gerhard O. "The Ordained Ministry." In *Called and Ordained: Lutheran Perspectives on the Office of the Ministry*, edited by Todd Nichol and Mark Kolden, 117–36. Minneapolis: Fortress, 1990.

France, R. T. *The Gospel of Mark: A Commentary on the Greek Text*. New International Greek Testament Commentary. Grand Rapids: Eerdmans, 2002.

Gadamer, Hans-Georg. *Truth and Method*. 2nd rev. ed. Translated by Joel Weinsheimer and Donald G. Marshall. London: Continuum, 2004.

Garlington, Don B. *Faith, Obedience and Perseverance*. Wissenschaftliche Untersuchungen zum Neuen Testament 79. Tübingen: Mohr Siebeck, 1994.

Goldsworthy, Graeme. *Gospel-Centred Hermeneutics: Biblical-Theological Foundations and Principles*. Nottingham, UK: Apollos, 2006.

———. *Preaching the Whole Bible as Christian Scripture: The Application of Biblical Theology to Expository Preaching*. Grand Rapids: Eerdmans, 2000.

Gregory the Great. *Pastoral Care*. Translated by Henry Davis. Ancient Christian Writers 11. Westminster, MD: Newman, 1950.

Greenhaw, David M. "As One *with* Authority: Rehabilitating Concepts for Preaching." In *Intersections: Post-Critical Studies in Preaching*, edited by Richard L. Eslinger, 105–22. Grand Rapids: Eerdmans, 2004.

Greidanus, Sidney. *The Modern Preacher and the Ancient Text: Interpreting and Preaching Biblical Literature*. Grand Rapids: Eerdmans, 1989.

———. *Preaching Christ from the Old Testament: A Contemporary Hermeneutical Method*. Grand Rapids: Eerdmans, 1999.

Griffith Thomas, W. H. *The Principles of Theology: An Introduction to the Thirty-Nine Articles*. 6th rev. ed. London: Vine, 1978.

Guibert de Nogent. *A Book about the Way a Sermon Ought to Be Given*. In *Readings in Medieval Rhetoric*, edited by Joseph M. Miller, Michael H. Prosser, and Thomas W. Benson, 162–81. Bloomington: Indiana University Press, 1973.

Hajdu, David. "Wynton's Blues." *Atlantic Monthly*, March 2003, 43–58.

Heath, Chip, and Dan Heath. *Made to Stick: Why Some Ideas Survive and Others Die*. New York: Random House, 2007.

———. *Switch: How to Change Things When Change Is Hard*. New York: Broadway, 2010.

Henderson, Suzanne Watts. *Discipleship and Christology in the Gospel of Mark*. Society for New Testament Studies Monograph Series 135. Cambridge: Cambridge University Press, 2006.

Hilber, John W. "Theology of Worship in Exodus 24." *Journal of the Evangelical Theological Society* 39 (1996): 177–89.

Hirsch, E. D. *The Aims of Interpretation*. Chicago: University of Chicago Press, 1976.

———. "Meaning and Significance Reinterpreted." *Critical Inquiry* 11 (1984): 202–25.

———. "Past Intentions and Present Meanings." *Essays in Criticism* 33 (1983): 79–98.

Hogan, Lucy Lind, and Robert Reid. *Connecting with the Congregation: Rhetoric and the Art of Preaching*. Nashville: Abingdon, 1999.

Hogue, Michael S. *The Promise of Religious Naturalism*. Lanham, MD: Rowman and Littlefield, 2010.

Holmberg, Bengt. *Paul and Power: The Structure of Authority in the Primitive Church as Reflected in the Pauline Epistles*. Philadelphia: Fortress, 1978.

Hugh of St. Victor. "Noah's Ark." In *Selected Spiritual Writings*, by Hugh of St. Victor, 45–182. New York: Harper and Row, 1962.

Hughes, Philip Edgcumbe. *Paul's Second Epistle to the Corinthians*. New International Commentary on the New Testament. Grand Rapids: Eerdmans, 1962.

Johnson, Dennis E. *Him We Proclaim: Preaching Christ from All the Scriptures*. Phillipsburg, NJ: P&R, 2007.

Johnstone, Keith. *Impro: Improvisation and the Theatre*. London: Methuen, 1981.

Kaiser, Walter C. *Toward an Exegetical Theology: Biblical Exegesis for Teaching and Preaching*. Grand Rapids: Baker, 1998.

Keir, Thomas H. *The Word in Worship: Preaching and Its Setting in Common Worship*. Oxford: Oxford University Press, 1962.

Kelly, J. N. D. *Golden Mouth: The Story of John Chrysostom—Ascetic, Preacher, Bishop*. London: Duckworth, 1995.

Klauck, Hans-Josef. "Lord's Supper." In vol. 4 of *The Anchor Bible Dictionary*, edited by D. N. Freedman, 366. New York: Doubleday, 1992.

Kodell, Jerome. *The Eucharist in the New Testament*. Collegeville, MN: Liturgical Press, 1991.

Kuruvilla, Abraham. *Ephesians: A Theological Commentary for Preachers*. Eugene, OR: Cascade, 2015.

———. *Genesis: A Theological Commentary for Preachers*. Eugene, OR: Resource Publications, 2014.

———. *Mark: A Theological Commentary for Preachers*. Eugene, OR: Cascade, 2012.

———. "The Naked Runaway and the Enrobed Reporter." *Journal of the Evangelical Theological Society* 54 (2011): 527–45.

———. *Privilege the Text! A Theological Hermeneutic for Preaching*. Chicago: Moody, 2013.

———. *Text to Praxis: Hermeneutics and Homiletics in Dialogue*. Library of New Testament Studies 393. London: T&T Clark, 2009.

Lapsley, Jacqueline E. *Can These Bones Live? The Problem of the Moral Self in the Book of Ezekiel*. Beihefte zur Zeitschrift für die alttestamentliche Wissenschaft 301. Berlin: Walter de Gruyter, 2000.

Lathrop, George Parsons. "Talks with Edison." *Harper's New Monthly Magazine* 80 (1890): 425–35.

Lathrop, Gordon. *Holy Things: A Liturgical Theology*. Minneapolis: Fortress, 1993.

Leithart, Peter J. "Synagogue or Temple? Models for the Christian Worship." *Westminster Theological Journal* 64 (2002): 119–33.

Lerner, Alan Jay, and Frederick Lowe. *My Fair Lady: A Musical Play in Two Acts Based on Pygmalion by Bernard Shaw*. New York: Coward-McCann, 1956.

Levin, Michael. "What Makes a Classic in Political Theory?" *Political Science Quarterly* 88 (1973): 462–76.

Locher, Gottfried. *Zwingli's Thought: New Perspectives*. Leiden: Brill, 1981.

Locke, Charles S. "Statement of Charles S. Locke, Chairman and Chief Executive Officer, Morton Thiokol, Inc., before the Science and Technology Committee, United States House of Representatives (June 17, 1986)." In *Investigation of the Challenger Accident (Volume 1, Part 2): Hearings before the Committee on Science and Technology, House of Representatives, Ninety-Ninth Congress, Second Session (June 10, 11, 12, 17, 18, 25, 1986)*, 329–34. Washington, DC: Committee on Science and Technology, 1986. http://www.gpo.gov/fdsys/pkg/GPO-CHRG-99hhrg64294-vol1/pdf/CHRG-101shrg1087-2.pdf.

Lohmann, Fred von. "Google Book Search Settlement: Updating the Numbers, Part 2." Electronic Frontier Foundation, February 23, 2010. https://www.eff.org/deeplinks/2010/02/google-book-search-settlement-updating-numbers-0.

Long, Thomas G. "The Distance We Have Traveled: Changing Trends in Preaching." In *A Reader on Preaching: Making Connections*, edited by David Day, Jeff Astley, and Leslie J. Francis, 11–16. Aldershot, UK: Ashgate, 2005.

———. "A New Focus for Teaching Preaching." In *Teaching Preaching as a Christian Practice: A New Approach to Homiletical Pedagogy*, edited by Thomas G. Long and Leonora Tubbs Tisdale, 3–17. Louisville: Westminster John Knox, 2008.

———. "The Preacher and the Beast: From Apocalyptic Text to Sermon." In *Intersections: Post-Critical Studies in Preaching*, edited by Richard L. Eslinger, 1–22. Grand Rapids: Eerdmans, 2004.

———. "The Use of Scripture in Contemporary Preaching." *Interpretation* 44 (1990): 341–52.

_____. *The Witness of Preaching*. 2nd ed. Louisville: Westminster John Knox, 2005.

Lowry, Eugene L. *The Homiletical Plot: The Sermon as Narrative Art Form*. Rev. ed. Louisville: Westminster John Knox, 2001.

Luther, Martin. "Concerning the Ministry." In *Luther's Works*, vol. 40, *Church and Ministry II*, translated by Conrad Bergendoff, edited by Helmut Lehmann and Jaroslav Pelikan, 4–44. Philadelphia: Muhlenberg, 1958.

_____. "Concerning the Order of Public Worship (1523)." In *Luther's Works*, vol. 53, *Liturgy and Hymns*, translated by Paul Zeller Strodach, revised by Ulrich S. Leupold, 7–14. Philadelphia: Fortress, 1965.

_____. *D. Martin Luthers sämtliche Schriften*, vol. 3, *Predigten über das erste Buch Mosis und Auslegungen über die folgenden biblischen Bücher bis zu den Psalmen*. Translated by Johann Georg Walch. St. Louis: Concordia, 1880–1910.

_____. "Prefaces to the Old Testament." In *Luther's Works*, vol. 35, *Word and Sacrament I*, translated by Charles M. Jacobs, revised by E. Theodore Bachmann, 233–333. Philadelphia: Muhlenberg, 1960.

MacArthur, John F., Jr. "The Mandate of Biblical Inerrancy: Expository Preaching." *The Master's Seminary Journal* 1 (1990): 3–17.

Mather, Cotton. *Student and Preacher*. London: Hindmarsh, 1789.

Mayer, Wendy, and Pauline Allen. *John Chrysostom*. London: Routledge, 2000.

Melville, Herman. *Moby-Dick, or The White Whale*. Boston: The St. Botolph Society, 1890.

Merida, Tony. *Faithful Preaching: Declaring Scripture with Responsibility, Passion, and Authenticity*. Nashville: Broadman and Holman, 2009.

Moule, H. C. G. "Statement by Professor Moule." In *The Doctrine of Holy Communion and Its Expression in Ritual: Report of a Conference Held at Fulham Palace in October 1900*, edited by Henry Wace, 91. London: Longmans, Green, 1900.

Murphy, James J. *Rhetoric in the Middle Ages: A History of Rhetorical Theory from St. Augustine to the Renaissance*. Berkeley: University of California Press, 1974.

Neusner, Jacob. *The Comparative Hermeneutics of Rabbinic Judaism*. Vol. 1, *Introduction and the Hermeneutics of Berakhot and Seder Mo'ed*. Binghamton, NY: Academic Studies in the History of Judaism, 2000.

The Nicene and Post-Nicene Fathers. Series 1. Edited by Philip Schaff. 1886–1889. 14 vols. Repr., Peabody, MA: Hendrickson, 1994.

The Nicene and Post-Nicene Fathers. Series 2. Edited by Philip Schaff and Henry Wace. 1886–1889. 14 vols. Repr., Peabody, MA: Hendrickson, 1994.

Oden, Thomas C. *Pastoral Theology: Essentials of Ministry*. San Francisco: HarperSanFrancisco, 1983.

Old, Hughes Oliphant. *The Medieval Church*. Vol. 3 of *The Reading and Preaching of the Scriptures in the Worship of the Christian Church*. Grand Rapids: Eerdmans, 1998–2010.

_____. *Worship: Reformed according to Scripture*. Louisville: Westminster John Knox, 2002.

Parunak, Henry Van Dyke. "Structural Studies in Ezekiel." PhD diss., Harvard University, 1978.

Pasquarello, Michael. *Christian Preaching: A Trinitarian Theology of Proclamation*. Grand Rapids: Baker Academic, 2006.

Pelikan, Jaroslav. *Divine Rhetoric: The Sermon on the Mount as Message and as Model in Augustine, Chrysostom and Luther*. Crestwood, NY: St. Vladimir's Seminary Press, 2001.

Perkins, William. *The Arte of Prophecying; or, A Treatise concerning the Sacred and Onely True Manner and Methode of Preaching*. Translated by Thomas Tuke. London: Felix Kyngston, 1607.

Peterson, Eugene H. *Working the Angles: The Shape of Pastoral Integrity*. Grand Rapids: Eerdmans, 1987.

Pfeiffer, Robert H. *One Hundred New Selected Nuzi Texts*. Translated by E. A. Speiser. New Haven: American Schools of Oriental Research, 1936.

Porter, Stanley E. "Hermeneutics, Biblical Interpretation, and Theology: Hunch, Holy Spirit, or Hard Work?" In *Beyond the Bible: Moving from Scripture to Theology*, by I. Howard Marshall, 97–127. Grand Rapids: Baker Academic, 2004.

Ralston, Timothy J. "Class Notes for PM101: Spiritual Life." Dallas Theological Seminary, Spring 2006.

Reumann, John. "A History of Lectionaries: From the Synagogue at Nazareth to Post–Vatican II." *Interpretation* 31 (1977): 116–30.

Reynolds, Kent A. *Torah as Teacher: The Exemplary Torah Student in Psalm 119*. Leiden: Brill, 2010.

Richard, Ramesh. *Preparing Expository Sermons: A Seven-Step Method for Biblical Preaching*. Grand Rapids: Baker Books, 2001.

Ricoeur, Paul. *Hermeneutics and the Human Sciences: Essays on Language, Action and Interpretation*. Edited and translated by John B. Thompson. Cambridge: Cambridge University Press, 1981.

———. "Naming God." *Union Seminary Quarterly Review* 34 (1979): 215–27.

———. "Philosophy and Religious Language." *Journal of Religion* 54 (1974): 71–85.

Ringgren, Helmer. *Sacrifice in the Bible*. World Christian Books 2.42. London: United Society for Christian Literature, 1962.

Robert of Basevorn. *The Form of Preaching*. In *Three Medieval Rhetorical Arts*, translated by Leopold Krul, edited by James J. Murphy, 114–215. Berkeley: University of California Press, 1971.

Robinson, Haddon W. *Biblical Preaching: The Development and Delivery of Expository Messages*. 3rd ed. Grand Rapids: Baker Academic, 2014.

Rose, Lucy Atkinson. *Sharing the Word: Preaching in the Roundtable Church*. Louisville: Westminster John Knox, 1996.

Ross, Allen P. *Creation and Blessing: A Guide to the Study and Exposition of Genesis*. Grand Rapids: Baker, 1997.

———. *Recalling the Hope of Glory: Biblical Worship from the Garden to the New Creation*. Grand Rapids: Kregel, 2006.

Rowling, J. K. *Harry Potter and the Deathly Hallows*. New York: Scholastic, 2007.

Ryrie, Charles C. *Basic Theology: A Popular Systematic Guide to Understanding Biblical Truth*. Chicago: Moody, 1999.

Schillebeeckx, Edward. *The Eucharist*. Translated by N. D. Smith. New York: Sheed and Ward, 1968.

Schneiders, Sandra M. "The Paschal Imagination: Objectivity and Subjectivity in New Testament Interpretation." *Theological Studies* 46 (1982): 52–68.

Schreiner, Thomas R. *Paul, Apostle of God's Glory in Christ: A Pauline Theology.* Downers Grove, IL: InterVarsity, 2001.

Smart, James D. *The Strange Silence of the Bible in the Church: A Study in Hermeneutics.* London: SCM, 1970.

Smith, James K. A. *Desiring the Kingdom: Worship, Worldview, and Cultural Formation.* Cultural Liturgies 1. Grand Rapids: Baker Academic, 2009.

———. *Imagining the Kingdom: How Worship Works.* Cultural Liturgies 2. Grand Rapids: Baker Academic, 2013.

Smyth, John. *The Works of John Smyth.* Vol. 1, edited by W. T. Whitley. Cambridge: Cambridge University Press, 1915.

Star Trek II: The Wrath of Khan. Written by Jack B. Sowards and Harve Bennett. Hollywood: Paramount Pictures, 1982. http://www.imsdb.com/scripts/Star-Trek-II-The -Wrath-of-Khan.html.

Stein, Robert H. *Mark.* Baker Exegetical Commentary on the New Testament. Grand Rapids: Baker Academic, 2008.

Stewart-Sykes, Alistair. *From Prophecy to Preaching: A Search for the Origins of the Christian Homily.* Supplement to *Vigiliae christianae* 59. Leiden: Brill, 2001.

Stott, John R. W. *Between Two Worlds: The Art of Preaching in the Twentieth Century.* Grand Rapids: Eerdmans, 1982.

Taycher, Leonid. "Books of the World, Stand Up and Be Counted! All 129,864,880 of You." *Google Books Search* (blog), August 5, 2010. http://booksearch.blogspot.com/2010/08 /books-of-world-stand-up-and-be-counted.html.

Thomas of Chobham. *Summa de arte praedicandi.* Corpus Christianorum: Continuatio Mediaevalis 82, edited by Franco Morenzoni. Turnhout, Belgium: Brepols, 1988.

Tyndale, William. "A Prologue by William Tyndale Shewing the Use of the Scripture, Which He Wrote before the Five Books of Moses." In *The Works of the English Reformers: William Tyndale and John Frith*, 3 vols., edited by Thomas Russell, 2:6–11. London: Ebenezer Palmer, 1831.

Van Dyk, Leanne. "The Reformed View." In *The Lord's Supper: Five Views*, edited by Gordon T. Smith, 66–82. Downers Grove, IL: InterVarsity, 2008.

Vawter, Bruce. *Biblical Inspiration.* Louisville: Westminster, 1972.

Volf, Miroslav. *After Our Likeness: The Church as the Image of the Trinity.* Grand Rapids: Eerdmans, 1998.

Warren, Timothy S. "The Theological Process in Sermon Preparation." *Bibliotheca sacra* 156 (1999): 336–56.

Watson, Thomas. *A Body of Practical Divinity, Consisting of above One Hundred Seventy Six Sermons on the Lesser Catechism.* London: Thomas Parkhurst, 1692.

White, Hayden. "The Value of Narrativity in the Representation of Reality." In *On Narrative*, edited by W. J. T. Mitchell, 1–23. Chicago: University of Chicago Press, 1981.

Willard, Dallas. *The Spirit of the Disciplines: Understanding How God Changes Lives.* San Francisco: Harper & Row, 1988.

Willimon, William H. *Conversations with Barth on Preaching*. Nashville: Abingdon, 2006.

Witherington, Ben. "Word as Sacrament." *Ben Witherington* (blog), November 9, 2007. http://benwitherington.blogspot.com/2007/11/word-as-sacrament.html.

Wolterstorff, Nicholas. *Divine Discourse: Philosophical Reflections on the Claim That God Speaks*. Cambridge: Cambridge University Press, 1995.

Wright, Christopher J. H. *Old Testament Ethics for the People of God*. Downers Grove, IL: InterVarsity, 2004.

Wycliffe, John. "On the Seven Deadly Sins." In *Select English Works of John Wyclif*. Vol. 3, *Miscellaneous Works*, edited by Thomas Arnold, 119–67. Oxford: Clarendon, 1871.

Yaguello, Marina. *Language through the Looking Glass: Exploring Language and Linguistics*. New York: Oxford University Press, 1998.

Subject Index

206

Scripture and Ancient Writings Index